PARTY AND FACTIONAL DIVISION

IN TEXAS

PARTY AND FACTIONAL DIVISION IN TEXAS

By James R. Soukup

Clifton McCleskey

Harry Holloway

UNIVERSITY OF TEXAS PRESS, AUSTIN

ACKNOWLEDGMENTS

During the course of our research several persons and organizations provided us with valuable assistance. A sizable portion of the funds needed for the collection and classification of data came from grants by the University of Texas Research Institute. The Bureau of Business Research, the Institute of Public Affairs, the Sociology Department at the University, and the Legislative Reference Division of the Texas State Library offered liberal use of their facilities. Three research assistants—Marvin Felder, Gary Dowis, Jr., and David Reagan—spent many hours helping us to record and to tabulate statistics on the state's 254 counties. Much of the specialized information about Bexar County politics was gathered by Professor Mitchell Grossman of San Antonio Junior College. Most rewarding, from both an informational and a personal standpoint, were our many interviews with officials of the Texas Manufacturers Association and the Texas State AFL-CIO, local and state leaders of the Negro and Latin American communities, members of the 1959 Texas Legislature, and newspaper correspondents at the State Capitol. To all of these persons and organizations we wish to express our sincere gratitude.

CONTENTS

LIST OF FIGURES

LIST OF TABLES

INTRODUCTION

The true nature of Texas is probably as much obscured as revealed by all that has been written and said about it. Its reputation for a cowboy culture, for wealthy oilmen with ostentatious manners and many Cadillacs, for emphasis on athletic prowess rather than on intellectual pre-eminence, for a politics that is colorful and chaotic yet vociferously conservative—these and other notions are features of the popular image of the state. It is possible that like most stereotypes these notions, if not false, are at least exaggerated and distorted reflections of reality. A conviction that such is the case for Texas politics provided the initial impetus for our research.

The authors hope that this study will reach both interested laymen and scholars in political science and related disciplines. Laymen, for all their interests in politics, often lack the lens for viewing political developments and personalities in clear perspective; this volume is an attempt to supply this lens. As far as academicians are concerned, our goal is to present significant election statistics in a form that facilitates more rigorous analysis. A number of works of varying quality have been published on Texas politics,[1] but so far there has been no comprehensive treatment of voting patterns—in depth and over a span of years. By examining the results of fourteen elections from 1946 through 1962—four presidential, three United States senatorial, and seven gubernatorial—we seek to meet the need for systematic categorization. In fact, the principal value of our labors may very well lie in such taxonomic efforts, for rigorous categorization is a necessary prerequisite to more specialized studies capable of doing much to refine our knowledge of political processes. At the same time our findings are relevant to several general hypotheses concerning the effects on voting behavior of geographic location, historical tradition, economic factors, racial-ethnic background, and, above all, urbanization.

[1] The most useful general discussions of Texas politics are "Texas: The Politics of Economics," by V. O. Key, Jr., Chap. 12 in *Southern Politics in State and Nation* and the series by O. Douglas Weeks, *Texas Presidential Politics in 1952, Texas One-Party Politics in 1956,* and *Texas in the 1960 Presidential Election.*

Although not directed specifically to Texas, such studies as Alexander Heard's *A Two-Party South?* and Donald Strong's *Urban Republicanism in the South* are also quite helpful.

Our overall framework of analysis is the state's organized political factions. Specifically, in the late 1930's and the early 1940's an ordered political competition along liberal-conservative lines developed in Texas. Continuing growth and other related changes reinforced that tendency. Although the broad trends of this evolution were already discernible by the late 1950's, so much remained blurred and confused that further examination was clearly warranted. It seemed especially vital to measure the continuity and consistency of underlying political patterns and to probe more deeply into the changes taking place.

Our findings lead us to assert that the political struggle in Texas is conducted within a loose, but increasingly explicit, *ideological* context and that perceptible *changes* are occurring in the nature, strength, and modes of operation of the competing political forces. We are, of course, mindful of the danger of oversimplification by ignoring individual deviations and the impact of specific personalities and events, but we are also impressed by the apparent decrease in importance of such factors due to the crystallization of political attitudes and the emergence of highly organized political action groups. Indeed, the greater danger is that many Texans, priding themselves as they do on their individuality and the colorfulness of their political characters, will fail to see and to understand the underlying group or ideological interests.

The use of ideological categories such as "conservative" and "liberal" should not be misunderstood. We have not attempted to define the "true" essence of any ideology; if we had done so, we would have run the risk of introducing value-oriented biases. We have sought instead to define the terms "liberal" and "conservative" in accordance with the operational position of each faction or party on issues that they themselves consider to be significant. In short, the viewpoints ascribed to liberals or conservatives may or may not be *truly* liberal or conservative; what really matters is that those who hold those views believe them to be.

Our procedures and methodology have purposely been kept simple, although the size and variety of the state have made the task a lengthy and time-consuming one. The obvious rivalry between the conservative and the liberal blocs within the Democratic Party as well as the challenges of the Republicans dictated the structure of the study. Was it possible to find sets of counties tending with considerable consistency to support one of these three major political groups? If such sets of counties could be identified by analysis of election returns over a period of time, was it not likely that differences in their social and economic characteristics had a direct bearing on those tendencies? And on the basis of the political record and the socio-economic profiles developed, could we not offer explanations for the past and present tendencies and predictions for the state's political future?

In attempting to answer these questions, we open with a background chapter which includes a discussion of the nature of the political struggle and of the institutional factors affecting it. The body of the analysis follows, with the Republicans, the conservative Democrats, and the liberal Democrats taken up in Chapters II, III, and IV, respectively. Each of these chapters opens with a brief history, then proceeds to an account of the particular party or faction being scrutinized. The pattern of support for each is developed by sifting county returns in a series of primaries and elections for national and state offices presenting a significant choice between the Republican Party and one or both Democratic factions, or between Democratic factions alone. The counties which show the most marked and consistent voting tendencies are then separated and examined with an eye to their outstanding social and economic features, such as regionalism, population size and change, ethnic composition, urban-rural balance, income levels, and predominant economic activities. These analyses, we believe, establish a basic pattern of electoral behavior and relate it to the socio-economic system of the state.

Whenever feasible, we have also included information about the effects of organizational techniques, community power structure, and relations between metropolitan areas and their surrounding counties. Unfortunately, the integration of such data with election figures is demanding in both time and effort and, consequently, only a beginning is made in this direction. Nevertheless, it is our firm conviction that unless such a combined approach is applied systematically to future studies—especially analyses of broadly defined metropolitan areas—voting-behavior research will fall short of attaining a definitive status.

The examination of Republicans, conservative Democrats, and liberal Democrats in Chapters II, III, and IV concentrates on the period from 1946 to 1961. The 1962 primaries and elections are analyzed separately in Chapter V, a separation for which several justifications can be offered. Much of our basic data-processing was completed prior to 1962, and inclusion of the results for that year in each chapter would have required a disproportionate effort. Too, the 1962 elections seemed in many ways to mark a turning point in Texas political history, as evidenced by an unusual number of contests for top offices, by the emergence of a great many new faces and the disappearance of many old ones, and by the sharp contest and high turnout of the general election. Separate treatment of the 1962 results also offered a chance to test the findings from the earlier period and to verify or qualify them as necessary.

The story of the 1962 elections brings the account to an end. A concluding section then briefly summarizes the findings and tentatively explores future problems and prospects in the state's interparty and intraparty warfare.

This volume does not pretend to be either the first or the last word on the subject of Texas politics, but we do hope that our readers will find the evidence clear and the reasoning persuasive. Lest there be misunderstandings, it is well to point out now the limitations built into this study. We present little or no information on the internal politics of the state's legislative, executive, and judicial branches and on local government. Only a portion of the political process in Texas is discussed, and that fact should be kept in mind at all times.

Given the tendency to think of politics in terms of the personalities involved, some laymen may wonder about the limited treatment of such factional and party leaders as Lyndon Johnson, Allan Shivers, Ralph Yarborough, John Tower, Mrs. R. D. Randolph, and many others. The role and activities of particular leaders are played down, not because such persons are deemed unimportant, but because our concern is with the context in which they operate. Personalities and campaigns certainly represent important variables in Texas elections, but our quest is for more constant factors. We believe we have identified some of them.

Our emphasis on ideology in Texas politics may be challenged on the grounds that the average American voter is not ideologically motivated. Such a challenge might seem to be supported by material reported in the much respected analysis of national electoral behavior in presidential elections, *The American Voter*. According to the authors of this work, only about 12 per cent of the respondents express what can be called an ideological motive in voting;[2] these people think consciously in some degree of the liberalism or conservatism of candidates in making their electoral choices. The remainder of the electorate, Campbell and his associates maintain, does not do so and its vote could not be described as ideologically structured.

We do not quarrel with that evidence from *The American Voter*, and do not believe we need to. The 12 per cent of the electorate who are conscious ideologues are also more likely to be the "actives"—the political leaders and workers who do so much to set the tone of the

[2] Angus Campbell, Phillip E. Converse, Warren E. Miller, and Donald E. Stokes, *The American Voter*, pp. 227–234.

political dialogue. Even if not political "actives," the conscious ideologues are likely to be influential in the community. It is significant, for example, that approximately one-third of all college-educated voters perceive politics in terms of liberal-conservative positions.[3] Furthermore, although only 12 per cent of all voters are conscious ideologues, another 45 per cent can be assigned to a category of "ideology by proxy," or unconscious ideology, meaning that their evaluations of politics are in terms of the interests of various population groupings (business, labor, ethnic origin), which interests can themselves be assigned some place along the liberal-conservative continuum.[4] And, finally, the authors of *The American Voter* themselves emphasize the importance of ideological considerations in political change:

. . . if we are interested primarily in political change, we may be willing to ignore sixty or eighty per cent of the population entirely, focusing upon the minority that appears to contribute to the tides of partisan victory and defeat. It is at the point of political change, then, that attitude structure partaking of ideology might loom important.[5]

In short, although the ideological element in party and factional warfare is stressed herein, this emphasis does not necessarily mean that all Texas voters are ideologically motivated. Some are, and we present evidence to show the highly developed ideological consciousness present among "influentials." Undoubtedly many of the voters at large are not consciously moved by such convictions. Yet the county returns do reveal for many of these ordinary voters a consistent preference for one party or faction, under conditions such that ideologically related factors were necessarily a prime factor. For these reasons, therefore, we are confident of the validity of our approach.

There is no claim here to sophistication in our statistical or research techniques. In attempting to correlate election results with socioeconomic data, we have incorporated, wherever possible, some precinct data, but generally we were forced to utilize county returns. The large number of Texas counties (254) and their great diversity made further fragmentation out of the question. The trouble with the use of county figures, of course, is that significant differences in voting patterns or socio-economic patterns within the county may be obscured by the use of the aggregate results. Despite this drawback our findings do demonstrate that significant numbers of counties have fairly clear-cut and

[3] *Ibid.*, p. 250.
[4] *Ibid.*, pp. 234–240.
[5] *Ibid.*, p. 215.

uniform characteristics and related voting habits. In any case, without preliminary sifting and classification of this sort, it is doubtful that future research—whether qualitative in nature or of the survey type—could be properly focused.

Throughout this study we have been forward rather than cautious in generalizing and speculating, an approach which may provoke dissent but which also helps to direct attention to meaningful questions. We know only too well that much more remains to be done in this subject area. The politics of Texas is fascinating to probe and ponder, and we will have accomplished not a little if we communicate to our readers some of this curiosity and excitement. Republicanism on the rise, the Confederate tradition fading, minority groups increasingly restless, cattle and oil challenged by industry and commerce, urbanization—it is a dynamic and dramatic development, politically as well as socially and economically. We believe that what follows will shed some light on the process; we hope it will stimulate even more fruitful analysis.

**PARTY AND FACTIONAL DIVISION
IN TEXAS**

I

BACKGROUND OF TEXAS POLITICS

Before a statistical analysis is made of the relative strength of the conservative Republicans, the conservative Democrats, and the liberal Democrats, certain background questions should be answered. How extensive is the conservative-liberal struggle in Texas? Which groups and political leaders are found in each of these ideological camps? What are the issues that most divide conservatives from liberals in Texas? What effect do election regulations have upon the distribution of power among the competing parties and factions? These are the questions with which this chapter is concerned.

IDEOLOGICAL SETTING

As early as 1949 V. O. Key commented: "In Texas the vague outlines of a politics are emerging in which irrelevances are pushed into the background and the people divide broadly along liberal and conservative lines." He attributed this development to the "personal insecurity of men suddenly made rich who are fearful lest they lose their wealth" and to the repercussions of the New Deal.[1]

Today the conservative-liberal rift is broader and deeper. Both sides have increased the tempo of their grass-roots activities. Such ideologically oriented organizational drives are especially evident in the fast-growing cities. Extreme ultraconservative organizations such as Freedom in Action and the John Birch Society are extremely vocal. Less dogmatically and more effectively, the Texas Manufacturers Association, local Chambers of Commerce, individual firms and corporations, and professional groups have been providing training and guidance in the art of politics.[2] With business and professional groups

[1] V. O. Key, Jr., *Southern Politics in State and Nation*, p. 255.
[2] *Austin Statesman*, February 19, 1961. Major oil companies have been especially active. Gulf and Phillips Oil Corporations were among the first to encourage their employees to participate in local, state, and national politics. More recently

as a nucleus, several conservative political organizations have been formed in metropolitan areas, the most noteworthy being the Dallas County Organization of Conservative Voters and the Democratic Precinct Organizations in Houston.[3] Such right-wing efforts were formerly confined to the Democratic Party, but, of late, new conservatives working with the Republican Party have also supplied organization and zeal.[4]

Liberal groups—organized labor, Negro and Latin American minorities, and assorted intellectuals—are engaged in similar activities.[5] Among the most effective liberal precinct organizations are the Harris County Democrats, the Bexar County Democratic Coalition, and the Nueces County Democratic Alliance. From 1958 to 1960 Mrs. Frankie

---

Humble Oil and Refining Company has adopted a similar policy. Such programs are referred to as nonpartisan, but it would be surprising if they did not strengthen the conservative cause.

[3] During the 1950's San Antonio conservatives maintained a highly effective organization entitled the Bexar County Legislative Group with the avowed objective of capturing the county's seven seats in the Texas House of Representatives. However, after several successful campaigns all but one member of the group's slate were defeated in the 1960 legislative races.

At a 1960 conference of top-level Texas business and professional people, Lee Smith, vice chairman of the Dallas County Democratic Executive Committee, offered his conservative colleagues the following ground rules for political success:

1. The first and usually the last political mistake a group of like minded persons can make is to band together into an organization . . . elect a Board of Directors, officers, establish by-laws, etc. . . . for example, Democrats of Texas, Southern Democratic Clubs, etc. . . . There are many of us here who know each other. Business leaders know us and we know them. When something needs to be done we caucus. There is no leader. We group loosely around our County Chairman. We don't need or use much money, but when we need it, it is easy to find. Out of 187 precincts we have about 140 and we know which ones and why.

2. Start with youth. They must be selfless people . . . interested in no personal gains or favors . . . young men under 35. Their first and continuing objective should be to take over the county executive committee by placing themselves and like minded persons in office as precinct chairmen.

3. A county must not be allowed to split into factions because factions are endless and wasteful. . . . We have had people who refused to compromise. They have wound up outside looking in and writing letters and pamphlets "For America," "For Texans." We won't allow them to wreck us.

The above quotations are from *Report on the Conference of Business and Professional Leaders*, pp. 46–48. Another example of business emphasis on precinct activities is the Texas Manufacturers Association publication entitled *How To Be Influential in Politics*.

[4] "The Young GOP Turks: A Political Composite," *Texas Observer*, March 30, 1962.

[5] As used here, the term "intellectual" is broad enough to cover such diverse groups as writers, scholars, administrators, and, in general, those who are occupied with intellectual matters both inside and outside the academic world.

Randolph's Democrats of Texas (DOT) attempted to weld these diverse elements into a statewide network, but failed because many liberals feared being "labelled" and wished to form broader alliances with moderate groups.[6] In most instances, however, this reluctance to join an overall liberal organization stemmed from tactical, not ideological, considerations. Specifically, the question of whether to oppose then Senator Johnson in his quest for the 1960 Democratic presidential nomination was probably the key point of division. When organized labor refused to join the fight against him, the DOT suffered irreparable damage. Despite the continuation of such tactical differences, liberals recently regrouped themselves loosely under the new and more flexible Democratic Coalition.[7]

Even the relatively disorganized state legislators are being affected by mounting ideological pressures. In prewar days there was little talk of a conservative-liberal showdown at the State Capitol. From 1920 to 1944 the handful of liberal legislators were surrounded—indeed smothered—by a vast array of conservatives and so-called "independents." A few governors occasionally championed measures of a "Populist" nature, but the biggest political battles were fought over personalities, not principles.[8] Today, however, legislators, lobbyists, and newsmen alike often refer to the legislative struggle as one between conservative and liberal elements. A considerable number of vacillating moderates remain, but they are under increasing pressure to take sides.[9]

All this does not mean, however, that the liberalism or the conservatism of a candidate or party is the only consideration in Texas politics. Such nonideological factors as family, friends, and the personalities of competing candidates still exert influence over many voters. Nevertheless, the importance of such nonideological variables is shrinking steadily. Indeed, their significance would have diminished even more were it not for the existence of a long-standing decentralized one-party system that contributes to ideological ambiguity. Until recently, only Democratic Party nominees had an opportunity to capture state offices, and, therefore, ambitious men representing all shades of opinion tried

[6] In August, 1960, the State Convention of the AFL-CIO expressed sympathy for the Democrats of Texas, but indicated that it would follow an "independent" course of action (*Texas Observer*, August 12, 1960). A majority of nonlabor liberals in San Antonio and Austin followed a similarly cautious path.

[7] *Texas Observer*, October 20, 1961.

[8] Key, *Southern Politics*, pp. 260–270.

[9] Unless otherwise specified, this and other information about legislative activities in Texas is based upon interviews with forty selected members of the State Legislature conducted during the 1957 and 1959 sessions.

to squeeze in under the same Democratic roof. The old-guard Republicans failed not only to win elections, but even to provide mild criticism. Consequently, many public officials saw little need for openly declaring themselves; in fact, they often felt that taking a stand would alienate rather than impress prospective voters. The resulting confusion of the general public reinforced the frequently observed American tendency to vote according to personalities rather than principles—thus making it difficult for political organizers to mobilize votes on the basis of well-defined policies.

Numerous examples of vacillation among the state's top political figures should be noted also. Despite endorsement by several conservative businessmen and ranchers and opposition from some labor union officials, Lyndon Johnson in 1948 received the support of many liberals in his successful senatorial campaign against conservative Coke Stevenson. A glance at Johnson's senatorial voting record reveals that he did often embrace "countryside" liberalism. Specifically, he supported spending for rural electrification, farm price supports, river development, water and soil conservation, and aid to the aged. Liberals have criticized him for not going far or fast on such issues as federal aid to education, health insurance, public housing, and racial integration; but, unlike many Southern conservatives, he has never closed the door on such proposals. Furthermore, though skeptical of disarmament, negotiation with Russia, and the efficacy of economic aid, Johnson as a senator more often than not preferred an internationalist approach to world politics.

Concomitant with Johnson's support of some liberal policies is his advocacy of certain conservative measures. He has frequently favored proposals to regulate organized labor and to provide tax relief for business corporations—especially the oil and gas industries. Above all, his *tactical* position in both national and state politics has angered the liberals. As Senate majority leader, Johnson made sizable concessions to conservative Democrats and Republicans, which he justified on the grounds that he was "the leader of the United States Senate and not of a particular political party" and that "half a loaf is better than none." A more serious liberal criticism is that in state Democratic conventions since 1956 Johnson has repeatedly thrown his weight in favor of conservative elements.

In contrast, United States Senator Ralph Yarborough is regarded as a pillar of liberalism. Just as is President Johnson, he is imbued with rural populism and, therefore, definitely inclined to endorse domestic welfare spending. Unlike Johnson, he is a defender of organized labor. Johnson has close personal ties with some minority group leaders, but

Yarborough unquestionably has been more open in his quest for the support of such groups, although recently he has been criticized by Latin and Negro leaders for not acting more rapidly and more vigorously on the issues of concern to them. Yet, he has frequently voted against liberal-backed foreign-aid measures. Furthermore, like Johnson, he has been careful not to attack the oil and gas industry, which often is a target for some liberals. Specifically, during the two sessions of the Eighty-Seventh Congress Yarborough voted with the Northern Democrats 70 per cent of the time and with the Southern Democrats only 30 per cent of the time.[10]

Former Governors Allan Shivers (1949–1956) and Price Daniel (1957–1963) are in the conservative camp. Of the two, Governor Shivers is considered to be more conservative—especially since he spearheaded Democrats-for-Eisenhower campaigns in 1952 and 1956 and the Democrats-for-Nixon drive in 1960. Nevertheless, during the Shivers' administrations spending for social welfare in general and public education in particular did rise substantially.

First as United States senator and then as governor, Price Daniel backed many business-supported programs. More significantly, in state convention politics he strongly endorsed conservatives and attacked liberals. However, in recent sessions of the Legislature he openly indicted the "interstate oil and gas lobby" and bitterly criticized bankers for opposing his proposals to shift unclaimed bank and utility-company funds to the state treasury. Thus, despite his conservative machinations within the Democratic Party apparatus, liberals occasionally found common ground with Governor Daniel.

Such illustrations serve to caution against oversimplification of Texas politics. They do not, however, disprove the thesis that Texas is fast becoming a key battlefield in the conservative-liberal struggle. Behind-the-scenes political organizers are often motivated by ideological sentiments. Moreover, with due allowances for tactical compromises and deviations, they are gradually insisting that prospective candidates deal with the basic issues. Like it or not, therefore, party nominees and voters alike will have to concern themselves with conservative-liberal arguments.

If, as many predict, the balance of power in Texas shifts from a right-wing to a moderate orientation, the move will probably be due more to a stalemate between organized conservatives and liberals than to the emergence of a large, philosophically consistent group of moderates. It is true, of course, that moderate Lyndon Johnson enjoys the

[10] As reported in *Congressional Quarterly Weekly*, Report No. 48 (November 30, 1962), p. 2216.

backing of many of the state's *top-level* officeholders. At the *grass-roots* level, however, he has been forced to make alliances with groups quite distinct from his own loyal precinct supporters[11] or, at the very least, to take advantage of divisions between and within established conservative and liberal organizations. Similarly, as will be demonstrated in the chapters to follow, independent candidates who have sought to play up their personality traits and play down ideological issues have seldom emerged victorious in recent statewide elections.

Granted that ideology is significant, what is the philosophical basis of the conservative-liberal struggle in Texas? Is it race or economics? Race is not the dominant issue in Texas politics as it is in many Southern states. True, conservatives in East Texas, Houston, and a number of other localities have tried to delay integration. Some Houston conservatives have even endeavored, with limited success, to use the race issue as a means of disrupting the coalition between Negroes and labor liberals. And, as yet, neither Negroes nor Mexican-Americans have attained a full measure of equality. But in the 1948 presidential election race-conscious Dixiecrats were able to garner only 10 per cent of the state's popular vote and this was concentrated in East Texas—an area with declining population and with a tendency to vote liberal on economic issues. In December, 1962, the Southern Regional Council estimated that Texas had 6,700 Negroes in integrated classrooms, whereas the entire figure for the rest of the old Confederacy was 5,647.[12] Informed Houston conservatives also contended that the extreme, segregationist White Citizens Council is fast losing ground among members of the local business community.

The biggest political battles in Texas are over economics. As V. O. Key aptly remarked, "The Lone Star State is concerned about money and how to make it, about oil and sulphur and gas, about cattle and

---

[11] In their strategy caucuses prior to the 1960 Travis County Democratic convention liberal activists observed that outright Johnsonites controlled but two or three precincts in the county. Other precincts were headed by either known liberals or known conservatives. Of course, Johnson's eventual endorsement was a foregone conclusion, but it resulted from a general, though by no means unanimous, consensus that it was unwise to oppose him for tactical reasons. In the September, 1960, state convention Johnson held the loyalty of Democratic electors but his forces were not strong enough to prevent a repudiation of the national Party platform.

This is not to say that Johnson is weak politically. Rather the point is that, in many localities, his own precinct organization is not as strong as one might suppose. His strength stems from his ability to sway *top* state officials and to "play off" liberal and conservative forces against one another. Moreover, his stature as Senate leader undoubtedly helped him pull together Southern leaders in a successful effort to elect the Democratic presidential ticket.

[12] *Southern School News*, December, 1962, p. 1.

dust storms and irrigation, about cotton and banking and Mexicans."[13] Among the conservatives this concern produces an intense opposition to big labor, "creeping socialism," concentration of power in the hands of the national government, and social-welfare spending. In state politics many conservatives still call themselves Democrats. In national elections, however, they have pronounced tendencies toward "presidential Republicanism."

The 1958 questionnaire responses of 52 specially selected officials of the Texas Manufacturers Association (TMA)—a stronghold of state conservatism—illustrate these attitudes.[14] When asked to specify the three most important problems facing the nation, 12 cited both "socialism" and "too much national government power"; another 16 referred to socialism only; and another 11 expressed fears about the national government. In other words, almost four-fifths of the TMA respondents were worried about socialism and/or national government control. In answer to the query "Do you think the national government should be given more, the same, or less power than it now has to deal with welfare problems?" 44 of these business leaders stated "less" power should be given to the federal government. Thirty-one also rejected both welfare aid (i.e., federal aid to education and medical programs) and subsidies to farmers and to transportation companies, while another 7 accepted subsidies but not welfare assistance.

The TMA respondents were most antagonistic toward organized labor. No fewer than half gave top priority to the problem of "controlling big labor unions." All but 4 stated that "unions are too powerful" and "the way they are organized now, unions do more harm than good."

In contrast, although 28 disapproved of the Supreme Court integration decision and another 16 approved only "with reservations," no more than 6 TMA leaders considered the race problem to be of "vital concern" and asserted that "Negroes have too much power for the welfare of the country." With specific reference to the United States Supreme Court, TMA officers' remarks and printed statements

---

[13] Key, *Southern Politics*, p. 254.

[14] This and subsequent commentaries on views of the Texas Manufacturers Association are based on a survey conducted by James R. Soukup in 1958. Questionnaires were sent to a sample of 50 of the TMA officers and directors, 35 replying, and to 30 of the approximately 450 Houston Chapter members, 17 answering. In both cases the sample was stratified according to type of industry and business. In the case of the officers and directors, an effort was also made to reflect possible regional differences. On questions of party preference, voting record, and general ideology no significant variations based on industrial or regional differences appeared.

found in the organization's policy statements definitely indicate that Texas businessmen are more upset by the Court's economic than its racial decisions.[15]

The inclinations of these businessmen toward "presidential Republicanism" are clearly illustrated in Table 1.

TABLE 1

Party Preference and Voting Record of Texas Manufacturers Association Members

Voting Record of 52 TMA Officers and Members	Stated Party Preference					Horizontal Totals
	Conservative Democrat	Moderate Democrat	Independent with Republican Leaning	Republican	Other	
Voted for all Republican presidential candidates but for Democrats in U.S. Senate and state gubernatorial races*	14	1	9	3	2	29
Voted for all Republican presidential candidates and U.S. senatorial candidates but voted for Democrats in state gubernatorial races*	1	1	7	6	1	16
Mixed presidential voting pattern but voted for Democrats in U.S. Senate and state gubernatorial races*	3	3	1	0	0	7
Totals	18	5	17	9	3	

* The presidential elections covered are those of 1948, 1952, and 1956; the U.S. Senate election is that of 1957; and the gubernatorial races are those of 1954, 1956, and 1958.

These conservative attitudes have not gone unchanged, however. In addition to shifts in party allegiance, slight alterations in conservative reactions to government spending have occurred. Some Texas conservatives are beginning to support limited expansion of state spending for educational and health facilities. For them, the issue is not so much "shall we spend more for such activities" but "where will we get the money?" On the latter, they lean toward general sales taxes, which

[15] Texas Manufacturers Association, *1958 Statement of Guiding Principles and Program* (mimeographed).

are hailed as "broad-based" taxes (condemned by liberals as "regressive" taxes).

Businessmen, who along with cattlemen and wealthy farmers form the hard core of Texas conservatism, also have occasional differences of opinion. The truck-rail fight still smolders within the Legislature and outside it. Most significant is the continuing rift between independent and major oil companies over oil and tax policies. During the 1959 and 1961 legislative sessions Texas Independent Producers and Royalty Owners Association (TIPRO), chief spokesman for the independents, refused to join the majors in their opposition to liberal efforts to pass a severance beneficiary tax directed at major oil companies and interstate natural-gas pipeline companies.

Basically, however, such disagreements, particularly apparent during legislative tax fights, are based on temporary clashes of economic self-interest. On broad, philosophical questions, such as opposition to socialism, national government supremacy, power of labor unions, and large-scale welfare spending, the conservatives are united. For example, when questioned about such issues, 22 TIPRO leaders[16] expressed the same sentiments as their counterparts in the Texas Manufacturers Association.

As opposed to conservatism, "pure" liberalism endorses welfare spending by means of deficit financing if necessary; equal treatment for Negroes, Latin Americans, and other minorities; increased government regulation of business activities; in accordance with the preceding aims, the expansion of national government powers; trade-union organization; and taxes on business—especially on large, interstate corporations—rather than on sales or individuals. Furthermore, many Texas liberals have made loyalty to the *national* Democratic Party a part of their political creed.

Among the groups and individuals who support all or most of these doctrines are (a) officials of the Texas AFL-CIO; (b) several, but by no means all, of the state's Negro and Latin American leaders, with United States Congressman Henry Gonzalez as an outstanding example; (c) independent liberals like Mrs. Frankie Randolph, Texas National Democratic Committeewoman until her ouster in 1960; the editors of the *Texas Observer*, a small but outspoken liberal newspaper published fortnightly; young and vigorous Don Yarborough; Maury Maverick, Jr., son of one of Texas' most colorful advocates of the

---

[16] In 1959 Soukup sent questionnaires to 10 members who "were generally called upon for political activities" and to a sample of 20 TIPRO members from the Midland-Odessa area. All 10 of the political activists and 12 from Midland-Odessa responded.

Roosevelt New Deal; (d) United States Senator Ralph Yarborough; and (e) scattered county precinct organizations that resemble California's political clubs in fervor though not effectiveness.

In practice, Texas liberalism is neither as pure nor as monolithic as Texas conservatism. Special problems have arisen as a result of the still powerful heritage of states' rights. Native Texas liberals have an inherent pride in their state and, hence, are sometimes more willing than their Northern counterparts to try first to resolve problems at the state level before turning to federal intervention. Accordingly, they eagerly endorse taxes on interstate corporations on the grounds that "it is a tax on *foreign concerns*." As in the case of Senator Yarborough, criticism of the oil and gas industry is also somewhat restrained.

Racial-ethnic questions are a more substantial source of liberal cleavages. Many East Texas politicians favor welfare aid and spending for public works, suspect big business, and oppose a general sales tax on one hand, but support segregationist proposals on the other. Despite reprimands from state AFL-CIO headquarters, several labor locals— especially in the skilled trades—have also rejected Negro appeals for union integration.

Negro and Latin leaders are disgruntled by Anglo-liberal delays in mounting full-scale drives for equal rights. They contend further that they have not been given a "full partnership" in the liberal coalition. Referring to Mexican-American discontent, the *Texas Observer* reported:

They feel, quite simply, that liberals and labor have ignored the burgeoning Latin political force, that they have been patronized, and that an aggressive show of discontent would dramatize their grievances within the historic liberal coalition. The DOT endorsement of Senator Yarborough in 1958 without a corresponding endorsement of Congressman Henry Gonzalez, the choice of labor and most liberals of Maverick over Gonzalez in 1961, patronage disagreements with Senator Yarborough all figure prominently.[17]

In accordance with such sentiments, Negro and Latin leaders have demanded that more of their people be included on candidate slates and that, at the very least, qualified members of their groups be considered for appointive offices. Tactically, a considerable number of Negro and Latin leaders are somewhat skeptical of liberal ability to deliver votes. Such cold appraisals of liberal chances combined with conservative promises of patronage have, on more than one occasion, led them to play it safe and to align themselves with conservative community leaders.[18]

[17] *Texas Observer*, February 16, 1962.
[18] In 1960 and again in 1962, had it not been for a sudden shift of several Negroes

Some intellectuals and East Texas liberals also have misgivings concerning labor's role in the liberal alliance. Intellectual reservations result largely from the fear that labor will seek to dominate leadership posts rather than from any lack of sympathy for the labor movement. East Texans, however, are uneasy about unionism as such, particularly "big labor."

Texas liberals are gradually overcoming these differences over goals. But since 1960 their disagreements over tactics have been increasing. Many leaders of the old DOT are convinced that the way to win is to remain ideologically pure, to crystallize political attitudes, and to drive all conservatives into the waiting arms of the Republican Party. In 1960 Mrs. Randolph's supporters held fast for Adlai Stevenson and bitterly fought Johnson's bid for Texas support in his efforts to attain the Democratic presidential nomination. During the 1961 senatorial campaign the *Texas Observer* supported Republican John Tower against conservative Democrat William Blakley with the argument that a Tower victory would lead Texas conservatives to rally around the Republican banner and, thereby, leave the Democratic Party machinery in liberal hands. In a more restrained but not dissimilar manner, Mrs. Randolph advised "either a write-in vote for a good Democrat or go fishing."[19]

Other liberal leaders—top union officials, leaders of moderate-liberal alliances in Bexar and Nueces Counties, and moderate intellectuals—advocate compromise and formation of broader coalitions. In 1960 the latter contended that it was futile to fight Johnson, and that "tactical" cooperation with Johnson moderates might prevent conservative control of the state Democratic convention. And in 1961 they reluctantly supported Blakley so as not to destroy their ability to use a plea for "party loyalty" in subsequent campaigns. Today there is reason to doubt that state labor officials would support an antiunion conservative Democrat like Blakley, but they still advocate broad, rather than narrow, coalitions. For example, Hank Brown, president of the Texas AFL-CIO, recently stated:

I feel a tremendous need for a political coalition of small businessmen, small farmers, the Latins, the Negroes, labor, organized perhaps on a congressional district or even a county basis. Until we have such a state organization, based at the local level and working year round, we're constantly going to have close elections in which we still finish second.[20]

---

from two key precincts to the conservative side, liberals would have controlled the Travis County Democratic Conventions for the first time in many years.

[19] Based on Mrs. Randolph's May 16, 1961, letter to liberal precinct workers.

[20] "Labor's President Views the Future," *Texas Observer*, June 23, 1962.

In summary, the conservative-liberal battle in Texas is largely over economics. Conservatives oppose—in order of intensity—organized labor, concentration of power in the hands of the federal government, and government welfare spending. When the government is forced to spend, they are inclined to raise the necessary funds by a general sales tax. In contrast, liberals—in order of intensity—advocate government welfare aid, accept national government expansion, and sympathize with the aims of organized labor. On tax questions they endorse levies on natural resources and business, and, in some instances, favor progressive income taxes. Many liberals also wish to promote the cause of Negro and Latin American equality with other citizens, but they frequently disagree over the rate and manner of doing so.

Both camps suffer from internal dissension. Conservative businessmen have temporary disagreements over matters affecting their individual competitive status. Of late, some conservatives have also become concerned—at least tactically—about ultraconservative dogmatism and extremism. And, most important, they now have serious doubts as to whether it is wiser to remain Democratic or to turn Republican.

Liberals are faced with greater discord. It is difficult, for example, to prevent divisions over racial issues. Though most liberals are vocally sympathetic to the Negro cause, East Texas "economic liberals" are not so disposed. To complicate matters, Negro and Latin American leaders are impatient with what they feel is a liberal tendency to promise but not deliver. Despite obvious labor efforts to avoid being accused of "taking over," East Texas "Populists" and assorted intellectuals have expressed concern that this might occur. Tactically, the liberals are further divided over the question of whether to moderate their stand and form coalitions with middle-of-the-roaders sympathetic to Lyndon Johnson.

In essence, the conservatives are more philosophically cohesive than liberals in Texas. This solidarity, combined with the state's tradition of conservatism, gives them a distinct advantage. Yet another edge can be derived from Texas election laws, which provide the institutional setting for political action in the state and affect the power of competing political parties and factions.

INSTITUTIONAL SETTING

In the not too distant past one could have argued that, in some respects at least, the Texas election system actually discouraged political competition of an ideological nature. Today, however, electoral institutions are being increasingly colored by ideological factors. One example of this fact is the changing nature of statewide primary elections.

Texas law generally requires that primaries rather than conventions be used to nominate candidates for state and local offices—including the position of United States senator. The task of conventions is largely confined to choosing delegates to the party's national convention, naming members of its State Executive Committee, and selecting presidential electors.[21] The major exception is the provision that parties whose gubernatorial candidate in the preceding general election received less than 200,000 votes may, if they desire, nominate their candidates by the convention method. Accordingly, the Republican Party until quite recently always selected its candidates in conventions.

As Professor O. Douglas Weeks pointed out after the 1952 elections, this extensive reliance on the direct primary in Texas has operated historically to prevent fundamental splits in the party or to minimize them, at least with respect to state and local politics. Specifically, he noted the tendency for primary campaigns to revolve around the candidates' personalities rather than around well-defined issues. Ideological rifts, he found, had generally been confined to presidential elections and to state conventions, which, by their very nature, are tied to national candidates and their ideological positions.[22]

In the late 1950's however, this situation began to change, at first gradually and then with increasing rapidity. There has been a considerable increase in the number and the activities of issue-oriented groups, and a similar increase in the concern with candidates' stands on issues. For example, though a staggering number of candidates ran for the United States Senate in 1961, all but a few of the votes were distributed among the six candidates with the most definable positions ranging along the ideological spectrum from conservative to liberal. Furthermore, Attorney General Will Wilson, who avoided talking about ideological issues and relied heavily upon a friendship-oriented campaign organization, finished a surprising fourth. In essence, personality factors still prevail in local races—especially in rural counties—but statewide contests have been increasingly colored by ideological considerations.

The direct primary and general state campaigns are not the only parts of the institutional system being flavored by ideological contro-

---

[21] For a detailed description of Texas election laws see any of the standard college texts on Texas government, or Wilbourn E. Benton, "Suffrage and Elections," Arnold Foundation Monograph VII.

[22] O. Douglas Weeks, *Texas Presidential Politics in 1952*, p. 5.

versies. Election regulations governing the form of ballots, methods of marking ballots, and qualifications for voting have also been drawn into the conservative-liberal struggle. In particular, Republicans and liberal Democrats—the two groups at the extreme ends of the political spectrum—are both complaining that certain features of the Election Code are partial to their opponents.

On the surface, Texas laws put the Republicans at a slight disadvantage. In special elections for United States senators or representatives, for example, 1957 and 1961 amendments to the Election Code now require an absolute majority of votes cast in order to win. If no candidate receives a majority, then a runoff election confined to the two top candidates is required. Although the Republicans have benefited from the conflicts among Democrats seeking such offices, they have not been able to take full advantage of the situation because the necessity of a runoff in which at least one candidate will be a Democrat provides an opportunity and an incentive for the Democrats to close ranks. In other words, full utilization of a "divide and conquer" strategy is prevented by the shift from plurality to majority election, a fact of which the Democrats in the Legislature were only too aware when they rewrote the laws.

More directly, the combined impact of a party-column ballot and the inconvenience of voting a split ticket has cost the Republicans votes. When voting a straight party ticket on a paper ballot Texans need only to draw a line through the columns provided for every party other than the one they are voting for, or, when using voting machines, to throw a single lever for one entire party column. If they wish to split their ticket, however, they must go through the tedious task of crossing out the names of all candidates except the desired one for each of the many offices listed on the ballot; when using voting machines, persons splitting their ticket must flip the lever beside the name of the favored candidate for each office. Moreover, when paper ballots are used a failure to mark out the names of all candidates from minor parties (e.g., Prohibition Party) renders the vote for such offices invalid. Republican feelings on a ballot that facilitates straight-ticket voting are perhaps best illustrated by the exchange following a resounding Republican victory in Dallas County in 1962. The shocked Democrats complained publicly of the "irresponsible straight-ticket voting" behind the Republican successes, to which a local GOP leader replied that he would be willing to join the Democrats at once if they wanted to launch a crusade to remove the party-column lever from voting machines.

Legal barriers to Republicanism should not be exaggerated, for other provisions of the Election Code can be helpful to them. By law Texas primaries are "closed" to all except party members, but the statutory definition of party membership is quite broad: any qualified voter who has not already voted in another party's primary on that day (or, possibly, during the same poll-tax period, depending on how the law is construed). Similarly, a pledge required of each voter in a primary to support the party's nominees in the general election has repeatedly been held to be only a moral commitment unenforceable legally. Therefore, it is a simple matter for conservative Democrats (and, of late, a few liberals as well) to cross over after the primary and vote Republican in general elections without fear of subsequently losing their right to participate in Democratic Party functions.

Liberal Democrats as well as Republicans feel that they have cause to complain. As noted above, conservative Democrats can vote for one of their number in the Democratic primary and, if he fails, switch to a Republican in the general election, thereby squeezing out liberal candidates. The absence of ceilings on campaign expenditures places further burdens on the financially weak liberals. Moreover, incomplete and inaccurate *pre*-election reporting on such spending deprives them of potential campaign ammunition.[23]

A more serious deterrent, in the view of the liberals, is the use of a long ballot and—in the primary elections and in general elections when the straight ticket is not voted—the attached requirement that the voter express his preference by marking out the names of all other candidates. Less educated, low-income groups—who provide many of the liberal votes—are constantly in danger of having their ballots declared invalid because of stray pencil marks or failure to mark out the names of minor-party candidates (even well-educated persons can make slips, but the rate of incidence is no doubt lower). Negroes and Latin Americans are particularly vulnerable. And, the vagaries characteristic of a long ballot provide a prejudiced election judge with ample excuse to invalidate their ballots if they are cast.

[23] Texas law designates certain unlawful expenditures and now holds both the campaign manager and the candidate responsible for violations. Direct contributions from labor unions and business corporations are forbidden, but this stipulation does not prevent individual, voluntary contributions from businessmen and laborers.

Preliminary campaign-expense reports must be filed seven days prior to the election, but final reports need not be in until after the election. Candidates often declare minimum expenses in the first report and wait until the final report to give a complete accounting. Hence, publicity concerning spending is too late to affect voter choices. Even then the reports are apt to understate the total amounts expended on behalf of the candidate, sometimes by tremendous margins. See the section entitled "Money in Texas Politics" by Clifton McCleskey, *The Government and Politics of Texas*, pp. 59–67.

The difficulty of assessing the overall impact of the legal and institutional arrangements for Texas elections is illustrated by the increasing pressure put on conservative Democrats by one provision of the Election Code: representation at county and state party conventions is in proportion to the vote in the respective counties and precincts for the party's gubernatorial nominee in the last general election. Since conservative Democrats are most likely to shift and vote for the Republican gubernatorial candidate in the general election, they penalize themselves each time they do so, insofar as representation in Democratic conventions is concerned.

Thus, each party or faction can point to some feature of the electoral system and complain of its injurious effects. Except in close elections, these features are unlikely to have decisive significance, although they may have some long-range consequences for the growth and stability of the organization. A glaring exception to this generalization is the requirement that the poll tax must be paid before qualifying to vote, for its impact is directed mostly against liberal Democrats, and it has fairly immediate and important consequences.

As of 1962 Texas was one of five states retaining the poll tax. Though the poll tax functions partially as a means of registering voters, Texas lacks a system of general registration.[24] Citizens pay their $1.75 poll tax[25] from October through January and are thereafter entitled to vote during the twelve-month period following the January 31 deadline for its purchase. Persons who are sixty or more years of age are exempt from paying;[26] in fact, in cities of less than 10,000 population they need not obtain an exemption certificate. (They simply show up and vote on oral affidavit, the theory being that since small-town officials will know the voters, registration would be superfluous.)

Under such circumstances, it is virtually impossible to make a full count of the state's voters. The 1959 and 1961 reports of the United States Civil Rights Commission provide the best estimates to date, but they too are incomplete and inaccurate.[27]

[24] Fagan Dickson, "The Texas Poll Tax," *Texas Bar Journal*, XI (1948), 1–12.

[25] The state levies a fee of $1.50. Counties may and normally do charge an additional $0.25. Cities may assess an added fee of $1.00 but seldom do.

[26] A few lesser categories are also exceptions but the over-sixty group is by far the most significant.

[27] The 1959 *Report of the United States Commission on Civil Rights* (hereinafter referred to as *Civil Rights Report*) contained the count for 165 counties (provided by the Long News Service in Austin) and estimates for the remainder of Texas' 254 counties. The 1961 *Civil Rights Report* covered 213 counties, but relied heavily upon information mailed by county officials. In some cases, the counts reported were of such a nature that more than 100 per cent of the Negroes who were of voting age were reported as having poll taxes. The *Texas Almanac* published by the *Dallas Morning News* also lists poll-tax receipts by county.

It is difficult to point to any single motive for establishment of the poll tax in Texas. The first such tax under the present Constitution was levied in 1877. However, it was not until 1902, twenty-six years after Reconstruction, that payment of the tax was made a prerequisite for voting. This lapse of years before this provision was enforced suggests that the move was directed as much against poor-white Populists as Negroes.[28] As a practical matter, the poll tax has also interfered with the political participation of Mexican-Americans. But, whatever its true origins, it has served—in the past at least—to reduce voting by members of three groups of citizens who are potential sources of liberal strength.

It is generally agreed that the poll tax cuts down participation by persons in the lower economic brackets—white persons of the working class or poor farmers, as well as most Negroes and Latin Americans. Exactly how much it cuts their participation is much harder to agree upon. County tax assessor-collectors seldom make official computations of qualified voters according to race or ethnic background. Educated guesses backed by scattered precinct figures indicate less than average participation in many Negro and Latin American districts. However, this thesis is much truer of these groups in rural than urban areas. In San Antonio, for example, 1961 and 1962 estimates indicate that many Latin precincts had a higher percentage of poll-tax payments than some moderate-income white districts. Furthermore, spurred on by their drive for civil rights and greater community recognition, Negro and Latin American leaders are beginning to organize with much greater vigor. It is by no means clear, even when participation by low-income whites and minority groups lags significantly, to what extent this is the result of the poll tax and to what extent it is the result of other forces. Even in states where the poll tax is not used participation by such groups tends to be smaller than that of high-income groups. And despite the fact that most criticism of the poll tax has been centered upon the deterrent effect of the sum involved, it seems highly probable that some of its impact stems from the January 31 deadline for poll-tax payment— long before the primaries and elections get under way. In other words, the Texans whose interest is stirred only after the campaign has begun

[28] Donald S. Strong, "The Poll Tax: The Case of Texas," *American Political Science Review*, XXXVIII (August, 1944), 693–695.

Arthur Dewitty, Secretary of the Travis County Voters League (chief Negro political organization in Austin) asserted that some Negroes buy the poll tax to display as a prestige sign, but they don't know how to vote and are embarrassed to ask. Therefore, the operation of voting clinics or workshops is high on the priority list of minority political organizations.

are too late to be placed upon the election rolls. The votes of many good, but unwary, citizens are often lost merely because they innocently "forgot" or were "too busy" to make the premature deadline.

On balance, it would appear that liberal Democrats are hurt more than Republicans by the nature of Texas election laws. Of course, the margin of disadvantage has been appreciably decreased by organizational activities—particularly among city minorities. Actually, social and economic changes and conflicts are likely to be more basic as determinants of electoral behavior. Consequently, it is with these latter factors that we will be primarily concerned in the pages to follow.

II

THE REPUBLICAN PARTY BEFORE 1962

After almost a century of political failure, the Texas GOP has made impressive gains in the past decade. "Presidential Republicanism" stemming from conservative opposition to the New Deal-Fair Deal policies of the national Democratic Party, bitter dissension within the Texas Democratic Party, recent social and economic changes conducive to Republican growth, and the streamlining of the GOP campaign organization have helped the Republicans reach a position from which they can now challenge the Democrats in presidential, congressional, and gubernatorial elections.

In terms of total elective offices throughout the state the present number of Republican officeholders is still quite small. Nevertheless, the following analysis of historical trends (ranging from the Reconstruction era to the 1960's) and the examination of the social and economic bases of Republican support in recent elections illustrate the Party's partial triumph over past adversities. Moreover, if Republicans adjust certain of their policies in the decade to follow, they should continue to improve their political fortunes in Texas.

HISTORICAL PERSPECTIVE

In a century of campaigning the Texas GOP has won the governorship but once (in 1869 under conditions which were such that a mere 380 Democratic votes were tallied)[1] and has polled a majority for president on only four occasions (1872, 1928, 1952, and 1956). The showing in congressional contests is equally disillusioning. Since the end of Reconstruction Texas Republicans have served no more than

[1] It might be argued that J. W. Throckmorton's election as governor in 1866 was also a Republican victory. However, the nature of his support, the chaos at the end of the Civil War, and the supervisory role of the Union Army during his tenure warrant omission of his name from the list of Republican officeholders.

fourteen full terms in the United States House of Representatives.[2] In the Senate they were totally absent from 1877 until 1961, when John Tower managed to win the seat vacated by Vice President-elect Lyndon Johnson.

During the Reconstruction sizable numbers of Republicans sat in both chambers of the State Legislature (available records do not make possible an exact count). Although not all Republicans were eliminated at once, GOP membership began to decline steadily at the end of the Reconstruction and continued to do so through the remainder of the nineteenth century. In the first quarter of the twentieth century the Party had only token representation. A single Republican was present in the Senate sessions of 1905, 1911, 1913, 1925, and 1927. Two GOP representatives served in the 1905 and 1909 House meetings; only one was there in 1903, 1911, 1913, 1915, and from 1919 to 1927. Thus from 1903 to 1927 Republicans never occupied more than one place in the Senate or more than two in the House during any given legislative session. There were no Republicans in either chamber of the State Legislature from 1927 to 1951, when a lone member of the Party from Dallas served a single term in the House of Representatives. Another decade of absence from the Capitol followed, until special elections in Potter and Galveston Counties to fill vacancies in the House of Representatives brought two Republican victories. Neither was able to retain his seat in the 1962 general elections, but seven other Republicans (six from Dallas County, one from Midland County) did capture seats in the lower chamber. Finally, in 1963 the Republican total in the House was raised to ten when GOP nominees won special elections in Corpus Christi and Dallas. Heartening as this is to the Party, the fact remains that it gives the Republicans only 6.7 per cent of the House seats and still leaves them totally without representation in the more powerful Senate.

Behind this history of frustration was the legacy of the Civil War; namely, the Republican Party came to Texas under circumstances that stamped it as the party of Unionist sentiment, military government, and Carpetbag rule. Under Reconstruction policies Republicans

[2] For the 1895–1897 term George Noonan served the San Antonio district; Robert Hawley of Galveston was elected for the two terms from 1897 to 1901. Harry Worzbach of San Antonio served from 1921 until his death early in his sixth term. In February, 1950, Ben Guill won a special election in the Panhandle district, serving until the term expired in January, 1951. Republican Bruce Alger of Dallas completes his fifth term in 1964. The 1962 election victory of Ed Foreman from Ector County brings the Republican total to fourteen full terms. These and other historical details were kindly supplied by Stephen Jones, former research director for the Republican Party of Texas.

briefly dominated legislative and executive positions, but their control was broken by the Democrats in the state elections of 1873. Thereafter, the Texas GOP wallowed in political misery. Its chief bloc of support—the Negro—was systematically disenfranchised; the Southern equivalent of the "bloody shirt" was waved with telling effect; the temporary but long-remembered Negro control of the Party alienated potential supporters;[3] and, on occasion, new political movements even threatened to usurp its claim as the "second" party.[4] As in most Southern states the Republican Party degenerated into a patronage-dispensing organization more concerned with intraparty rivalries than with winning elections. Grass-roots support all but disappeared, and the number of candidates offered steadily declined, as did the number of votes they received.[5]

Degeneration took only a few years, but several decades elapsed before revival was possible. Indeed, appreciable and lasting rejuvenation of the Texas GOP did not take place until the 1950's, when the effects of the mutations which had been gradually taking place in the body politic became clearly visible.

At an early stage of their development V. O. Key attributed these changes to the emergence of a new breed of political animal:

Indigenous to the South is a strange political schizophrenic, the Presidential Republican. He votes in Democratic primaries to have a voice in state and local matters, but when the Presidential election rolls around, he casts a ballot for the Republican presidential nominee. Locally he is a Democrat; nationally, a Republican.[6]

The 1928 presidential election might be taken as an example of this phenomenon in Texas since the Republican presidential candidate obtained 51.8 per cent of the popular vote while the Party's gubernatorial nominee garnered only 17.4 per cent. Several good reasons can be mustered, however, for hesitating to say that the 1928 election fits

[3] Although the failure of Norris Gurney and his fellow Negroes to support McKinley in the Party's presidential nominating convention of 1896 was the beginning of their end as Republican Party leaders in Texas, it was not until 1900 that the so-called "Lily-Whites" managed to wrest control of the Party from its Negro leadership.

[4] The People's Party in the 1890's and the Socialist Party in the pre-World War I days were especially successful in bids for ranking as the second party in Texas. In several elections their candidates outpolled the GOP nominees.

[5] This brief historical survey draws upon materials presented in H. E. Budd, "The Negro in Texas Politics, 1867–1898" (unpublished M.A. thesis); V. O. Key, Jr., *Southern Politics in State and Nation*; Office of the Chief Clerk, Texas House of Representatives, *Members of the Legislature of Texas from 1846–1939*; William R. Sanford, "History of the Republican Party of Texas" (unpublished M.A. thesis); *Texas Almanac*; O. D. Weeks, *Texas Presidential Politics in 1952*.

[6] Key, *Southern Politics*, p. 278.

Key's description (e.g., the injection of religious issues into the campaign). Rather, it would seem that, in Texas, "presidential Republicans" have been produced largely by the changes wrought by the New Deal. This is not the place to review the details of the state's conservative revolt against the national Democratic Party and the Roosevelt and Truman administrations; suffice it to say that a large, influential segment of the conservative camp carefully cultivated a distinction between state and national Democratic parties, with the implicit understanding that they could not care less what happened to the *national* Democratic Party as long as it retained its New Deal-Fair Deal flavor.

During the postwar era, therefore, the Texas GOP's greatest opportunity has arisen out of the bitter divisions within Democratic ranks. Related to this dissension is the presence of several social and economic conditions that are conducive to Republican growth. Among them are the social dislocations and psychological tensions that inevitably accompany transition from agrarian to industrial society, the weakness of organized labor, the growing size and influence of middle-class white-collar groups, and the heavy influx of young managerial, professional, and technical people from Republican states. Moreover, all these transitions are taking place within the context of rapid urbanization. In the presence of such tradition-shattering changes it is not at all surprising that the one-party mold should also be cracked.

Yet, it should not be inferred that the Republicans have only to hold up the political basket in order to have the ripened fruit of socio-economic change drop into it automatically. To capitalize on these opportunities they have been compelled to overhaul their party organization. Some observers mark the year 1948 as the turning point for organizational change, for in that year Republican Jack Porter capitalized on the dissatisfaction of some Democrats with the results of the Democratic senatorial primary (won by Lyndon Johnson by a margin of eighty-seven votes, under conditions which made charges of fraud and corruption inevitable and unending) to make a better than usual GOP showing. In the opinion of one observer this election provided Porter a springboard for the launching of the 1952 revolt against the Old Guard Republicans.[7] It is more likely, however, that 1952 was the true turning point, when thousands of Democrats crusaded for Eisenhower and invaded Republican precinct conventions to swamp old Party regulars who generally endorsed Senator Robert Taft.[8] The "new" Republican did not rest on his laurels, but continued to work—though somewhat

[7] See Allen Duckworth's article in the *Dallas Morning News*, June 18, 1961.
[8] The 1952 story can be followed in O. Douglas Weeks, *Texas Presidential Politics in 1952.*

sporadically—to build a younger and stronger party machinery. Particularly in the large metropolitan areas these labors have produced grass-roots organizations of unsurpassed zeal and, on occasion, great effectiveness. The Party's improved chances of victory are in no small measure traceable to this better organization.

Of course, organizational reforms would be of little avail unless the voters could be persuaded to break the habits binding them to the Democratic Party. Republican efforts to do so have been directed almost entirely at the conservative Democrats. GOP candidates are often billed simply as "conservatives" with their party affiliation unmentioned; all their campaign speeches echo conservative refrains. Thus, in recent years the Republican Party in Texas has hoisted high the banners of the "Old Guard," now led by Senator Barry Goldwater of Arizona, thereby all but trampling those of "Modern Republicanism" in the dirt; this development is not without its irony since the original architects of Republican revival in Texas were apostles of Eisenhower Republicanism who snatched control of the Party away from the Taft Old Guard in the early 1950's. In essence, conservative Democrats appear to be the most likely source of Republican votes and conservatism seems to be the magic word in Texas of today; so the GOP tunes its campaigns to that frequency. While the Republican Party in Texas—and nationally as well—is more conservative than the national Democratic Party, it is doubtful that the center of gravity is as far right as depicted. At present, clarification along such lines is not deemed expedient and so the GOP continues to court the conservative Democratic vote. Nevertheless, one cannot avoid wondering what would happen to this alliance of convenience if someone like Governor Rockefeller should be nominated as the Republican presidential candidate.

The extent to which this quest for Democratic support has borne fruit can only be judged by careful examination of the ledger. On the credit side, the GOP has in presidential elections the victories of 1952 and 1956 and the near-miss of 1960, and in United States Senate contests it has the triumph in 1961. Furthermore, on five consecutive occasions Republican Bruce Alger has won the right to represent the Fifth Congressional District (Dallas) in the House of Representatives, and in 1963 he was joined by newly elected Ed Foreman from Odessa in the Sixteenth Congressional District. Four other congressional seats seem also to be within reach of the GOP: the Twenty-Second District (Southern Harris County), the Twentieth (Bexar County), the Eighteenth (Panhandle), and the Third (East Texas). A near-miss in 1960 contests for the State Legislature encouraged Dallas Republicans to try again in 1962, with the previously mentioned result that six representatives were elected to the Texas House from that county. At the same time Midland added a seventh representative, and 1963 special elections brought one from Corpus and two others from Dallas. In Dallas County a Republican won the key local office of county commissioner in 1960, and in the 1962 elections another Republican captured a place on the County Court at Law. Finally, as a result of election victories in 1962, other Republicans hold the following elective offices: county judges in Kerr, Midland, and Harrison Counties; county commissioners in Pecos, Hutchinson, Ector, Zavala, Kenedy, Starr, and Randall Counties; four justices of the peace, two of them in Bexar County and the others in Kenedy and Starr Counties; two constables, one in Brewster and the other in Potter County; one county superintendent of schools in El Paso County; one district attorney in Smith County; and two county attorneys, one in Kerr and the other in Kendall County.[9]

Nevertheless, a quick review of overall election returns is a reminder that Texas Republicans still have a way to go before they constitute a consistent top-to-bottom threat to the state's Democratic Party. As cited earlier, Democratic precinct and county leaders of conservative persuasion often do not discourage voting for Republican presidential and senatorial candidates in their bailiwicks, but they do work to keep up the Democratic vote for governor in order to retain their delegate strength in Democratic conventions. This factor operates to keep the GOP percentage of the vote lower in gubernatorial than in presidential and senatorial elections. Table 2, for example, reveals this obvious lag in the Republican vote for governor, and less markedly in United States Senate elections. In the 1961 Senate runoff the Republicans finally emerged victorious, but this triumph was with a voter turnout only one-third that of the 1960 presidential election, and came only after a first heat in which five Democratic candidates made a shambles of their party's unity. Had the parties nominated candidates in the usual manner, and had the respective winners then been identified by party affiliation on the special election ballot, it is unlikely that Republican Tower would have been elected. Though there is no denying the Republican showing in presidential and a few congressional, state legislative, and local government contests, the fact remains that these victories involve only a fraction of the total number of offices held by Democrats. As of 1961 the fairest assessment of the situation was the following made by Allen Duckworth, the perceptive political editor of

9 Memorandum distributed by Republican state headquarters dated January 28, 1963.

TABLE 2

Votes Cast for Republican Party Candidates in Texas, 1920–1962

Year	Presidential Vote Total (Thousands)	Presidential Vote Repub. % of Total	Senatorial Vote Total (Thousands)	Senatorial Vote Repub. % of Total	Gubernatorial Vote Total (Thousands)	Gubernatorial Vote Repub. % of Total
1920	486	23.7			482[c]	24.1
1922			395	33.1	408	18.0
1924	656[a]	19.8	693	14.6	718	41.1
1926					265	11.9
1928	708	51.8	689	18.8	706	17.5
1930			304	12.8	315	19.7
1932	856	11.4			847	37.5
1934			452	2.8	442	3.2
1936	850	12.1	834	7.1	841	7.0
1938					370	3.0
1940	1,117	18.9	1,037	6.1	1,079	5.5
1942			272	4.4	290	3.2
1944	1,144	16.7			1,108	9.0
1946			381	11.5	379	8.8
1948	1,147[b]	24.5	1,166	32.7	1,202	14.8
1950					395	10.1
1952	2,076	53.1	1,895	24.8	......[d]	
1954			633	14.9	636	10.4
1956	1,955	55.3			1,722	15.2
1958			787	23.6	790	11.8
1960	2,290	48.9	2,254	41.1	2,238	27.2
1961[e]			886	50.6		
1962					1,569	45.8

Sources: Totals in presidential elections are from the U.S. Bureau of the Census, *Historical Statistics of the United States from Colonial Times to 1957*, except for 1960, when an official release of the Texas Secretary of State was used. The senatorial and gubernatorial totals are from Heard and Strong, *Southern Primaries and Elections, 1920–1949*, with those for post-1949 years coming from the *Texas Almanac*. Unless otherwise indicated, the totals shown are the two-party totals, and the percentages are based on them.

[a] Includes 43,000 Progressive Party votes.

[b] Includes 107,000 States' Rights votes.

[c] Includes 6,796 Socialist and 69,380 American Party votes. Republican percentage includes both the regular (90,217) and Black-and-Tan (26,091) tallies.

[d] The Republican Party did not have its own gubernatorial nominee in 1952, but instead cross-filed Allan Shivers, the Democratic nominee for the office.

[e] Figures reported here are for the runoff between Republican John Tower and conservative Democrat William Blakley.

the *Dallas Morning News*: "The Republicans of Texas are a long, long way from conquering the state, but they have established a small beachhead."[10]

[10] *Dallas Morning News*, June 18, 1961.

It is with this Republican "beachhead"—its location and the conditions that made it possible—that we will concern ourselves in the succeeding pages. By investigating the geographic dispersal and the social-economic sources of GOP support, we hope to contribute to an understanding of the Republican Party's past gains and future prospects in state as well as in national elections.

LOCATION OF REPUBLICAN COUNTIES

The first step in analyzing Republicanism in Texas is to identify the hard core of support which can be counted on in the most trying days. For this task the returns of the last three presidential elections are not completely reliable, involving as they do unusual factors of personality (Eisenhower in 1952, 1956) and religion (Kennedy in 1960). On the other hand, until 1962, Republicans generally avoided putting much money or effort in gubernatorial campaigns. It appears, therefore, that bedrock Republicanism can best be studied by analyzing the two special United States Senate contests of 1957 and 1961 respectively— elections, it might be added, that still have pitfalls for the unwary analyst. With a low voter turnout in each case—due largely to the out-of-season date—and with a wide range of viewpoints represented by the numerous Democratic candidates, it seems clear that the votes cast for the Republican nominees in these two elections could have come only from loyal adherents.

In 1957 more than twenty candidates tried to fill the vacancy created when Price Daniel left the United States Senate to take over as Texas governor, but the three principal protagonists were (1) Ralph Yarborough, liberal Democrat and the eventual victor with a plurality of 38 per cent of the total vote; (2) Martin Dies, conservative Democrat who attracted 30 per cent of the ballots; and (3) Thad Hutcheson, Republican who finished third with 23 per cent of the total. In 1961 more than seventy hopefuls paid the nominal $50 filing fee which entitled them to a place on the ballot, but the contest was actually between six contenders who finally collected 96.14 per cent of the votes cast: (1) John Tower, conservative Republican who garnered 30.93 per cent of the total vote; (2) William Blakley, interim appointee and conservative Democrat who finished second with 18.03 per cent; (3) Jim Wright, moderate-liberal Democratic congressman who captured 16.9 per cent of the votes; (4) Will Wilson, incumbent attorney general and moderate-conservative Democrat, who received 11.53 per cent; (5) Maury Maverick, Jr., liberal Democrat who tallied 9.52 per cent; and (6) Henry Gonzalez, liberal Democrat and state senator with a special appeal to Latin American voters, who finished sixth with 9.23 per cent of the ballots. Subsequently, Tower won the Senate seat in a runoff with Blakley, but the first-round vote is more useful here because it represents a wider range of choice for the voters. Under such conditions only confirmed Republicans could have voted for Tower.

Our first concern is with the geographical distribution of the votes amassed by Hutcheson and Tower in these two senatorial elections. For easier analysis the state's 254 counties were ranked from high to low according to the percentage of the total vote given to the Republican candidate in each of these elections. Each of the arrays thus obtained was then divided into four equal parts or quarters. Such "quartiles" provide distinctions of general significance that are, at the same time, sufficiently limited in number to permit rapid comparison.[11] It must be emphasized, however, that the results do not necessarily reflect the absolute level of the Republican vote. They simply represent the counties in which the Republicans made their best showing, even though in some of these counties the GOP candidates actually received less than a majority of the ballots cast.

In 1957 counties in the highest quarter of the vote for Republican Hutcheson provided him with 24.4 per cent or more of their support, while in 1961 the first-quartile counties gave Tower 35.8 per cent or more of their votes. Comparison of the top quartiles in each of these years reveals 39 counties which were so ranked in *both* elections. This observation alone would justify classifying them as the most Republican counties in the state, but, as it happens, this judgment is reinforced by their records in other elections. No less than 20 of these 39 counties were in the first-quarter Republican vote in all four postwar presidential races; another 13 were so ranked in three of the four contests; 5 more were in that category in two such elections; and one was there in a single instance. Hence, every one of the 39 counties ranked at least once in the first quartile of the Republican presidential vote and, of those counties that occasionally failed to make the first quarter, only one (Galveston) ever dropped below the second quarter of the Republican tally. Moreover, all but 9 of the 39 were in the first quartile of the Republican vote in the 1962 gubernatorial race.

These 39 hard-core Republican counties are shown in Figure A. Closer inspection reveals two distinct clusters: the first in the Panhandle and the second in a broader area of western and southern Texas below a diagonal line drawn between the northeast corner of Midland

[11] For the sake of greater convenience the percentage breakdowns for each of the four quarters of the Party votes in each election have been divided and assembled in Appendix A.

County and the northeast corner of Harris County. Within the latter area a Republican concentration appears in the Hill Country-Edwards Plateau section northwest of Bexar County, with a much looser aggregation along the Coastal Plain of South Texas. With one exception, therefore, the 39 most Republican counties are located in two noncontiguous parts of the state containing less than half of its counties. By contrast, within the broad belt stretching from East Texas through Central Texas to the West Texas Plains—containing over half of Texas' counties—only Dallas County has a place in the Republican first quartile for both the 1957 and 1961 elections.

The suspicions aroused by such clusters are confirmed when one adds other counties which were in the first quarter of the Republican vote in *either* of the two Senate elections. Twenty-three such additional counties were in the Republican first quartile in 1957, but failed to maintain this standing in 1961. Of these 23, 8 were in the Republican first quarter in three of the four presidential elections, only 5 had not been so ranked at least once, and none of them had failed to appear in the Republican first or second quarter at least once in the four races. Even in their 1961 fall-off more than half of the 23 could still be found in the Republican second quartile. Moreover, this decline in 1961 was often the result of a draining off of otherwise Republican votes to Henry Gonzalez, favorite of the Latin Americans, and to Will Wilson, who has long had close personal ties with a number of South-Southwest Texas politicians. In Figure A, for example, 22 of the 23 were below our NW-SE line in the general area of greatest Mexican-American population. (The Republican drop in the remaining North Texas county of Parker was probably due to the candidacy of its well-regarded native son, Democratic Congressman Jim Wright.)

The 25 counties which were ranked in the Republican first quarter in 1961 but not in 1957 are of even greater interest because they indicate that things may be looking up for the GOP in some areas where it has heretofore found the going rough.[12] This is not to say that the 1961 results were a radical departure from the past; all but 8 of these counties were ranked in the Republican second quarter in 1957 and in presidential elections they often registered in the top half of the Republican tally (not one failed to appear at least once in either the first or second quarter of that vote, although 7 were not in the first quarter in any of the four presidential contests). The 1961 results do suggest,

[12] Not too much significance should be attached to the presence of Wichita County in the 1961 Republican first quarter, inasmuch as Republican candidate John Tower had resided there for several years in his capacity as an instructor at Midwestern University.

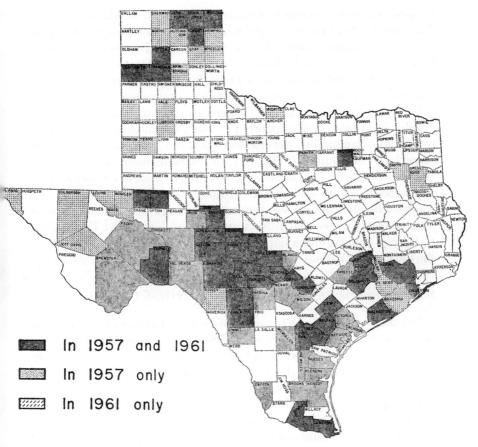

In 1957 and 1961

In 1957 only

In 1961 only

Figure A. First-quartile Republican counties in Texas:
1957 and 1961 senatorial elections.

however, that the political map of Texas is slowly being redrawn. Such a judgment is not based on the geographic distribution of these 25 counties; 17 are located in areas where Republican strength has been observed previously. Rather, it is derived from the fact that 5 of the remaining one-third are situated in the South Plains around Lubbock, while 2 are found in the heart of East Texas.

The trend in the South Plains, involving some of the area's most populous counties, is not without significance. But more arresting are the developments involving the two East Texas counties. To those who were unaware of the changes of political interest occurring in certain East Texas communities, it must have come as a shock that a leading conservative Democrat (William Blakley)—who proudly associated himself with such Southern Senators as Eastland of Mississippi and Thurmond of South Carolina and who ran with the warm endorsement of the White Citizens Council—was defeated by a Republican in Smith County (2½ to 1) and in Rusk County (almost 1½ to 1). Smith and Rusk are by no means all of East Texas, but they do exemplify what is happening in portions of a once solidly Democratic area.

In short, the following observations can be made about the geographic location of GOP support: (1) The Republican appeal is greatest in the Panhandle and western-southern portions of the state (especially in Southwest Texas); (2) outside these areas there is sizable strength in the Dallas-Fort Worth area and, to a lesser extent, in the South Plains and the Smith-Rusk oasis of East Texas; (3) in contrast, Republicans are weakest in the Rolling Plains of West Central Texas, scattered counties in Northwest Texas, lower East Texas, Central Texas proper, and a handful of counties on the westward side of the Rio Grande Plain.

Socio-Economic Characteristics of Republican Counties

Beyond a doubt, the geographic areas of Republican concentration can be located. More important, however, are the reasons why they are so disposed. Although not all the areas delineated lend themselves to a general discussion of the sources of Republican strength, two of them do.

One of these geographical areas is the Panhandle, the twenty northernmost counties of the state. Inasmuch as this area is part of the celebrated Great Plains stretching north all the way into Canada, it is hardly surprising that Panhandle counties are primarily agricultural, with emphasis on cattle raising and large-scale farming, principally dry-land cultivation of wheat and sorghums, but with increasing growth in importance of irrigated crops as well. The percentages of urban, nonfarm rural, and farm rural population vary from county to county, but sixteen of the twenty counties involved had no cities with as many as 10,000 population in 1950, and, of the remaining four, only Potter (Amarillo) had a city with 100,000 or more people.

For such a heavily rural region Panhandle residents have surprisingly high levels of income. In 1950 several counties were well above the median family income for the state as a whole, and only three were below it. The character and scale of agricultural production is an important part of the explanation, but it should also be remembered that a number of these counties have natural gas and/or oil production, a few in impressive quantities.

Significantly the Panhandle has been geographically isolated from the main currents of Texas history and culture. Physically, Panhandle voters are much closer to staunch Republicans in Kansas and northern Oklahoma. Spiritually also they have an affinity with these northern neighbors—an affinity stemming from close cultural as well as economic and topographic similarities. (Detailed evidence is not at hand, but there is good reason to believe that a substantial part of the Texas Panhandle was originally settled by people from the Middle West rather than other regions in Texas or the South.)[13] Specifically, these counties are overwhelmingly white, Anglo-Saxon, and Protestant ("WASP"). While the Republican Party has no monopoly on the support of this group, it often receives a disproportionate share of such a vote.[14]

Whatever the positive motivations of the WASP, the predominance of this group in the Panhandle is a negative force of some importance. Without a "minorities" problem (the area has only a tiny percentage of Latin Americans and even fewer Negroes) and without a Confederate heritage, Panhandle citizens are less firmly tied to the Democratic tradition than are those from other parts of Texas, and can respond more readily to a Republican program. Their traumatic experiences have been dust storms and droughts, not the Civil War and Reconstruction. Thus, the residents of the Panhandle have less built-in resistance to the tug in the direction of Republicanism.

The economic status of the region is probably the biggest factor pulling it toward Republican conservatism. While the political significance of economic forces has long been appreciated, the nexus is not always easy to perceive because of shortcomings of our techniques and the presence of other noneconomic influences. However, in the case at hand, there is a correlation between certain economic characteristics and the voting record which is too strong to be coincidental or explained away by other factors.

If one examines the average percentages presented in Table 3 (of course, they must be used cautiously), it will be discovered that the 5

[13] A similar influence in the more Republican counties of northern Oklahoma has been noted by V. O. Key, Jr., *American State Politics: An Introduction*, pp. 220–222.

[14] Thus, Eisenhower in 1956 won 64 per cent of the Protestant vote; Nixon in 1960 won 63 per cent. Phillip E. Converse *et al.*, "Stability and Change in 1960: A Reinstating Election," *American Political Science Review*, LV (June, 1961), 272. The preference of Protestants outside the South for the Republican Party is, of course, much stronger than these 1956 figures indicate, because a considerable part of the remaining 36 per cent of the Protestant vote is located in the Democratic South. The article just cited does an excellent job of evaluating the impact of the religious issue in the 1960 presidential election.

Panhandle counties with the lowest Republican averages are Armstrong, Collingsworth, Donley, Hartley, and Wheeler. In 1950 the percentages of the population earning over $5,000 annually in 4 of these counties (no figures were available for Hartley) were the lowest

TABLE 3

Republican Voting in the Texas Panhandle, 1948–1961

County	Republican Percentages of Total Vote and Quartile Rank[a]						Average Republican Vote (% of Total) Six
	1948	1952	1956	1957	1960	1961	Elections
	%QR	%QR	%QR	%QR	%QR	%QR	%
Armstrong	12(4)	57(2)	47(3)	11(4)	55(1)	38(1)	37
Carson	24(2)	58(2)	52(2)	20(2)	58(1)	29(2)	40
Collingsworth	10(4)	50(3)	40(4)	10(4)	61(1)	29(2)	34
Dallam	21(2)	55(2)	49(3)	21(2)	53(1)	33(2)	39
Deaf Smith	26(1)	71(1)	55(2)	26(1)	61(1)	42(1)	47
Donley	14(3)	55(2)	48(3)	16(3)	55(1)	31(2)	36
Gray	27(1)	62(1)	62(1)	24(2)	69(1)	56(1)	50
Hansford	18(2)	73(1)	63(1)	25(1)	72(1)	59(1)	52
Hartley	15(3)	54(2)	44(3)	19(2)	51(2)	34(2)	36
Hemphill	17(2)	60(1)	61(1)	19(2)	72(1)	49(1)	46
Hutchinson	23(2)	51(3)	55(2)	23(2)	66(1)	46(1)	44
Lipscomb	34(1)	85(1)	70(1)	33(1)	78(1)	58(1)	60
Moore	15(3)	47(3)	45(3)	20(2)	61(1)	41(1)	38
Ochiltree	25( )	80(1)	70(1)	24(1)	78(1)	67(1)	57
Oldham	22(2)	55(2)	49(3)	22(2)	49(2)	28(2)	38
Potter	29(1)	62(1)	58(2)	25(1)	61(1)	42(1)	44
Randall	27( )	69(1)	62(1)	29(1)	68(1)	47(1)	50
Roberts	18(2)	81(1)	70(1)	31(1)	76(1)	54(1)	55
Sherman	17(2)	68(1)	56(2)	15(3)	69(1)	50(1)	46
Wheeler	15(3)	51(3)	48(3)	16(3)	58(1)	36(1)	37

Sources: Percentages calculated from election statistics as reported in the *Texas Almanac*, except those for Ochiltree and Randall Counties in 1948, which were taken from Heard and Strong, *Southern Primaries and Elections, 1920–1949*, pp. 186–189. Since no official returns were made for these counties and for several others not in this group (the source just cited relied on unofficial materials), they were not ranked for quartiling purposes.

[a] All data are for presidential elections, except those for 1957 and 1961, which are for special Senate elections held those years (the preliminary rather than the runoff contest was used for 1961). Percentages in the presidential elections are based on the two-party total except for 1948, when the "States' Rights" vote was included.

of all the Panhandle counties (their range was 12–16 per cent). In contrast, the other 15 counties had much higher percentages earning over $5,000 (ranging from 20–43 per cent). Similar differences emerge from a comparison of median family income in 1950. The per-annum amounts ranged from $2,200 to $2,500 in the 4 *least* Republican counties, while they varied from $2,800 to $4,100 in the *more* Republican counties (9 of the 15 had median incomes of $3,500 or more).[15]

To some extent these income differentials are rooted in petroleum geology (some of the more Republican counties are better endowed than the less Republican ones). In large part, however, they are a result of topography. Four of the five less Republican counties (Hartley excepted) are in the southeastern portion of the Panhandle and, thereby, wholly or partially on the Rolling Plains below the "Cap Rock" (edge of Great Plains). Like the Great Plains, the Rolling Plains area has an agricultural economy, but its terrain and soils make for a much smaller scale of operations. Of course, farm or ranch size by itself is not an entirely reliable index. One needs to know also whether the land is devoted to ranching, dry farming, or irrigated cultivation; one hundred acres of irrigated land in Deaf Smith may be worth one thousand or more acres of ranchland in Armstrong County. But it is of some interest that the county with the poorest Republican showing (Collingsworth) is also the county with the smallest average farm size (550 acres), and that three of the least Republican counties have the lowest average farm sizes in the Panhandle.

More significant is the fact that the three least Republican counties derive most of their income from crops rather than livestock and livestock products; whereas, in the three most Republican counties, livestock production plays a much bigger role. Of course, this pattern varies somewhat when one contrasts intermediate ranges of partisanship rather than just the extremes; hence, it must not be urged too strenuously.[16]

The observation that political variations do not entirely parallel

[15] For the state as a whole, the 1950 Census reported 17.2 per cent earning over $5,000 annually; median income was $2,680. The 1960 Census reported 48.7 per cent of all families earned over $5,000 annually; the median income for families in the state was $4,884. Because the 1960 figures are reported by the Census Bureau most conveniently in terms of the percentage of families earning below $3,000 annually and the percentage earning $10,000 or more annually, those figures will be used henceforth for 1960 instead of the more elusive percentage earning over $5,000 (the 1950 method of presentation).

[16] Unless otherwise indicated, economic data—such as median income, manufacturing employment, or size of farms—presented in this study are from the United States Census Bureau. Another convenient but less detailed source is the *Texas Almanac*.

economic differences warns us that other factors are also present—
though they are probably less significant than economic considerations.
For example, the figures for the 1960 presidential election (Table 3)
leave little doubt that the Protestantism of the Panhandle helped to
swell the Republican vote. Quite likely it also affected the 1961 special
Senate election by causing some Panhandle residents to feel that a vote
for Republican John Tower was somehow a vote against the Catholic
President in office. Furthermore, as already indicated, Midwesterners
played a considerable part in the early settlement of the Panhandle.
Since one's most lasting political impressions are often colored by the
family, this too may be of importance in explaining the area's patterns.
Accordingly, the three most Republican counties are located in the
northeastern portion of the Panhandle—where Midwestern migration
would be most likely to leave its mark. In contrast, the three most
Democratic counties are in the southeastern Panhandle where emi-
gration from Texas and southern Oklahoma was probably stronger.

In substance, inhabitants of the Panhandle counties are tempted to
vote Republican for much the same reasons as those motivating Midwestern farmers. The temptations may be weaker in the Panhandle
than in Kansas, but there can be little doubt that causal similarities
are present.

The complexities of Panhandle politics are nothing compared to the
variegated patterns prevailing in the other and much larger area of
relative Republican strength. The West Texas and South Texas counties, with about half of the state's land mass and a good share of its
population, present an analytical challenge of no small dimensions.
The most striking fact illustrated by Figure A is that many of the
counties with strong Republican tendencies are clustered in the Hill
Country-Edwards Plateau region northwest of San Antonio. It is best,
therefore, to concentrate on the features of this particular area rather
than to attempt to characterize the entire West Texas-South Texas
region.

The Hill Country-Edwards Plateau area is historically noted for its
original settlement by German immigrants. (By 1860 they numbered
approximately 20,000.) Often imbued with the "liberal" German
thought of the period, alienated in a strange country, and holding lands
ill-suited to a slave economy, the Texas Germans tended to be Union-
ists or at least neutralists when the issue of secession came to the fore.
Harassed and oppressed by hot-headed Secessionists during the war,
after hostilities ceased they quite naturally received the triumphant
Republican Party with open arms. Traditionally, they have not yet
extricated themselves from that political embrace.

Just how strong is the Republicanism of the "German" area today? In making an effort to answer, one is immediately confronted with the problem of identifying the so-called "German" counties. There was a time, of course, when the German immigrants and their descendants could be quickly assigned a place on the map, but this day has long since passed. Since the German counties cannot be accurately specified today, we have relied on the original counties. (This serious if unavoidable drawback must be remembered when interpreting the figures presented in Table 4.)[17]

According to Table 4, 13 of the 16 counties classified as "German" (including Calhoun) were in the Republican first quarter in the presidential elections of 1948, 1952, and 1956 and in the special Senate election of 1957. Only 2 of the remaining 3 counties were consistently out of the first quartile, and then they were found mostly in the second quarter. None of the 16 ever dropped as low as the fourth quartile of the Republican tally until 1960.

In absolute terms a Republican presidential nominee can expect to receive 60 per cent or more of the vote in 5 or 6 German counties (perhaps a great deal more, if he happens to be a popular military figure); in another half dozen German counties a Republican majority is virtually assured; and in another 4 or 5 such counties Republicans can acquire up to 40 per cent of the total without too much effort. Such figures seem to substantiate the traditional view that the German counties remain a sharply defined island in the midst of a Democratic sea.

However, a more careful reading of their postwar record indicates that the German counties are gradually becoming less of a special case. Even in the 1948 presidential election, only 5 of these counties (Gillespie, Kendall, Comal, Guadalupe, and Washington) distinguished themselves by giving the Republican candidate 51 per cent or more of their vote; the remainder returned percentages not much different from those produced in a dozen counties lacking the German tradition. Moreover, in the 1952 presidential race only Gillespie and Kendall yielded Republican majorities head and shoulders above the rest of the state; the next 4 highest German counties produced Republican percentages that were equalled by a score or more counties elsewhere; and the lower-ranking German counties could not in any sense be distinguished from a host of others. This trend was continued in the 1960 and 1961 contests. In the 1960 presidential sweepstakes 6 of the 16

[17] The 1960 Census figures for Texas confirm that all but five of the original sixteen still contain many people of German origin (the exceptions are Calhoun, Goliad, Kimble, Mason, and Victoria).

TABLE 4

Republican Voting in Texas German Counties, 1948–1961

| Percentage of German Population[a] | Republican Percentage of Two-Party Total Vote[b] | | | | | | | | | | Average Republican Vote, Six Elections |
| | Presidential & Senatorial Elections[c] | | | | | | Gubernatorial Elections | | | | |
	1948	1952	1956	1957	1960	1961	1948	1950	1954	1956	
20–34%	%	%	%	%	%	%	%	%	%	%	%
Colorado	29	61	62	34	45[d]	44	24	9	7	11	46
Goliad	42	70	73	44	51[d]	50	35	18	12	12	55
Lee	22[d]	49[e]	53[d]	19[d]	43[e]	35[d]	10	3	5	6	37
Kerr	48	73	78	47	71	55	26	17	8	16	62
Mason	37	64	64	39	59	44	22	13	11	6	51
Washington	51	72	76	33	58	53	33	8	6	6	57
35–49%											
Calhoun	..[f]	63	64	25	45[e]	22[e]	12	7	8	8	44
De Witt	44	68	70	35	55	44	22	16	8	10	53
Guadalupe	51	65	67	46	54	46	34	19	13	21	56
Lavaca[g]	26[d]	57[d]	51[e]	20[d]	27[h]	22[e]	12	7	5	7	35
Victoria	31	58[d]	63	33	44[e]	32[d]	15	17	9	10	43
50–74%											
Austin	44	67	67	26	53	38	21	7	7	8	49
Fayette[g]	33	62	61	25	39[e]	27[d]	11	7	5	8	41
Gillespie	60	92	93	70	77	69	59	46	22	28	63
Kendall	68	83	82	61	74	70	50	37	22	27	60
75% and over											
Comal	57	60	75	47	62	50	24	9	9	16	58

[a] Based on Roscoe Martin's classification in *The People's Party in Texas*, p. 102. Travis and Bexar Counties are omitted from this list because of fundamental transformations in population character.

[b] All percentages for gubernatorial elections were made available by Professor James R. Jensen of the University of Houston. The three-party rather than the two-party total was used for the 1948 presidential election.

[c] Except as noted, all counties were in the first quarter of the Republican vote in presidential and senatorial elections (gubernatorial elections were not quartiled).

[d] Second quarter.

[e] Third quarter.

[f] No returns available.

[g] Includes some of Czech background.

[h] Fourth quarter.

German counties were missing from the Republican first quarter, 4 dropping to the third quarter and one to the fourth. In the 1961 Senate election 5 of these remained outside the Republican first quarter (3 in the second; 2 in the third quarter).

Of course, the results in 1960 and 1961 are colored by the fact that a sizable number of Catholics live in the German counties. Without question some of these German Catholics switched from the Republican to Democratic ticket in 1960. Likewise, lingering resentment of the way in which a tinge of anti-Catholicism manifested itself in the 1960 Republican campaign and the presence in some German counties of Mexican-Americans predisposed to support Henry Gonzalez probably cost Republican John Tower several votes in the first 1961 election.

More startling is the observation that—like the rest of Texas—the German counties have expressed less sentiment for Republican gubernatorial candidates (see Table 4). Only 4 counties—Guadalupe, Gillespie, Kerr, and Kendall—can be regarded as outstanding for their Republicanism in such elections; the remaining 12 were typically tepid, providing Republican percentages not much different from those found in several other areas of the state. The 1962 gubernatorial election results, it might be added, do not change this picture, for the Republican percentages were much higher all over the state as well as in the German counties.

Thus, on the basis of their present voting records, two-thirds of the traditionally German counties cannot be distinguished easily from a large number of other counties lacking their peculiar background. Of course, it is not so much that their Republican sentiment has declined; rather, the other counties have increased their Republican voting to a much greater rate.

According to tradition, the Republicanism of the German counties is a continuation of sympathies aroused during the Civil War. Certainly, such a socio-political heritage is important. Moreover, it is clear that economic factors have considerably less to do with German counties than with Panhandle Republicanism. In 1949 only one of the sixteen German counties had a median family income higher than that of the statewide average. Specifically, their incomes ranged from a low of $1,288 to a high of $2,849. And, rather surprisingly, the county with the lowest median income in 1949 has been among the five German counties with the highest Republican percentage in presidential and United States senatorial races (Washington County).

The foregoing facts notwithstanding, the thesis that tradition alone explains German-county Republicanism should be viewed with some skepticism. Many of the non-German counties of the Edwards Plateau area—especially those just to the west and northwest of Kerr, Gillespie, Kendall, and Comal Counties—have similar Republican records. One might assert that such similarities are the result of nothing more than the expansion of German influence from the original counties, but sober second thought dictates otherwise. There is, after all, a limit to the area and population that can be influenced by a comparative handful of immigrants and their descendants.

Actually, a closer check indicates that in many such contiguous non-

German counties the appeal of the Republican Party depends more on its present economic philosophy than on traditional ties. Moreover, several of the German counties do not have similar Republican records, and the inconsistencies that are present indicate that something other than history affects voting within them. The high percentages of German population (determined historically, however) frequently do not correlate with high percentages of Republican votes. Of the six most Republican counties of the group, two are in the category 20–34-per-cent German, one is in the 35–49-per-cent category, two are in the 50–74-per-cent, and one is in the 75-per-cent-and-over category. It is also significant that each of the three counties weakest in Republican sentiment (Fayette, Lavaca, Lee) falls in a different category.

Of the twelve counties giving Eisenhower more than 70 per cent of their vote in 1952, only five are on the list of German counties. The Republican increase in that election over 1948 was 40–50 per cent in many other counties of the state, but only 20–30 per cent in those with German population; thus, most of the latter counties were at about the same level of Republicanism as that established in other parts of the state in 1952.

Two conclusions can be drawn from the foregoing observations. First, the Republicanism of Texas Germans tends to be of the "presidential" variety; the contrast between percentages given the gubernatorial and those given presidential candidates does not bespeak any great attachment to the GOP as a party—at least not as a *state* party. The second and related point is that these German counties are becoming less and less distinguishable as a group. In part, this development indicates gradual dispersion of the group and the consequent dilution of views, but it reflects also greatly increased Republican support in other counties.

URBANIZATION AND THE REPUBLICAN PARTY

Interesting as they may be, the Panhandle and German counties—particularly the latter—are not sources of decisive votes (the sixteen German counties contributed only 3.9 per cent of the Tower total in 1961). After all, most of these counties are predominantly rural; and in Texas, as elsewhere, the growth and political potential is in the metropolitan areas. (The state was 62.7 per cent urban in 1950 and 75 per cent in 1960.)

To what extent are the Republicans registering significant gains in the fast-growing cities? What is the nature of the urban vote, and how does it differ from rural or small-town patterns? In an effort to shed more light on these queries, an elaborate urban-rural classification system was devised, based on the absolute size of urban centers and the respective proportions of urban, nonfarm rural, and farm rural population in each county.

The counties were assigned to their respective categories in the urban-rural classification on the basis of 1950 Census data, with certain exceptions involving five counties in Category I. The 1950 Census recorded the chief cities in Potter, Jefferson, Lubbock, McLennan, and Wichita Counties as being below the 100,000-population mark specified in the description for Category I, but by the time this study commenced it appeared that those cities had attained that level of population (the estimate was in error only for Waco—McLennan County—which had only 97,898 population according to the 1960 Census). Since the cities involved were and still are among the twelve largest cities in the state, it seemed best to place them in the category into which they grew shortly after the 1950 Census, rather than in one they had outgrown. No doubt rigid adherence to this rule would have affected counties in other categories as well, but the greater importance of these largest ones, and the availability of reliable data on them prior to the 1960 Census, justified a limited application of the rule.

The patterns produced by such a breakdown of Texas election returns are revealed in Table 5. Our interest focuses especially on the

URBAN-RURAL CLASSIFICATION[18]

Category	Description
I Metropolitan (12)	70% or more urban; one or more cities of 100,000 or more.
II Large Urban (17)	50% or more urban; one or more cities of 25,000–99,999.
III Intermediate Urban (22)	50% or more urban; one or more cities of 10,000–24,999.
IV Small Urban (7)	30–49% urban; less than 20% farm rural; one or more cities of 10,000 or more.
V Agri-Urban (20)	30–49% urban; 20% or more farm rural; one or more cities of 10,000 or more.
VI Nonfarm Rural-Urban (27)	80% or more nonfarm rural and urban; less than 20% farm rural; no city of 10,000.
VII Nonfarm Rural (65)	20–39% farm rural; no city of 10,000.
VIII Farm Rural (84)	40% or more farm rural; no city of 10,000.

[18] The number of counties in each category is indicated in parentheses; the counties in each category are listed in Appendix E.

profile for the twelve counties in Category I (70 per cent or more urban; one or more cities of 100,000 or more), for this group appears to be most consistently sympathetic to the Republican Party. These Category I counties provided from 50 to 60 per cent of the votes gathered by Republican nominees in the four presidential and two key senatorial elections from 1948–1961. During these six elections only one such county (McLennan in 1961) fell into the Republican fourth quarter; and approximately 78 per cent of the possible appearances of these metropolitan areas were recorded in the first two quartiles of the Republican vote.

From an absolute standpoint the Republican showing is much less impressive. Eisenhower did obtain majorities in 8 of these 12 metropolitan centers in 1952 and from 10 of 12 in 1956, but in 1960 the Kennedy-Johnson ticket forged ahead in all but 5 of the counties involved (Dallas, Harris, Lubbock, Potter, and Tarrant). In 1957 the Republican candidate for United States Senator managed to obtain 30

TABLE 5

Republican Patterns in Urban-Rural Categories, 1948–1961[a]

Urban-Rural Category	Republican Vote Accounted for				[b]Appearances in Indicated Quarter Republican Vote					1961 Total Vote as % of 1960 Total Vote	1961 Rep. Vote as % of 1960 Rep. Vote	1961 Rep. Vote as % of 1960 Total Vote
	'48	'57	'60	'61	Total	1st	2nd	3rd	4th			
	%	%	%	%		%	%	%	%	%	%	%
I(12)	56.0	61.4	54.2	58.0	72	39	39	21	1	46.6	31.2	35.0
II(17)	11.1	11.5	12.8	13.1	101	37	30	17	17	37.7	29.8	36.9
III(22)	5.2	4.4	5.3	5.0	126	33	30	29	7	43.4	27.7	31.5
IV(7)	2.4	2.3	2.6	2.5	42	17	38	36	9	40.3	27.7	31.6
V(20)	5.9	3.9	5.9	4.5	118	13	27	30	30	42.6	22.2	23.6
VI(27)	2.1	2.9	3.0	3.1	153	36	35	16	12	42.3	29.2	33.3
VII(65)	6.9	6.7	7.8	7.3	376	29	24	25	21	45.4	27.4	27.5
VIII(84)	10.3	6.6	8.3	6.6	497	16	16	26	42	38.9	23.4	24.8

[a] The 1948, 1952, 1956, and 1960 presidential elections and the 1957 and 1961 (first) special Senate elections were used in constructing this table. The figures for all of the six elections are given in the columns on "Appearances in Indicated Quarter Republican Vote," but, since the figures for each of the four presidential elections are quite similar, only the statistics for the first (1948) and the last (1960) of these four contests are shown in the the the columns for "Republican Vote Accounted For."

[b] Calculated on the basis of a multiplication of the number of counties in each category by the number of elections (6). In a few cases counties failed to make returns, in which case the number of such omissions was subtracted from the product to get the total shown. Rounding of the percentages shown for the four quarters is responsible for failure to total 100 per cent.

per cent or better of the vote in only 3 counties (Bexar, Dallas, and Harris) and in no case did he receive more than 39 per cent of the tally. Tower did exceed the 30 per cent mark in 8 of the 12 counties during the first heat of the 1961 Senate race, but only Harris, Lubbock, and Potter Counties gave him pluralities of better than 40 per cent. (In the runoff with William Blakley, Tower carried 7 of the 12 metropolitan counties—the exceptions being Jefferson, McLennan, Nueces, Travis, and Wichita. However, for reasons noted earlier, the runoff race is not an accurate measure of true Republican sentiment.) Finally, with the exception of the 1962 contest, Republican percentages in the state's gubernatorial contests were barely respectable.

Despite Republican failures to win absolute majorities in United States senatorial and gubernatorial elections, the patterns that do emerge, when viewed in context, invite favorable comment. After all, these counties in the past have been an integral part of Democratic Party hegemony, and their political heritage impels them to continue this role. Why then does it happen that the one-party mold has first been cracked—a few would say "shattered"—in the twelve most urban counties? And how does one square their tendencies with the lore of American national politics which calls for cities—at least the largest ones—to be heavily Democratic?

Final and complete answers to such questions cannot be given here. The explanatory offerings are intended to open rather than close discussion. There is no reason to suppose that a single factor can be found which will explain everything. This is unlikely enough in any political system, and even more so in one that has several economic and geographic groupings, as well as numerous subcultures. How perplexing it can be even to prominent participants is perhaps illustrated by the response of Senator Barry Goldwater when asked why Republicans do well in Southern cities but lose the rural areas while the reverse is true in the North: "I can't answer that."[19]

That industrialization has been of great significance in turning some parts of Texas toward the Republican Party is generally agreed upon, but the area of consensus does not include an explanation of why the process strengthens Republicanism in Texas while it turns older industrial states Democratic. Part of the answer, no doubt, lies in the fact that it is not actually the same process. Industrialization in Texas has not been a story of mass-production industries employing large percentages of unskilled, immigrant labor; rather, it has been distinguished by its relatively high ratio of skilled to unskilled, white-

[19] *U.S. News and World Report*, October 22, 1962.

collar to blue-collar, native-born white to nonnative, nonwhite personnel. Plants are smaller, managerial and professional personnel more numerous, automation much more practiced and practicable.

Hence, the process in Texas has resulted in a small percentage of employment in manufacturing, a fact well illustrated by 1960 statistics. Compare, for example, the percentages of the labor force employed in manufacturing at Cleveland (40.8 per cent), Detroit (37.4 per cent), Chicago (33.5 per cent), and Philadelphia (33.2 per cent) with the percentages in Houston (19.6 per cent), Dallas (20.4 per cent), and San Antonio (11.3 per cent). Similarly, at a smaller level, the manufacturing employment percentages for strongly Democratic Evansville, South Bend, and Toledo are 30.6, 39.4, and 34.4 per cent, respectively, while in the more Republican-prone Texas cities of Amarillo and Lubbock the percentages are 11.9 and 10.6 per cent respectively. Of the Texas cities in Category I only Port Arthur (36.9 per cent) has an employment in manufacturing percentage comparable to the percentages of Northern and Midwestern cities—and it also has a similar voting pattern. The Texas metropolis closest to Port Arthur in rating is Fort Worth with 23.6 per cent employed in manufacturing.[20]

Finally, even within the ranks of manufacturing employment Texas has a smaller percentage of union members than that found elsewhere. Since organized labor in the industrial areas of Texas, as elsewhere in the nation, often provides much of the organization, work, and money involved in systematic Democratic politics, its relative weakness in the state limits its effectiveness as a counterweight to the positive Republican forces released by industrialization.

These released forces are in no small measure a function of the prevailing value system. The American value system, according to one of the better recent textbooks on state government, has been deeply influenced by three myths: frontier individualism, industrial individualism, and the social-service state.[21] While the latter myth may not have won total acceptance anywhere, it has met especially stiff resistance in Texas, where the first two myths are still treasured. Like the other states of the Confederacy in its fundamentalist religion, Texas is also fundamentalist in its economics. This devotion to the "American

[20] The figures given are for the core cities and do not include fringe areas. If one were to include fringe areas, the manufacturing employment percentages for such cities as Detroit and Chicago would be slightly higher as would the percentage for Houston, Texas.

[21] Charles R. Adrian, *State and Local Governments*, pp. 38–76. The sense in which he—and we—use the term "myth" is explained in his study on pages 39 and 40.

Creed"—or at least to one of its facets—has made it difficult for some to adjust to the changes in economic policies and relations which have come in the last thirty or so years. Aspects of the welfare state which have won rather general acceptance elsewhere are in Texas still the subject of arguments possessing an ideological tone reminiscent of the 1930's. While such attitudes are not unknown in rural and small-town areas, they are apt to be expressed more shrilly and more emphatically in the metropolitan centers.

But, since these views are not at all incompatible with the position of the conservative Southern Democrat, why do they produce Republican votes? Presumably a partial explanation is that in presidential elections no Democrat—Southern or otherwise—who supports this view appears on the ballot, because the elements controlling the national Democratic Party have long since moved away from it. The only choice, as a practical matter, is thus between a liberal Democrat and a Republican, and while the record of Republican congresses and Presidents alike shows no great variation from the national Democratic Party's position, at least the Republican articles of faith still honor the old verities. Furthermore, such a record produces Republican voting in other elections, not only because it weakens the old Democratic habit, but also because the ideologue concludes that the conservative Southern Democrat has become contaminated by his association with the national Party. Precisely this argument was used repeatedly in the Tower-Blakley Senate runoff in 1961; Blakley, although by all other signs a conservative Southern Democrat of the old school, had supported the Kennedy-Johnson ticket in 1960, so how could he possibly be the defender of the faith he claimed to be?

Republican success in the metropolitan counties of Texas may have ideological roots, but it also has been nurtured inadvertently by voter-qualification requirements, which have less of a deterrent effect upon educated, ideologically motivated middle and upper classes than upon the lower class. One such requirement—the poll tax—is less of a barrier today than in the past—inflation has seen to that—but, even so, it limits the participation of tightly budgeted low-income groups (or so some who are deputized to sell poll taxes have reported). An even more important restraint is the provision that the poll tax must be paid by January 31, some four months before the primary and nine months before the election—a time when political interest is low among the less concerned. Thus, a small portion of the Republican success can be attributed to partial discouragement of voting among Democratic-prone lower-income groups.

Closely related to this is another phenomenon. Traditionally, Texas politics has been largely unorganized in the sense of block-by-block, precinct-by-precinct partisan activities designed to drum up support and turn out the vote. The old Latin American machines of South Texas and the Negro machines of East Texas are (were) in their own way exceptions, but, by and large, the Texas heritage does not call for political practices considered an essential part of politics in other urban states, nor does it approve of them. In metropolitan centers both the Democrats and the Republicans are gradually becoming aware of the need for grass-roots organization, but, as yet, Democratic organizers have been unable to mobilize completely and continuously the votes of their likeliest supporters. This is not to say the Republicans invariably have superior organizations in urban counties; only occasionally is such the case. The disorganized state of the electorate, however, has worked to the advantage of the Republicans, particularly when they stress their conservatism rather than their Republicanism.

But remote, impersonal factors cannot be made to bear all the blame for the organizational failures of city Democrats. The fact is that the Democratic Party machinery at local levels—and, on occasion, at the state level as well—has repeatedly been immobilized because it has fallen into the hands of either avowed Republicans or conservative Democrats so close to the Republicans ideologically that they were willing to sit on their hands or even to work actively for GOP nominees. This kind of assistance has been invaluable to the Republicans, for it made it easier for rank-and-file Democratic voters to switch their support merely by following old leaders; and, simultaneously, it kept official Democratic organs from functioning properly. Such practices may decline in the future, at least if developments in Dallas offer any clue. There, the Republican audacity in electing a county commissioner in 1960—thus violating the old working agreement that kept Republicans out of local races in exchange for conservative Democratic support in national contests—produced in 1961 and 1962 a sudden lather of enthusiasm for the Democratic Party from "the courthouse crowd" that, if it leads to cooperation with other elements in the Party, may do much to contain Republican strength in the county.

Finally, the psychological impact of rapid urbanization may be a future asset to the Republican Party. For many who have migrated from farms and small towns to the new cities, the new life results in some severance of old customs, practices, and beliefs. Initially at least they are likely to experience a period of disorientation and political indecision. Under such conditions the newcomers are likely to be more susceptible to the blandishments of leaders in the community's social, economic, and political life—especially if these leaders succeed in identifying their cause with some of the more enduring and endearing symbols of national and state tradition. Hence, the gradual growth of Republican "respectability" among such community leaders, or at least their increasing participation in the popular parlor game of sniping at Democratic Party practices, may have a great deal to do with new developments in Texas politics. In time, another reorientation may occur that will firm up Democratic ranks, but, for the moment, it would appear that many new urbanites are ripe targets for Republican recruiters.

The tone of the discussion to this point might lead one to suppose that all of the metropolitan counties are affected by much the same forces. Common characteristics are present, but others of a more particular nature give each of these urban centers somewhat of a distinctive political style (see Table 6).

The relatively low support of the Republican Party in McLennan (Waco) and Wichita (Wichita Falls) Counties is no doubt related to their setting amidst the more rural and more traditionally Democratic counties of Central and North Texas. Economic conditions in McLennan County are hardly conducive to Republican voting (median family income of $2,553 with 14.6 per cent earning over $5,000 annually in 1950 while in 1960 the median family income was $4,684—below the state average of $4,884—with only 9.3 per cent earning over $10,000 annually). However, economics cannot be stressed too much, for a decidedly better climate prevailed in Wichita County (median family income $3,173 with 19.0 per cent earning over $5,000 in 1950, while in 1960 the median family income was $5,322 with 12.3 per cent earning over $10,000). A similar example of the influences of surrounding areas upon urban politics is Potter County, where Republican undercurrents in the surrounding Panhandle counties reinforce the Republican tendencies of Amarillo, or at least reduce impediments to them.

On the other hand, the fact that agricultural and once traditionally Democratic Lubbock County has recently had a higher percentage of Republican votes than either McLennan or Wichita Counties suggests that economics is the primary motivating factor. With a rapid rate of growth (95.1 per cent from 1940 to 1950, and 54.7 per cent in the period from 1950 to 1960) and with relatively high levels of income (median family income of $3,283 with 25.3 per cent earning over $5,000 annually in 1950, and in 1960 a median family income of $5,425 with 14.6 per cent earning over $10,000), Lubbock County might be even more susceptible to Republican appeals were it not for the fact that its source of prosperity is built on its location in the heart of a great irrigated farm region where Republican farm policies have never enjoyed great popularity.

Similarly, the weaker Republican showing in Jefferson County seems to be much less due to its position in the southeast corner of the state amid traditional Democratic influences than to the character of its economy. The county has one of the state's most industrialized economies in that 31.5 per cent of the labor force in 1954 was employed in manufacturing, and at least three-fourths of them worked for firms employing one hundred or more persons. Furthermore, the area has economically strong and politically active labor unions. Whether for these or other reasons, Jefferson County is also prosperous by Texas standards, since the 1950 figures showed a median family income of $3,624 and 22.4 per cent earning over $5,000 annually, and the 1960 data revealed a median family income of $6,001 with 13.8 per cent earning over $10,000 annually. Any stimulus toward Republicanism resulting from these relatively high levels of income, however, seems to have been dampened by the political efforts and impact of organized labor.[22] There is reason to believe that the same factor also influences to a lesser degree the vote in much larger Tarrant County (Fort Worth), where in 1950 manufacturing employment was 25.2 per cent of the total and the ratio employed in manufacturing firms of one hundred or more employees was 55 per cent (the 1960 figure for manufacturing employment was 26.5 per cent).[23]

The most intriguing questions relate to the three most populous counties: Harris, Dallas, and Bexar. Representing some 24.9 per cent of the population in 1950 and 30.1 per cent in 1960, the Republican voting averages of these three counties are the highest among those found in Category I. Yet the reasons for their Republican tendencies and their degree of consistency vary considerably.

Harris County, the state's largest with a 1960 population of 1,243,158, occupies a prominent position in the booming Gulf Coast area—the "Golden Crescent," in Chamber of Commerce vernacular. Boasting of Houston as the state's largest city and the nation's seventh

[22] The importance of the organized labor movement in Jefferson County is attested by the use of one of its principal industrial cities as the subject of a skillfully executed, bitterly antiunion film prepared for television audiences by followers of conservative Democrat Allan Shivers in his bid for renomination in 1954. Supporters of his labor-backed opponent, Ralph Yarborough, still froth when forced to recall the contest and the impact of "The Port Arthur Story." The film forcefully attempted to demonstrate—with what degree of reliability we will not here attempt to assay—the fate of labor-dominated communities.

[23] Income figures for Tarrant County in 1950: median income of $3,256; 20.6 per cent earning over $5,000 annually. Figures for 1960: median income of $5,697; 14.0 per cent earning over $10,000 annually.

TABLE 6

Republican Voting in Texas Counties in Category I, 1948–1961

Metropolitan Counties	Republican Percentages of Total Vote and Quartile Rank[a]						Average Republican Vote (% of Total) Six
	1948	1952	1956	1957	1960	1961	Elections
	%QR	%QR	%QR	%QR	%QR	%QR	%
Bexar	40(1)	57(2)	58(2)	39(1)	46(2)	30(2)	45
Dallas	38(1)	63(1)	65(1)	34(1)	63(1)	36(1)	49
El Paso	26(1)	58(2)	55(2)	24(2)	45(2)	36(1)	41
Harris	35(1)	58(1)	62(1)	30(1)	53(1)	45(1)	47
Jefferson	17(2)	46(3)	55(2)	18(2)	42(3)	26(2)	32
Lubbock	19(2)	58(2)	53(2)	23(2)	57(1)	41(1)	41
McLennan	15(3)	46(3)	39(3)	16(3)	43(3)	19(4)	30
Nueces	26(1)	49(3)	51(3)	27(1)	39(3)	25(3)	36
Potter	29(1)	62(1)	58(2)	25(1)	61(1)	42(1)	46
Tarrant	28(1)	58(2)	60(1)	23(2)	55(1)	30(2)	42
Travis	22(2)	52(2)	54(2)	22(2)	45(3)	25(3)	37
Wichita	18(2)	47(3)	49(3)	23(2)	46(2)	37(1)	37

a All are presidential elections except those of 1957 and 1961, which are special Senate elections (the preliminary rather than the runoff contest was used for 1961). All presidential percentages are based on the two-party total except for the 1948 total, which includes the "States' Rights" vote. The 1957 percentages are based on the votes for the five leading candidates, and those for 1961 on the votes for the six leading candidates.

largest (596,163 in 1950; 938,219 in 1960), Harris County typifies the new economy of the region. Industrial production figures prominently (manufacturing employment in 1954 was 22.3 per cent of the total); also important are commerce and finance, shipping (Houston is the nation's third largest port, in terms of total tonnage), the production, processing, and distribution of petroleum and agricultural commodities, and, most recently, the activities of the National Aeronautics and Space Administration. Stimulated by highly favorable economic conditions (the county had a median income of $3,476 in 1950, with 25.2 per cent earning over $5,000 annually, and, in 1960, the median income was $6,040 with 17.6 per cent earning over $10,000 annually), Houston and the smaller cities in Harris County have grown rapidly in the past twenty years. From 1940 to 1950 alone the county's population increased by 52.5 per cent; from 1950 to 1960 by 54.1 per cent. The area's rapid growth, the opportunities afforded by years of boom, the importance of the petroleum industry—all these have produced many *nouveaux riches*, and they in turn have contributed the antics and the foibles that make appropriate the local columnist's somewhat derisive description of Houston as "the land of the big rich." This factor is not without political significance, for new wealth is by nature fretful, suspicious, and uneasy, especially when it rests on an economically volatile petroleum base.[24]

This climate has, of course, drawn many persons from other states, as indicated by the census reports showing that 29.9 per cent of the Harris County population in 1960 was born in some other state. Since many of them are engaged in managerial and professional pursuits offering opportunities to influence others, added importance is given to their out-of-state origins. At the same time, however, the favorable economic climate has had a great attraction for those at the other end of the socio-economic scale. In addition to the white working-class immigrants from East and Central Texas and from nearby Southern states, Latin Americans in 1950 comprised an estimated 6.6 per cent of the population and Negroes represented another 18.5 per cent—a figure that had grown to 19.8 per cent by the time of the 1960 Census.

Some clues as to the dominant motivational themes at work in Harris County politics can be found in a comparison of precinct returns. In the 1956 presidential election, 3 Houston precincts in the highest-income category gave the Republican candidate a staggering 94.3 per cent of the two-party vote.[25] In 9 middle-income, middle-class precincts the Republican vote dropped slightly but still remained a little more than 80 per cent. Not until some of the lowest-income precincts are singled out and examined does anything resembling a balance reveal itself. Examination of 9 such precincts showed that in them the Republican presidential candidate received only 43.9 per cent of the two-party vote. Significantly, the GOP total percentage in 36 Houston Negro precincts was only 36 per cent.

Unfortunately for Houston Republicans, they simply cannot count upon enough precincts to deliver 80–90 per cent majorities; success requires votes from working-class and Negro neighborhoods. Proof of this may be found in the Eisenhower saga. In 1956 in Harris County the Eisenhower-Nixon ticket carried some 150 of 259 precincts. Of the 150, a total of 37 were carried by margins of 66.7 to 74.9 per cent; 19 were carried by margins of 75–79.9 per cent; and 28 were carried by margins of 80 per cent or more. In the last two categories alone (i.e., precincts returning 75 per cent or more Republican votes) 60,000 votes were for Eisenhower, or approximately 40 per cent of his total in Harris County. Obviously, the candidate was receiving considerable

---

[24] See Key, *Southern Politics*, p. 255.
[25] But these same three precincts gave the Republican nominee for governor only 33 per cent of their vote in that same election.

lower-class support, for—contemporary folklore notwithstanding—
great and even moderate wealth is not that widely distributed over
Houston, or any other part of Texas.

The fluctuations in the Houston Republican vote in the elections of
1952, 1956, and 1960 suggest some difficulty in nailing down these
supplementary sources, primarily because of determined if somewhat
episodic liberal Democratic opposition. Indeed, the *degree of organization among liberal Democrats helps to distinguish Harris County
from Dallas County*. Such liberal organization was in large part responsible for the sag in the Harris County Republican percentage in
the 1960 presidential election—8.9 points below the 1956 vote and 9.6
points below the 1960 Republican percentage for Dallas County. To
be sure, the coalition of minorities, labor, intellectual liberals, and
Democratic loyalists does not always function effectively, but as of
1961 it is the state of this coalition—more than the state of the Republican movement—that was reflected by the ebb and flow of GOP fortunes in Harris County.

Dallas County has likewise seen its greatest growth during the past
two decades with a 54.3 per cent increase in county population from
1940 to 1950; 54.8 per cent from 1950 to 1960. Yet, in a number of
significant respects, Dallas differs from Harris County. Though manufacturing is present in significant amounts, as indicated by the 18.6
per cent employed in this activity in 1954, Dallas County is more dis-
tinctively "white collar" as a result of its standing as the Southwest
center of finance, commerce, insurance, and management in general.
Like Harris, Dallas County has high levels of income with a median
family income of $3,433 and 26.5 per cent earning over $5,000 annually in 1950, and a median family income of $6,188, with 19.1 per cent
earning over $10,000 in 1960. However, while not without its *nouveaux
riches*, Dallas is slightly more staid and sedate. As in Houston, its managerial atmosphere has attracted many immigrants (28.8 per cent of
total population in 1960) from other states, particularly those with
strong Republican tendencies. But, on the whole, Dallas County is
markedly more homogeneous than Harris County. Out of the entire
population, Latin Americans represented but 3.5 per cent in 1950, and
only 13.4 per cent Negroes in 1960.

In Dallas County the Republicans have what is probably their most
dedicated and well-led organization. Its effectiveness is illustrated by
the facts that it has elected the state's first recent GOP congressman,
has broken the Democratic monopoly on the County Commissioners' Court, and has regularly returned high Republican percentages in
presidential elections (see Table 6). The Republicans have also

received valuable assistance from conservative Democrats—some of whom are top community leaders and members of what is surely one of the most influential oligarchies in any American city. This success in winning support among important elements of the community power structure has no doubt been a key factor enabling the Republican Party to obtain better candidates, forceful leadership, and important financial assistance.

No less important is the disorganization of the opposition. With much of the regular Democratic Party machinery collaborating with the Republicans, effective opposition requires some sort of extraparty organization. To date this simply has not been forthcoming. In any case such an opposition would have a formidable task, for the most likely bases of support are too limited; that is, the Negro community has been impotent, and organized labor is weak.

Nevertheless, a better organized opposition could cut into the substantial Republican presidential majorities. It is significant that the most effective challenge to Republican Congressman Bruce Alger was provided by a Democrat with the colorful name of Barefoot Sanders, who managed to piece together a temporary coalition of assorted elements to the left of the ultraconservative Alger. "Harmony" is today a much more frequent plea among Dallas Democrats, and perhaps they will, in the future, provide stronger opposition—though, for the moment, the existence of a Republican-minded majority in Dallas is indisputable.

Even to the trained observer of American urban politics, Bexar County is quite puzzling. Its rate of growth, although somewhat less than that of Harris and Dallas Counties, resembles that of other metropolitan areas of Texas. From 1940 to 1950 the increase was 48.0 per cent and from 1950 to 1960 it was 37.3 per cent. In addition to the modest amount of manufacturing indicated by the 11.4 per cent so employed in 1954, the county's economy is geared to agricultural production and processing, regional commercial and distribution activities, military installations—and tourism. But when one digs deeper, the politics of the county seems incomprehensible. In 1950 Bexar County's median income was $2,724 and its percentage earning over $5,000 was 16.9 per cent (the first barely above the statewide figure and the second just below it). In 1960 its median income was $4,766 and only 11 per cent of its inhabitants were earning over $10,000. These figures leave no doubt that Bexar County is a relatively poor metropolitan area—indeed, of the twelve metropolitan counties in Category I, only McLennan and Nueces fell below the Bexar income level. Furthermore, its population in 1950 included an estimated 38.8 per cent Latin Americans and 6.5 per cent Negroes.

In most other cities of the United States low incomes plus large minority groups would equal liberal Democratic majorities, but not in Bexar County, Texas. As Table 6 indicates, it has treated Republican candidates well. Were it not for the decline of Republican votes in 1960 and 1961, Bexar County might edge out Potter County as the third most Republican of the Category I areas. Why this is so is not easily comprehensible. One factor perhaps is regional influence, for as Figure A shows, Bexar County is situated in a general area noted for its Republican tendencies. The influence of the military, which is important in the San Antonio area and which probably leans to the conservative side, could be another factor. Too, some observers report a paternalism on the part of some of the local elite, which makes mobilization of lower-income groups difficult. For example, in contrast to several other counties where labor has economic if not political strength, Bexar County union organization has not progressed far enough to make even the first step a reality yet.

Moreover, until recently, the politics of the Latin Americans has not been conducive to building a strongly liberal and Democratic bloc. The Latin Americans are not shut out of city and county politics, but their leaders have, in the past at least, failed to steer them sharply away from the Republican Party. The emergence of a strong, liberal Democratic leader in the person of United States Congressman Henry Gonzalez is a notable exception, but even some of his supporters fear that his undoubted appeal is largely personal and ethnic, so that an equally personable Latin American of the opposite persuasion might cut deeply into his following. At the moment some signs suggest the development of better teamwork among moderate and liberal Democrats, including the capture of a majority of the Bexar County delegation to the Texas House of Representatives in 1960 and 1962, the election of the state senator, and the unopposed re-election of Congressman Henry Gonzalez in 1962. In all likelihood, however, this is the same sort of polarization that took place in Harris County several years earlier. Therefore, although this consolidation of liberal Democratic strength produces primary victories at present, it may also help the Republicans by driving the conservative Democrats into their waiting arms. If the sizable liberal potential in Bexar is realized, this consequent consolidation of conservative strength still may not suffice to produce Republican victories, but it will enable the GOP to continue to poll impressive percentages.

The importance of the 12 metropolitan counties in Category I for the Texas Republican Party cannot be questioned. As demonstrated in Table 5, this group regularly provides from 50 to 60 per cent of the Republican vote in the state. In presidential elections the tendency is for their share of the Republican vote to fall into the lower part of that range as counties in other categories show a great tendency toward "presidential Republicanism." For example, in 1952 the Republican presidential candidate received 60 per cent or more of the vote in some fifty counties, but only two of these fall in Category I. In 1956 sixty or so counties were in the 60-per-cent-or-more Republican bracket, but only three were in Category I. In 1960 some twenty-three counties gave the Republican presidential candidate 60 per cent or more of the vote, but only two were in this group. Evidence of this sort prompts the generalization that just as some forces inherent in Texas urbanization are conducive to Republican voting, other forces impede the growth of that vote beyond certain levels. In oversimplified terms, the first 40–50 per cent of the vote in presidential elections comes easily to Republicans in the populous, urbanized counties; to go much beyond that point is more difficult.

In the special Senate elections, however, the urban counties' portion of the Republican vote climbed (61.4 per cent in 1957), thereby indicating that, although the Republicans may experience difficulty beyond a certain point, the big-city support for the Republicans is on a firmer basis than that in the rural areas. The same conclusion can be drawn from the fact that the Republican vote in these 12 counties in 1961 fell less precipitously from the 1960 presidential level than did the vote in other categories of counties.

The obvious correlation between urbanization and Republicanism in Texas immediately raises the question of how well the GOP has been faring in rural areas. The Category VIII counties, at the opposite end of the scale, have no city of 10,000 and 40 per cent or more farm rural population. The data provided in Table 5 show that they are, as a group, the least Republican of the various groupings.[26] Similarly, it is noteworthy that only 16 per cent of their possible appearances were in the top quarter of the Republican vote, while 42 per cent were in the fourth quarter alone. Too, the fact that the 1961 Republican senatorial vote was only 23.4 per cent of what it had been in the 1960 presidential election suggests less success in permanently capturing rural voters from the Democratic Party. One also sees a situation just the reverse of that observed for Category I counties, in that these rural counties'

[26] See Appendix E, Category VIII.

share of the total Republican vote tends to go up in presidential elections, the high point being 10.3 per cent of the GOP total in 1948. In other elections the percentage of total vote accounted for by Category VIII counties declines, the low point being 6.6 per cent of the total in each of the special Senate elections of 1957 and 1961. This decline in Category VIII Republican strength since 1948 is no doubt due in part to the population shift which has reduced the proportion of the total number of voters. Similarly, the increase in the Category I proportion of Republican strength is due in part to population gain.[27] But despite such qualifications and despite the fact that there are notable exceptions, particularly among the South Texas German counties falling in this category, the inescapable conclusion is that rural counties are considerably less inclined to vote Republican than their metropolitan counterparts.

Even so, it is apparent that the GOP has made some headway in the rural areas. As revealed in Table 7, some 71 of the 84 Category VIII counties gave the Republican presidential ticket less than 30 per cent of their vote in 1948; in 1960 only 13 of them were below this mark; in 1956 only 7 of the 84 fell below the 30 per cent figure. The slight rise in Republicanism is also demonstrated by the increase in the number of such rural counties giving the Republican presidential nominee 40 per cent or more of their vote. In 1948 only 6 of them yielded percentages of 40 per cent or more for the Republican candidates; in 1956

TABLE 7

Republican Voting in Texas Counties in Category VIII, 1948–1961

Republican Percentage	Number of Counties[a]					
	1948	1952	1956	1957	1960	1961
0– 9.9	23	0	0	26	0	4
10–19.9	41	0	0	39	0	33
20–29.9	7	5	7	10	13	26
30–39.9	5	22	16	4	23	13
40–49.9	2	20	32	2	26	3
50–59.9	2	22	16	0	17	3
60–69.9	1	8	7	1	3	1
70 and over	1	7	6	2	2	1

a Eighty-four counties are recorded for all except the 1948 election, when the failure of two counties in the group to make proper election returns reduced the total to eighty-two. All elections are presidential, except those in 1957 and 1961, which are special Senate elections. The 1961 election used was the preliminary rather than runoff contest.

27 See Table 27 in Chapter IV.

61 counties and in 1960 48 counties had such a record. The tentativeness of this Republican voting is, of course, fully established by a comparison of data for the two special Senate elections, which shows that many counties lapsed back into their indifference to the Republican Party after the presidential elections of 1956 and 1960. Still, there is a glimmer of consolation for the Republicans in even these Senate races because the record for 1961, when only 37 Category VIII counties were below the 20 per cent Republican mark, is patently brighter than that for 1957, when 65 counties were below it.

On the basis of the findings concerning the metropolitan counties of Category I and the farm rural counties of Category VIII, it would be easy to leap to the conclusion that the distinguishing factor in their voting patterns is urbanization. Any such inference immediately runs into the peculiarities of Category VII counties—those having 20–39 per cent farm rural population with no city of 10,000 or more. If lack of urbanization had any such determinative powers, one would expect the Republican voting of these counties to hew rather closely to the line of Category VIII counties. Table 5 reveals, however, considerably more Republican sentiment in the former than in the latter category. This difference might be due to the lower percentage of farm rural population characteristic of Category VII, but a much more likely explanation is simply the influence of economic, regional, and historical factors associated with the counties in that category.[28]

These counties tend to be concentrated in the Panhandle and in South and Southwest Texas, where Republican inclinations have already been pointed out, and the cleavage in the voting of Category VII counties located in these areas and those outside them is fairly clear, with the former showing much stronger Republican feeling. Economically, large-scale farming and ranching activities are predominant in the Panhandle; in some, but not all, of the South and Southwest counties the scale of agricultural operations equals or exceeds that of the Panhandle, although they may be of a rather different type.

The point that the mere existence or nonexistence of urbanization is not always a sufficient explanation of differences in voting patterns is made even more emphatically by the data for Category VI, consisting of counties with less than 20 per cent farm rural population and no city of 10,000 or more.[29] Of their total appearances in various quarters of the Republican vote in the six elections covered by Table 5, 71 per cent were in the first half and only 12.4 per cent in the fourth quarter. The frequency distribution of Republican percentages in the

[28] See Appendix E, Category VII.
[29] See Appendix E, Category VI.

six elections shown in Table 8 has little resemblance to that of Category VIII shown in Table 7, the most noticeable difference occurring in 1961, when some three-fourths of all Category VIII counties provided Republican votes of less than 30 per cent, compared to only about two-fifths of the counties in Category VI. Other differences that stand out involve the 1952 and 1956 presidential elections, when about three-tenths of the Category VIII counties produced a Republican vote of less than 40 per cent compared to around one-tenth of the Category VI counties. However, it is unlikely that these differences have very much to do with the fact that the bulk of Category VI population is in small cities, towns, and villages rather than on the land, as in Category VIII. Although a few of these counties are scattered over other areas of the state, their concentration in Far West Texas and on the Rio Grande Plain suggests what fuller investigation verifies: In these counties the rancher, his ethics, and his politics reign supreme. Twenty-two of the 27 counties in this category have 40 per cent or more of the value of agricultural production coming from livestock and its products, and in 12 of these 22 counties the figure was 70 per cent or more.

To be sure, in a number of these counties the acreage devoted to irrigated cropping is increasing, and in others oil and gas production is important; but these methods of livelihood need not and seemingly do not have any corrosive effect on the conservative tone of traditional political orientation. The implication of a comparison of the 1960 with the 1952 and 1956 presidential election returns is, however, that this tradition can be affected whenever the issues produce—as did the

TABLE 8

Republican Voting in Texas Counties in Category VI, 1948–1961

Republican Percentage	Number of Counties[a]					
	1948	1952	1956	1957	1960	1961
0– 9.9	2	0	0	1	0	0
10–19.9	8	0	0	8	1	4
20–29.9	10	1	0	13	1	7
30–39.9	4	2	1	3	5	13
40–49.9	1	2	6	2	13	2
50–59.9	0	13	6	0	5	1
60–69.9	0	8	12	0	1	0
70 and over	0	1	2	0	1	0

[a] Twenty-seven counties are recorded for all except the 1948 election, when the failure of two counties in the group to make proper election returns reduced the total to twenty-five. All elections are presidential, except those of 1957 and 1961, which are special Senate elections. The 1961 election used was the preliminary rather than the runoff contest.

religious issue in 1960—resentment from the Latin Americans, found in sizable numbers in many of these counties.

The fact that the Republican vote in Category VI is shown by Table 5 to resemble that of the more urban counties is no more surprising than the parallel shown there between voting in Categories V and VIII. Category V counties are those with over 20 per cent farm rural population, 30–49 per cent urban, and one or more cities of 10,000 or more. They ranked in the first-quarter Republican vote in the six elections covered by Table 5 only 12.7 per cent of the time. The comparable figure for Category VIII was 15.6 per cent. In the 1961 Senate race the Republican vote in Category V counties fell the greatest relative distance from the absolute level of the 1960 presidential vote, amounting to only 22.2 per cent as compared with 23.4 per cent for Category VIII.

Finally, a comparison of the distribution by percentages of Republican vote in Categories V (Table 9) and VIII (Table 7) reveals some similarity in the voting of the two sets of counties, particularly in the two special Senate elections. In part, this similarity is the result of regional factors, for many of the Category V counties are located in the same general areas of Central, East, and Northeast Texas, where one finds many Category VIII counties—and where one also finds strong traditional attachment to the Democratic Party.[30] The relatively large farm rural population of Category V probably has a direct bearing upon this similarity as well, in part because this rural population constitutes a not unimportant part of the total electorate in these

TABLE 9

Republican Voting in Texas Counties in Category V, 1948–1961

Republican Percentage	Number of Counties[a]					
	1948	1952	1956	1957	1960	1961
0– 9.9	1	0	0	6	0	0
10–19.9	14	0	0	11	0	9
20–29.9	4	1	0	2	0	6
30–39.9	0	1	1	0	4	4
40–49.9	0	11	8	1	12	1
50–59.9	1	6	7	0	4	0
60–69.9	0	1	4	0	0	0
70 and over	0	0	0	0	0	0

[a] Twenty counties are recorded for each election. All elections are presidential except those of 1957 and 1961, which are special Senate elections. The 1961 election used was the preliminary rather than the runoff contest.

[30] See Appendix E, Category V.

counties. An additional and perhaps more important explanation is the closeness of the tie between city and county. With perhaps a few exceptions the urban centers which put these counties into Category V have an agricultural focus; they are built upon and are dependent upon the countryside, serving as farm supply and market centers. The banker, the implement dealer, the purveyors of the ingredients represented as the stuff of the "good life"—all have a vested interest in the prosperity and welfare of the rural residents. Under such circumstances it would be surprising if the voting of these agricultural-urban counties were not similar to the more rural ones.

In many respects the counties constituting Categories II, III, and IV present the most difficult analytical tasks. The counties of Category II, composed of those having 50 per cent or more urban population and one or more cities of 25,000 to 99,999 population in 1950,[31] are shown by Table 5 to bear considerable resemblance to the patterns prevailing in the metropolitan counties of Category I. This is especially true with respect to the Republican vote as a percentage of the total, and also with respect to the appearances in the various quarters of the Republican vote over the years. The same table shows a significant easing of Republican strength in the counties of Category III, composed of those having 50 per cent or more urban population and one or more cities of 10,000 to 24,999 population,[32] and of Category IV, composed of counties having 30–49 per cent urban population, less than 20 per cent farm rural, and one or more cities of 10,000 or more.[33] Interpretation of these results is rendered difficult, however, because the analysis is based on county returns in which the votes from urban precincts are scrambled with those from rural ones.

There is an additional reason for caution in dealing with these three categories. The discerning reader will have observed that the more rural categories of VI, VII, and VIII were set apart by geographic and economic differences as well as differences in their urban-rural profiles. No such distinctions are in evidence for the counties in the intermediate categories with the exception of Category V; the counties in Categories II, III, and IV are not metropolitan enough to have the variety of socio-economic characteristics associated with modern industrialization and urbanization, nor are they homogeneous enough to be closely identified with other counties in the same category. Instead, each of the counties in these three classes tends to have some dominant social or economic characteristic that sets it apart from the other counties in

[31] See Appendix E, Category II.
[32] See Appendix E, Category III.
[33] See Appendix E, Category IV.

that category and imparts to it at the same time a definite and somewhat unique political flavor. The result is the creation of so many
subclasses, cutting so freely across the lines of prior categorization, that
the standards employed lose much of their meaning. In Categories
II, III, and IV, one may find East Texas counties with expanding industrial plants; counties where the oil and gas industry has left its
indelible imprint; German counties; counties under the influence
of nearby metropolitan centers—in short, a variety of influences that
greatly exceeds in degree if not in kind the variations within the other
categories.

These counties of Categories II, III, and IV ordinarily produce
around 18–20 per cent of the total Republican vote in Texas. Although
some of them may be encountered when other facets of the Republican
vote are scrutinized, an analytical gap necessarily results from our
inability to deal with them in meaningful terms on the basis of urbanization. The consequent setback to better comprehension of political
patterns can only be overcome by other and more elaborate approaches
than those employed in this study, but some notice of the rich lodes
awaiting more specialized prospecting can be posted.

For example, a complex of factors influences voters in the lower Rio
Grande Valley, particularly Cameron County, to lean in surprising
degree toward the GOP. That county was in the first quarter of the
Republican vote in four of the six elections covered by Table 5 and in
the second quarter in the other two; as early as the presidential election of 1948 it cast 40 per cent and as late as the 1961 special senatorial
election it cast 41 per cent of its vote for the Republican candidates.
Conditions there are unique: a large Latin American population estimated at 66 per cent of the total; an agricultural economy based on
irrigation and on intensely cultivated crops; substantial migration into
the county from Northern states either for retirement purposes or for
extended winter vacations; extremes of wealth and poverty (Cameron
County in 1950 had a median income of only $1,888—some $800
below the statewide figure—and had 13.0 per cent earning over $5,000
annually). This set of conditions could not be duplicated in any other
county in Texas; even the adjacent counties are no more than crudely
comparable. One supposes that the remnants of the patron system now
so firmly held by conservative elements, the impact of immigrants
from areas where Republicanism is respectability, the prosperity so
lumpy at the upper end of the income scale, along with other factors,
are the dyes from which the county's political hues are blended in
some as-yet undetermined process.

To take another example, it is doubtful that Midland and Ector

Counties could justifiably and profitably be compared with any other in the state. To be sure, their respective cities of Midland and Odessa are not unique because they happen to be the West Texas headquarters for the petroleum industry in West Texas; too many other cities serve in a like capacity over the state. What does make these two stand out is the utter lack of counterweights to the influences associated with the petroleum industry and its satellites. Especially in Midland the population is heavily weighted with professional, managerial, and white-collar personnel—the accountants, lawyers, geologists, engineers, clerks, and typists who are indispensable parties to the production of oil and gas. The expansion of the petroleum industry in West Texas after World War II saw almost overnight a new class and a new society superimposed upon the sparsely populated ranching and dry-land farming country. With an economy geared almost exclusively to oil, with no effective counterweights from a previous era, with no sizable minorities, with little organized labor, with high levels of income and education, Midland and Ector Counties have provided fertile soil for the growth of Republican strength. Midland County has been in the first quarter of the Republican vote in every one of the six postwar elections covered by Table 5; Ector has been so ranked in all except one—the presidential election of 1948, when it ranked in the second quarter. In the 1961 special Senate election Republican John Tower received in these two counties more votes than all five of the leading Democratic candidates, registering 56.23 per cent of the total in Midland County and 50.28 per cent of the total in Ector County. This is in Texas an impressive accomplishment by anyone's yardstick.

Our findings regarding urbanization and the Republican Party can be summarized in terms of three general propositions. First, some of the greatest gains of Texas Republicans have been recorded—somewhat unevenly—in the twelve counties with large urban centers. These include the cities of Houston, Dallas, San Antonio, and Fort Worth, as well as such smaller cities as Amarillo, Lubbock, El Paso, and Beaumont. Republican growth in the cities is not in keeping with nationwide tendencies, but it does follow the pattern of other Southern states. In Texas the urban strength of the Republican Party seems to be most directly related to the relative weakness of groups that are normally heavily Democratic—labor unions and minority groups. In part because of the character of the Texas economy and in part because of the climate of opinion, labor unions in Texas are weaker and smaller than in Northern and Midwestern industrial cities. Minority groups in Texas cities tend toward the Democratic Party, but they very often are poorly mobilized and poorly led. Other factors that help to boost Republican percentages in the larger cities include the psychological impact of urbanization and the deep divisions within the Democratic Party itself.

Second, in the most heavily rural counties, those with the highest proportion of farm population and the lowest proportion of urban folk, the Republican Party has been gaining at a far slower rate, but it has nonetheless been gaining.

Third, when one leaves the extremes of large metropolitan areas on the one hand and rural counties on the other, the impact of urbanization becomes much more difficult to assess. The tendency is for counties with more urban strength to be more Republican than others, but the exceptions are so numerous that one is forced to conclude that urbanization in intermediate-size categories is only one of several influences at work on the voters. Others include geographical factors, the nature of the local economy, and local history.

The problem of categorizing counties at intermediate levels of urbanization and population may be most acute in Texas, with its vast areas, cultural extremes, and economic diversities, but even so the germ of a more general principle emerges from the foregoing discussion. A classification based on urban percentages and/or size of urban place may suffice to delineate the extremes of rural-urban electoral differences, but it is not overly helpful in assessing voting in counties with small and medium-sized cities.

An Overview

The effort to this point has been to cover some of the salient facets of the Republican vote in Texas. The assorted quantitative and impressionistic material bearing on the Party and its prospects leads to two general conclusions about the GOP status: from 1952 to 1961 the Party made substantial progress, but as of 1961, it still had a considerable way to go before becoming an equal contender for offices high and low in Texas.

The Republican Party can justifiably be encouraged by its impressive gains recorded from 1957 to 1961. The comparison of percentage distributions for the 1957 and 1961 special Senate elections provided in Table 10 illustrates the point nicely. The number of counties giving the Republican candidate 30 per cent or more of the vote almost tripled from 1957 to 1961; there were more than 50 per cent fewer counties giving the Republican 20 per cent or less of the vote in 1961 as compared to 1957. Inasmuch as the gains in the higher percentage brackets involved virtually all of the more populous counties, this development is of great importance.

Yet the gains of the GOP should not cause one to lose sight of its general weakness in the state. Concern with the distinctive features of the Republican vote led to concentration on relative rather than on absolute party strength, but helpful as that course of analysis may be, it does make it easy to forget that the vote under scrutiny is that of a party still much in the minority. So far as state and local elections are concerned, the Republican Party has hardly dented the Democratic monopoly on offices; in terms of the number of offices held, the improvement over the 1920's is not striking. This poor showing of the GOP in most state elections may be in part a result of its postwar policy of concentrating resources on the election believed to offer the most hope, to the detriment of others. This is a relevant consideration, but it follows that had the poor showings been improved by an equal division of resources, the results in the favored elections would have shown less Republican strength. In the final analysis, despite the fact that the voter attachment to the GOP is today stronger and better distributed over the state than it has ever been, despite the rise of "presidential Republicanism" and the victories and near-victories of recent years, the Republican Party has not yet brought an end to one-party rule in Texas.

The truth of the matter is that the Texas GOP has a rather narrow basis of political support, except when candidates or issues seeming to transcend partisan politics can be associated with it. The Party in Texas is primarily a middle-class party whose firm support, year in and year out, is drawn from certain elements in the urban community, spearheaded by conservative and sometimes reactionary business and professional groups. To these supporters are added the groups historically conditioned to vote Republican, such as those in the Texas German tradition, those in the Panhandle with a background of Midwestern Republicanism, and those who have migrated here from states with a strong Republican Party. These, plus what Schattschneider called the "unearned increment of politics,"[34] make up the bulk of the normal Republican vote. Their ranks will be augmented from time to time, of course, by others—liberals expressing their unhap-

---

[34] The term is explained by the following quotation: "The corollary of the proposition that no party can win the unanimous support of any social group courted by its managers is that the party may hope to get some support from all groups whether they have been solicited or not; this is the unearned increment of politics" (E. E. Schattschneider, *Party Government*, p. 87).

TABLE 10

Distribution of Texas Counties According to Republican Percentages
in Two Special Senate Elections

Republican Percentage	Number of Counties	
	1957[a]	1961[b]
0– 9.9	44	9
10–19.9	113	57
20–29.9	59	92
30–39.9	24	53
40–49.9	10	26
50–59.9	0	13
60 and over	3	4

[a] Special Senate election of April, 1957 (based on vote for Thad Hutcheson). One of the 254 counties made no return.

[b] Special (first) Senate election of April, 1961 (based on vote for John Tower).

piness with the outcome of the Democratic primaries, ultraconservatives seeking to punish unresponsive Democrats, as well as some who resemble Levin's "alienated voter."[35] Recruits of these types, however, are untrustworthy. Support from such quarters is likely to be unstable and unpredictable, and hence should not be given too much weight in assessing firm Republican strength.

Behind this narrowness is an element of deliberate choice. As indicated by their conduct and pronouncements, state and local Republican leaders have virtually written off that one-fourth of the electorate composed of Negroes and Latin Americans. They have also chosen not to appeal to organized laborers, except perhaps to that small segment responsive to "union-busting" and "right-to-work" campaigns. Nor have they chosen to court the numerous small farmers wedded by circumstances and history alike to the Democratic Party. It is, of course, the prerogative of a political organization to make decisions of this sort, but they seem ill-adapted to attainment of major-party status and to shattering the one-party mold.

There is reason to believe that the GOP in Texas has a much greater potential than has been realized. While this study is concerned not so much with political attitudes as with their crystallized results in the form of election returns, anyone with an understanding of the citizenry in Texas would grant that there are some widespread political attitudes and values ripe for exploitation by Republicans. The

[35] For a study of voter alienation in one of America's largest cities, see Murray B. Levin, *The Alienated Voter: Politics in Boston.*

prevalence in the state of what Max Weber called "the Protestant Ethic," for example, surely represents a GOP asset. Also the great rents in the traditional social fabric induced by industrialization and the closely related attitudinal by-products of rapid and extensive urbanization could be exploited. The alterations over the past thirty years in the nature of the national parties themselves suggest further strains on traditional loyalties. Indeed, when one begins to review them, the opportunities seem so favorable for overthrow of the one-party system in Texas that its continuation seems incredible.

Frequently, the Republican leaders seem to have shown little interest or inadequate skill in seizing these opportunities, but it would be manifestly unfair to lay at their feet all the blame for the continued domination of the Democratic Party. Indeed, for reasons related to the existing community power structures, early and successful escape from that domination may depend upon developments largely out of the hands of Republican leaders. As analysts of the one-party system in the South have elsewhere pointed out,[36] that system tends to build up a momentum which may continue long after the circumstances prompting its emergence have faded. One of the most important instances of this self-perpetuating capacity involves the Democratic monopoly of public office at all levels of Texas government.

The consequence of this is a double handicap for the Republicans. First of all, segments of the community crucial to Republican success, especially those in some manner engaged in serving the public, are often reluctant to become too closely associated with the GOP because of the fear—no doubt sometimes well-founded—that such an identification would lead to erosion of their economic and even social position in that community. Particularly in the smaller cities and in the rural areas, the reluctance to ascertain empirically the consequences of political nonconformity is apparent.

The second handicap arises because the Democratic grip on public affairs in the period under discussion has been predominantly a conservative one. Although conservative Democrats are logically the proper supporters of the GOP, they are unlikely to be interested in joining Republicans in stalking two birds in the bush until and unless the bird in hand has clearly escaped.[37] Concerned as they are pri-

[36] See, for example, Alexander Heard, *A Two-Party South?*, Chap. 5 ("Shackles on the Minority").

[37] "As in all societies, those who have ruled and prospered in the South naturally want to continue to do so. In the final analysis, however, it matters little to them whether they do so under a one-party system or a two-party system. Which means that economic, social or political changes of sufficient magnitude to threaten the

marily with maintaining conservatism in public policies, the right-wing Democrats are not inclined to make common cause with the Republicans unless the occasion demands. As a matter of fact, such successes as the Republicans have had in recent years stem from this willingness on the part of conservative Democrats to throw their influence to the opposition party. Few would argue, for example, that General Eisenhower could have carried the state as he did in 1952 and 1956 had it not been for the support of then Governor Shivers and numerous other state officials and politicians—all nominally Democrats.

Yet, while impressive victories may be achieved in that fashion, a little reflection will show some inherent dangers and limitations. The bolt to the opposition party in presidential elections may cause, in time, a weakening of party loyalty in all elections and thereby undermine the homogeneous one-party base that has served the conservatives in the past. The conservative Democratic leaders have become increasingly aware that a division of their strength between the Democratic and Republican parties might very well result in liberal-moderate domination of the state. For the Republicans the satisfaction of having a winner is doubtless tempered by the knowledge that those who were in fact responsible for victory refuse to be identified with the "winning" party. Building up grass-roots support and political organizations for partisan purposes is difficult enough any time; when much of the real work is done by persons operating under another party label, then the task is harder than ever.

Hence, the future of the Republican Party in Texas depends not only upon improvements in leadership and organization and a broader appeal to the mass of the electorate, but also upon what happens in the Democratic Party. Paradoxically enough, if the liberal faction in that Party should emerge as an unmistakable victor, the stock of the Republican Party should soar, for one of the consequences of such a liberal triumph would be a wholesale desertion of conservatives from the Democratic Party. On the other hand, if the conservative element maintains its supremacy in the Democratic Party in Texas, then Republican growth will be much slower and more difficult. A key issue to the Republicans is thus the outcome of the factional fight in the Democratic Party. To that battleground and its ceaseless engagements we now turn.

---

position of these people would lead them to seek a revision of the one-party system. Correspondingly, they would resist a revision when the alternative appeared unfavorable" (Heard, *A Two-Party South?*, p. 146).

III

THE CONSERVATIVE DEMOCRATS BEFORE 1962

Conservative attitudes are deeply rooted in the history of Texas. Brief status as an independent Republic, participation in the Confederacy, and the traumatic experience of the Reconstruction have all contributed to the development of a states' rights orientation. Frontier individualism—carried over from an earlier era and still evident among ranchers and city descendants of pioneer settlers—has further nourished conservative values. More recently, both states' rights sentiments and individualism have been reinforced by the successes of private enterprise, particularly those of the oil and gas industry.

Although Texans still hold conservative values in high esteem, their traditional political conservatism is in a state of transition. The most obvious change is that many conservatives are now undecided about their party allegiances. Sizable numbers of former conservative Democrats are now realigning themselves with the Republican Party, others are fighting to maintain their traditional leadership within the Democratic Party, and many have not yet made up their minds about which course of action is best.

As the Republican Party lures more and more conservative Democrats into its fold, and as the liberal Democrats strengthen their organization, a serious question arises as to whether conservatives can maintain their control over the Democratic Party apparatus or, at least, whether they can do so without making substantial changes in their tactics and policies. This chapter, in its analysis of the sources of conservative Democratic support in the 1950's and of the impact of recent social and economic changes upon conservative Democratic strength, focuses on this question.

GENERAL PERSPECTIVE

Conservative Democrats have been enjoying political victories throughout the twentieth century, and still function as the political leaders of the state. Postwar liberals have yet to win a Democratic primary for governor or lieutenant governor. Moreover, neither of the two liberal candidates (Henry Gonzalez and Maury Maverick, Jr.,) reached the runoff for United States Senator in 1961, with the result that the voters were forced to choose between conservative Democrat William Blakley and conservative Republican John Tower. And, as indicated in Table 11, conservatives have long held the upper hand in the Texas Legislature.

It is obvious, therefore, that conservatives have an *overall* edge in the state's political battles. However, the question is whether they can continue to win *within the Democratic Party*. By 1957 the liberal Democrats had transformed themselves from a sputtering protest movement into a formidable foe. Ralph Yarborough's victories in the United States Senate races of 1957 and 1958 testify to this fact. As demonstrated by Table 11, general conservative Democratic hegemony in the Legislature has gradually eroded in the decade from 1951 to 1961. To complicate matters, conservatives are deserting to the Republican Party in ever-increasing numbers. Such shifts in party

TABLE 11

Estimated Strength of Conservative and Liberal Democratic
Factions in the Texas Legislature, 1951–1961

Year and Session	House of Representatives		Senate	
	Conservative	Liberal-Moderate	Conservative	Liberal-Moderate
1951 (52nd)	105	45	28	3
1953 (53rd)	91	59	23	8
1955 (54th)[1]	85	61	22	9
1957 (55th)	86	64	22	9
1959 (56th)	80	70	19	12
1961 (57th)	75	75	19	12

Sources: Estimates for the years 1951 through 1959 are from the previously cited *Report on the Conference of Business and Professional Leaders* and probably underestimate conservative strength since only "pure" conservatives are so categorized. The figures for 1961 are based on the *Texas Observer*, July 1, 1959, and Texas Manufacturers Association calculations. In all cases, and particularly in 1959, 1961, and 1962, closer scrutiny of roll-call voting reveals that from 30 to 40 per cent of the liberal-moderate group is composed of moderates.

Special Note: Following the June, 1962, Democratic Party runoff primary, the Texas Manufacturers Association concluded that the fifty-eighth session of the Legislature would have 79 conservatives, 50 liberals, and 21 moderates in the House and 14 conservatives, 14 liberals, and three middle-of-the-roaders in the Senate (*Texas Observer*, June 15, 1962).

[1] Evidently, the business and professional leaders felt that 4 legislators defied classification.

loyalties have not led as yet to liberal victories in gubernatorial primaries, but they have meant that more moderate conservatives such as Price Daniel and John Connally are likely to come to the forefront.

Hence, changes in the strength and nature of conservative forces within the Democratic Party are already evident. The 1962 election results indicate that Texas is now confronted with a three-way battle between almost equally matched conservative Republicans, moderate-conservative Democrats, and liberal Democrats—a three-way tussle which emerged from conservative-liberal Democratic struggles of the 1950's. Because the results of elections during the 1950's most clearly reveal each group's core sources of support and the socio-economic factors responsible for recent changes in Texas politics, we will concentrate on identifying the state's most conservative Democratic counties and describing their characteristics during the fateful fifties. It should be noted, however, that by 1962 almost half of the 58 conservative Democratic counties identified below had switched to the Republican column.

LOCATION AND GEOGRAPHIC COHESIVENESS OF CONSERVATIVE DEMOCRATIC COUNTIES

Gubernatorial and senatorial contests are the truest tests of strength for the state's competing political factions. Accordingly, for purposes of identifying the most conservative Democratic counties, the returns of the 1952, 1954, and 1956 gubernatorial and the 1957 and 1958 United States Senate races were utilized.[1] More specifically, on the basis of these returns three types of conservative counties are distinguished: consistently conservative Democrat, usually conservative Democrat, and usually conservative Democrat with Republican tendencies. The criteria for this distinction are as follows:

[1] In the chapter on the liberal Democrats the take-off point will be the special Senate election of 1957; much use will be made also of quartile rankings. The 1957 election was chosen to delineate liberal counties after it was seen to have a relatively high correlation with other elections offering a test of liberal Democratic voting. However, to utilize only the 1957 election to pinpoint conservative Democratic counties involves some serious problems not present with other alignments, particularly as a result of the Dies vote in East Texas, which reflects less an ideological inclination than loyalty to a native son and appreciation of his long service from an East Texas congressional district. Furthermore, while the use of quartile rankings helps to indicate *relative* party or factional strength it does not provide a sound basis for determining *absolute* strength. Accordingly, by using data covering several elections and giving some attention to percentage as well as quartile figures, an effort is made in this chapter to get a more exact picture of alignments.

For the full list of counties falling in the first quartile of the vote for conservative Democrat Dies in the 1957 special Senate election, see Appendix B.

Consistently Conservative Democrat

Majority for the conservative Democrat in the 1952, 1954, and 1956 gubernatorial primaries and in the 1958 United States Senate election; plurality or better for the conservative Democrat in the 1957 United States Senate contest; first quartile of conservative Democratic vote in at least three races and never below second quartile in any of the five races.

Usually Conservative Democrat

Majority or plurality for the conservative Democrat in four of five contests above; conservative majority in the 1957 Senate race with conservative Democrat receiving more votes than conservative Republican; never below second quartile of conservative Democratic vote in at least four of five designated elections.

Usually Conservative Democrat with Republican Tendencies

Majority for conservative Democrat in the 1952, 1954, and 1956 gubernatorial primaries and in the 1958 United States Senate election; conservative majority in the 1957 Senate race but conservative Republican received more votes than conservative Democrat; never below second quartile of conservative Democratic vote in at least four of five specified contests.

In accord with such criteria 58 "most conservative Democratic" counties are shown in Figure B. Of these, 12 are classified as consistently conservative Democrat, 35 as usually conservative Democrat, and the remaining 11 as usually conservative Democrat with Republican tendencies. Small clusters of these 58 conservative Democratic counties are found in the Panhandle, East Texas proper, and along the Gulf Coast; but the bulk are concentrated in a broad belt encompassing the western, southwestern, and south central portions of the state.

The existence of such geographic patterns is generally confirmed by an investigation of voting behavior in the Texas Legislature. Namely, a comprehensive analysis of roll-call votes during the 1953, 1957, and 1959 legislative sessions reveals that Democratic legislators from the Southwest-South Central, Panhandle, and Rio Grande regions had a strong conservative bias (see Table 12). To a lesser degree, West Texas representatives also displayed conservative leanings.

Closer scrutiny, however, suggests that geographic loyalties per se are gradually eroding. For example, the roll-call voting patterns of Gulf Coast solons are obviously more liberal than one might have expected on the basis of Figure B. Actually, the Gulf Coast contingent has swung back and forth between conservative and liberal tendencies

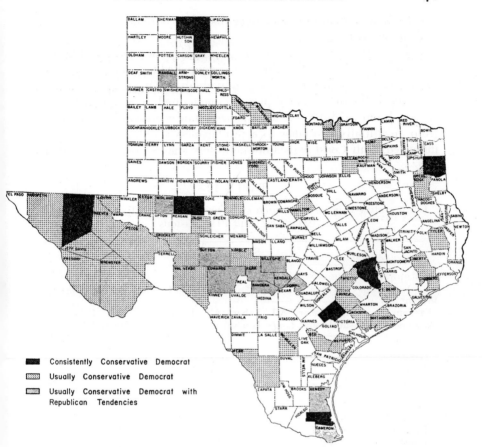

Consistently Conservative Democrat

Usually Conservative Democrat

Usually Conservative Democrat with
Republican Tendencies

Figure B. Most conservative Democratic counties in Texas: 1952–1958.

—depending upon which faction controls the crucial Houston delegation. Even more revealing are the statistics on East Texas representatives. Traditional political lore maintains that the Legislature is dominated by a *cohesive* "East Texas bloc." (The term "East Texas bloc"
includes legislators from both the East Central and East Texas proper
areas noted in Table 12.) But the figures in Table 12 contradict such
assertions. If the conservative Dallas delegation is excluded, within
the East Texas contingent conservative and liberal sentiments are
almost equally represented, with several moderates present as well.

Complicating matters and yet bearing out our doubts about regionalism is the tendency of legislators to shift according to the specific issues
at hand. East Texans, for instance, tend to be more liberal on tax issues
and more conservative on racial and labor questions. In contrast, Gulf

Coast solons are more inclined to be liberal on pure labor than on general welfare issues.

One explanation for this lack of geographic cohesiveness is that in a one-party state legislators seldom feel compelled to band together and, in fact, take pride in voicing their individualism. Of equal significance, however, is the multitude of pressures generated by economic interest groups. From 1953–1959 at least a dozen state representatives switched from an initially pro-labor to a pro-business stand. And, as already indicated, Gulf Coast legislators definitely showed respect for labor's

TABLE 12

Conservative-Liberal Alignments of Texas Representatives by Region:
1953, 1957, and 1959 Sessions

Region[a] and Factional Alignment	Session and Type of Issue[f]									
	1953		1957[e]		1959[e]			Total All Three Sessions		
	All Issues	Labor Issues	All Issues	Labor Issues	All Issues	Labor Issues	Tax Issues	All Issues	Labor Issues	Tax Issues
Panhandle										
Conserv.[b]	6	6	4	4	5	6	6	15	16	6
Moderate[c]	1	0	1	1	0	0	0	2	1	0
Liberal[d]	1	2	3	3	3	2	2	7	7	2
West Texas										
Conserv.	7	6	5	6	7	7	8	19	19	8
Moderate	0	0	5	1	0	2	0	5	3	0
Liberal	6	7	2	5	5	3	4	13	15	4
Southwest-South Central										
Conserv.	7	9	10	10	12	12	12	29	31	12
Moderate	3	0	3	3	0	1	0	6	4	0
Liberal	5	6	2	2	3	2	3	10	10	3
Lower Rio Grande Valley										
Conserv.	2	2	6	6	5	4	5	13	12	5
Moderate	1	0	0	0	0	0	0	1	0	0
Liberal	3	4	0	0	1	2	1	4	6	1
Gulf Coast										
Conserv.	10	5	7	6	5	5	8	22	16	8
Moderate	1	2	10	4	3	0	0	14	6	0
Liberal	13	17	7	14	16	19	16	36	50	16
South Texas										
Conserv.	3	2	1	1	2	2	2	6	5	2
Moderate	1	1	1	1	0	0	0	2	2	0
Liberal	1	2	3	3	3	3	3	7	8	3
West Central										
Conserv.	4	3	4	3	6	5	5	14	11	5
Moderate	2	3	3	1	1	2	1	6	6	1
Liberal	4	4	3	6	3	3	4	10	13	4

TABLE 12 (Continued)

Conservative-Liberal Alignments of Texas Representatives by Region:
1953, 1957, and 1959 Sessions

	Session and Type of Issue[f]									
	1953		1957[e]		1959[e]			Total All Three Sessions		
Region[a] and Factional Alignment	All Issues	Labor Issues	All Issues	Labor Issues	All Issues	Labor Issues	Tax Issues	All Issues	Labor Issues	Tax Issues
East Central										
Conserv.	10	9	11	11	12	11	10	33	31	10
Moderate	1	1	4	2	3	5	0	8	8	0
Liberal	8	9	4	6	4	3	9	16	18	9
East Texas Proper										
Conserv.	8	9	4	3	8	10	8	20	22	8
Moderate	5	6	10	5	6	4	3	21	15	3
Liberal	9	7	8	14	8	8	11	25	29	11

[a] See Appendix F for a map showing which counties are included in each of the designated regions. Though the results are generally comparable, due to the manner in which electoral district lines are drawn for the purpose of electing members to the Texas House of Representatives, a slight discrepancy between the senatorial and gubernatorial elections is apparent. Most of this slight discrepancy is limited, however, to the Panhandle area.

[b] Rated "bad" on 60 per cent or more of roll-call votes according to the AFL-CIO scorecard.

[c] Rated "good" on 41–59 per cent of roll-call votes according to the AFL-CIO scorecard.

[d] Rated "good" on 60 per cent or more of roll-call votes according to the AFL-CIO scorecard.

[e] Only the more crucial votes are used to classify legislators on labor and tax issues during the 1957 and 1959 sessions. During the 1957 and 1959 sessions conservative Waggoner Carr from Lubbock served as speaker and, therefore, he seldom, if ever, voted. This explains why the total number of West Texas representatives is only 12 in 1957 and 1959 as compared with 13 in the 1953 session.

[f] "All Issues" for the three sessions includes the other issues listed for each respective session.

numerical strength in their districts—at least on strictly working-class issues.

When interviewed in 1959, several key legislative leaders remarked that—allowing for some continuation of individualistic behavior—the legislative struggle was becoming more ideological each day, and, in any case, rarely revolved around traditional geographic rivalries. A seasoned West Texas conservative stated that, with the exception of the 1959 speakership race in which West Texas representatives endorsed Waggoner Carr because he hailed from their area, they more often consulted with fellow conservatives from the Gulf Coast than among themselves. Liberals reported that they too conferred more frequently with like-minded legislators from other sections of the state rather than with representatives from their own particular region. The increasing sharpness of this ideological battle is further illustrated by the relatively small number of moderates recorded in Table 12—even when the basis for classification allows ample opportunity for legislators to be so categorized.

In a similar vein, it is noteworthy that county-by-county variations in successful gubernatorial candidates' voting strength have gradually diminished with the passage of time. Specifically, as indicated by the accompanying figures,[2] the county percentages for Jester in 1946 and Daniel in 1956 clustered more around their overall state percentages in contrast to percentage variations associated with Moody's victory in 1926.

Gubernatorial Primary Election	Variation from State Percentage (No. of Counties)			
	Under 5%	5–9.9%	10–14.9%	15% and Over
Daniel (1956)	108	64	48	34
Jester (1946)	121	67	38	27
Moody (1926)	88	67	22	72

This increasing evenness-of-vote distribution also suggests a decrease in the influence of local or traditional geographic factors and a rise in the significance of generalized economic and social forces.

To be sure, regional sentiments affect voting behavior in Texas— more so than in most Northern states. But this premise is less true of Texas than of many Southern states. At the very least, it can be concluded that regionally defined voting forces exist only when *both* traditional historical forces *and* newer, more generalized socio-economic factors combine to exert pressure in the same direction. This conclusion was certainly suggested by the data presented in Chapter II and will become more evident in this and subsequent chapters.

ECONOMIC CHARACTERISTICS OF CONSERVATIVE DEMOCRATIC COUNTIES

The most conservative Democratic counties are not the most industrialized. This interesting fact is revealed by the figures in Table 13. As of 1950 only 11 counties, or 19 per cent, had 10 per cent or more of

[2] The figures for 1926 and 1946 were derived from V. O. Key, *Southern Politics* (p. 261), and those for 1956 were calculated by the authors.

their labor force employed in manufacturing, while in 50 or 86.2 per cent of such counties the value added by manufacturing was less than ten million dollars annually. In comparison, the figures for all of the state's 254 counties were 25.2 and 84.2 per cent respectively. This is not to say that the conservatives are losing ground in the industrial cities. If anything, they have an edge in such places. Rather, it merely signifies that the "safest" votes, though not the largest sources of conservative Democratic support, are located in agricultural areas (a fact that is likewise true for the liberals).

Significantly, 37.9 per cent of the 58 conservative Democratic counties derived the bulk of their income from livestock and livestock products as contrasted with a figure of 22.8 per cent for all counties. But only 27.6 per cent of the most conservative Democratic counties received most of their agricultural income from crop sales as compared with a 34.6 per cent figure for all of the state's counties. Thus, conservatism is much stronger in ranching than in crop-raising areas.

Less markedly, the most conservative Democratic counties tend to enjoy a higher farm standard of living than do the other counties in the state. No less than 17.2 per cent of the 58 conservative Democratic counties had an index number of 180 or above, whereas only 10.6 per cent of all counties were at a similar level. Likewise, the percentage of these 58 conservative counties in the lower-income bracket was decidedly smaller than the percentage figure for the state as a whole.

In order to test these observations more thoroughly our data were rearranged to see whether such economic tracers consistently show up in depth across the entire state. The results, shown in Table 14, generally confirm our earlier findings—except for deviations that can be readily explained.

Table 14 demonstrates that livestock counties are heavily conservative. In the 1954 gubernatorial primary an overwhelming majority of such counties gave high proportions of their vote to conservative Democrat Allan Shivers while crop counties, though not necessarily liberal, were decidedly less disposed to do so. In the 1957 Senate race the livestock counties were somewhat less enthusiastic for conservative Democrat Martin Dies than they were for Shivers in 1954; in fact, crop counties backed Dies with almost equal intensity. But under no circumstances do such discrepancies signify that livestock counties are leaving the conservative fold in substantial numbers. Rather, the situation in 1957 resulted from a set of special circumstances. On one hand, Republican Thad Hutcheson siphoned off some normally conservative Democratic votes in the livestock counties. On the other hand,

TABLE 13

Economic Characteristics of Most Conservative
Democratic Counties in Texas, 1950–1958

	Number and Per Cent of 58 Most Conservative Democratic Counties		Number and Per Cent of All Counties (254)	
	No.	%	No.	%
Per cent employed in manufacturing (1950)				
10% or more	11	19	64	25.2
Value added by manufacturing (1958)				
Above $50 million annually	1	1.7	10	3.9
Below $10 million annually	50	86.2	214	84.2
Pattern of agricultural sales (1954)ᵃ				
Predominantly livestock	22	37.9	58	22.8
Predominantly crops	16	27.6	88	34.6
Farm standard-of-living index (1954)				
180 and over	10	17.2	27	10.6
150–179	18	31.0	70	27.6
120–149	20	34.5	95	37.4
Below 120	10	17.2	62	24.4
Median family income (1949)ᵇ				
$3000 and over	10	20.4	45	18.8
$2000–$2999	22	44.9	99	41.2
Below $2000	17	34.7	96	40.0
Percentage of families earning $5,000 or more annually (1949)ᵇ				
20% and over	10	20.4	55	22.9
10% or less	15	30.6	90	37.5

Sources: The statistics on value added by manufacturing were taken from the United States Department of Commerce, Bureau of the Census, *Census of Manufactures: 1958*, Volume III. All other economic data were derived from the U.S. Bureau of the Census, *County and City Data Book: 1956*.

ᵃ The terms "predominantly livestock" or "predominantly crops" mean that 60 per cent or more of a county's agricultural income was derived from sales of that type of commodity. Among the most conservative Democratic counties 5 were oriented toward dairy and poultry farming and the remaining 15 had a "mixed" agricultural pattern. Similarly, for the state as a whole, 19 counties leaned toward dairy and poultry farming and 89 were engaged in "mixed" agricultural activities.

ᵇ No income statistics were available for 9 of the most conservative Democratic counties and for 5 of the others. Therefore, the income percentages given above are percentages of "classifiable" counties. Specifically, 49 was the base figure for calculating the percentages for the most conservative Democratic and 240 was the base number used in doing the same for all counties.

Dies did better than conservative Democrats usually do in the crop counties because of his personal following in a sizable number of such counties in East Texas, an area that he had previously served in the

TABLE 14

Relation of Agricultural Income and Sales to Conservative
Democratic Vote in 1954 and 1957

| Income and Sales | Percentage of Counties Giving Indicated Share of Vote to Conservative Democratic Candidates | | | | | | | |
| | 1954 Gubernatorial Primary[1] | | | | 1957 Special Senate Election[2] | | | |
	Under 40%	40–49.9%	50–59.9%	60% and over	Under 20%	20–29.9%	30–39.9%	40% and over
Farm standard-of living index (1954)								
180 and over (27 counties)	3.7	3.7	48.1	44.5	7.4	33.3	40.7	18.5
150–179 (70 counties)	1.4	15.7	40.0	42.9	7.1	44.3	41.4	7.1
120–149 (95 counties)	10.6	36.2	29.8	23.4	4.2	30.5	44.2	21.0
Under 120 (62 counties)	21.0	40.3	27.4	11.3	6.4	19.4	21.0	53.2
Pattern of agricultural sales (1954)								
Predominantly livestock (58 counties)	5.2	8.6	34.5	51.7	10.3	29.3	41.4	19.0
Predominantly crops (88 counties)	11.3	30.7	35.2	22.7	6.8	36.4	39.8	17.0

Sources: All percentages calculated by the authors; farm standard-of-living index
and agricultural sales patterns from U.S. Bureau of the Census, *County and City
Data Book: 1956.*
[1] Vote for Allan Shivers in the runoff primary.
[2] Vote for Martin Dies.

United States Congress. When the votes for the conservative Democrat
and conservative Republican are tallied *together*, 74.1 per cent of the
livestock counties went 50 per cent or more "conservative" in 1957
as compared with 86.2 per cent in 1954—a fairly sizable but by no
means discouraging drop of only 12.1 per cent. Likewise, only 39.8
per cent of the crop counties gave majorities to the two conservatives in
1957, as contrasted with a larger figure of 57.9 per cent in 1954—
thus demonstrating that their vote was more for Dies than for conservatism.

Counties with high incomes also are prone to vote conservative.
Such tendencies, however, appear to be less pronounced and decidedly
more unstable than those associated with livestock counties.

According to Table 14, in 1954 93 per cent of the counties with a farm standard-of-living index of 180 and above gave majorities to conservative Democrat Allan Shivers; 63 per cent of the counties with a standard of 150–179 and 53 per cent of those with an index of 120–149 did likewise; and only 39 per cent of the counties at the below-120 level gave their support to Shivers. Similarly, a glance at income data irrespective of agricultural-industrial distinctions (see Table 15) reveals that three-fourths of the counties with a median family income of $3,000 and above gave Shivers 50 per cent or more of their votes; two-thirds of the counties at the $2,000–$2,999 level did likewise; and among those counties with an under-$2,000 figure the number giving him over 50 per cent of the vote barely exceeded the number giving him less.

The figures for 1957, however, depart from the usual patterns. With a 30 per cent mark used as a dividing point—an arbitrary yet a reasonable figure since this contest featured three strong competitors—69 per cent of the counties with a farm standard-of-living index of 180 or better and 60 per cent of those with a median family income of $3,000 and above gave conservative Democrat Dies more than 30 per cent of their votes. Although in many such cases Dies emerged with a plurality, these percentages are decidedly below what one might expect on the basis of the 1954 figures. When the conservative Democratic

TABLE 15

Relation of Income Distribution to Conservative
Democratic Vote in 1954 and 1957

| Median Family Income (1949) | Percentage of Counties Giving Indicated Share of Vote to Conservative Democratic Candidates | | | | | | | |
| | 1954 Gubernatorial Primary[1] | | | | 1957 Special Senate Election[2] | | | |
	Under 40%	40–49.9%	50–59.9%	60% and Over	Under 20%	20–29.9%	30–39.9%	40% and Over
$3,000 and over (45 counties)	4.4	22.2	44.5	28.9	2.2	37.7	48.9	11.1
$2,000– $2,999 (99)	9.1	24.2	40.4	26.3	7.1	38.4	38.4	16.2
Below $2,000 (96)	12.8	33.9	23.9	29.4	7.3	22.9	31.2	38.5

Source: Income figures from U.S. Bureau of Census, *County and City Data Book: 1956;* percentages calculated by the authors. Income figures for 14 counties were not available.
[1] Vote for Allan Shivers in the runoff primary.
[2] Vote for Martin Dies.

and Republican totals are lumped together, only 78 per cent of the counties with a farm living index of 180-plus gave him 50 per cent or more of their support—a figure 15 per cent below that of 1954.

Hence, there was a *slight* though not damaging decline of conservative strength in the wealthier counties. More startling, however, is the fact that the lowest-income counties rather than those with the highest income most consistently supported Dies. No less than 74 per cent of the counties with a farm standard-of-living level of less than 120 and 70 per cent of those with a median family income of less than $2,000 gave him 30 per cent or more of their votes.

Though somewhat surprising at first, the 1957 deviation can be explained. As noted earlier, Dies had served as a congressman from an East Texas district; accordingly, he capitalized on regional sentiments to capture several of the lower-income counties within that area. In part, the instability of income patterns may also result from the methodological weaknesses inherent in using data from county units. As suggested by earlier information on Republican voting in Houston's silk-stocking areas, precinct returns would probably show more clearly the strong tendency of high-income groups to endorse conservative candidates.[3]

In summary, the "safe" conservative Democratic counties are primarily engaged in agricultural pursuits, are more oriented toward livestock ranching than crop farming, and generally, though not markedly so, enjoy a higher farm standard of living. Irrespective of agricultural-industrial distinctions, the median family incomes in these conservative Democratic counties are also a shade better than average.

URBANIZATION AND THE CONSERVATIVE DEMOCRATS

Political scientists frequently stress urban-rural differences as well as economic cleavages in their explanations of voting behavior. They point specifically to the tendency of big cities—especially their cores— to be liberal and Democratic and of rural districts to go conservative and Republican. Texas voting, however, does not conform to such

[3] Lubell's report indicates the clarifications made possible by sub-county data. In 1952 Eisenhower received about 75 per cent of the vote in Houston precincts with home valuations over $10,000 (94 per cent in the over-$30,000 areas) whereas in precincts with home valuations of $5,000 or less the general obtained only 40 per cent of the ballots cast (Samuel Lubell, *The Revolt of the Moderates*, p. 186). Donald Strong turned up equally interesting patterns when he calculated that within the 25 Dallas precincts in the first quartile of income levels some 79 per cent of the voters favored Eisenhower while in 11 precincts in the fourth quarter of income only 48 per cent supported him (Donald Strong, *Urban Republicanism in the South*, p. 24).

ready-made patterns. Distinctions between the political preferences of
urban and rural voters exist, but they are neither sharp nor consistent.
Furthermore, the metropolitan centers show the most conservative
strength while the more rural counties tend to sympathize with liberal and Democratic candidates. Such conclusions were suggested in
the preceding chapter and are even more clearly demonstrated by the
following analyses of the results of Democratic primaries and state
legislative sessions from 1956 to 1959.

Utilizing the urban-rural scale described in Chapter II, we find that
in the 1956 Democratic gubernatorial primary there was a 7.5 per
cent differential between the preferences of voters in the most urban
and those from the most rural counties. However, as indicated in
Table 16, conservative Democrat Price Daniel received his highest
ratio (52.5 per cent) from the urban areas and his lowest percentage
(45 per cent) from the rural sections. To complicate matters, the
figures for the other categories do not represent a consistent scaling
from these extremes. For example, the next lowest percentages for the
conservative candidate are not found in the next-to-the-most-rural
counties, but in the small-urban and agri-urban categories near the
center of the scale. And the next-to-the-most-rural counties (nonfarm
rural-urban and nonfarm rural) are almost as conservative as the
most urban counties.

Close scrutiny of roll-call votes in the 1957 and 1959 legislative
sessions reveals a similar lack of depth and of consistency in urban-
rural distinctions. As shown in Table 17, during the 1957 session another differential emerged. But, once again, it did not fit traditional

TABLE 16

Urban-Rural Differences in Voting for Conservative Candidate
in 1956 Democratic Gubernatorial Primary

Type and Number of Counties	Total Vote	Percentage of Total Vote for Conservative Candidate
Metropolitan (12)	591,174	52.5
Large Urban (17)	187,602	50.6
Intermediate Urban (22)	77,684	50.8
Small Urban (7)	42,207	46.2
Agri-Urban (20)	114,878	46.3
Nonfarm Rural-Urban (27)	43,068	51.4
Nonfarm Rural (65)	146,054	50.3
Farm Rural (84)	183,814	45.0

Source: Calculated by the authors from county election returns.

expectations, for the big-city delegations were more conservative than their colleagues from the countryside. In 1959 urban-rural cleavages were even less pronounced. On one hand, the metropolitan-based solons were closely divided between conservative and liberal leanings. Rural legislators, on the other hand, vacillated according to the nature of the problem—almost evenly divided on all issues, predominantly conservative on pure labor questions, and liberal in tax controversies. In actuality, sharp battles along urban-rural lines occur only on such issues as reapportionment of legislative seats, reduction of farm-to-market-road programs, and, to a lesser degree, utilization of water resources.

When added to the gradual loosening of traditional geographic loyalties, this relative absence of urban-rural clashes tends to confirm the thesis that Texas voting patterns are increasingly influenced by more generalized ideological forces of an economic nature. Interestingly enough, it also suggests that more attention should be devoted to an examination of mutual ties between residents of cities and their neighboring rural counties.

A full-fledged analysis of the interrelationships between metropolitan areas and their surrounding countrysides would require the sifting of data on a scale that is not feasible here. But limited investigation indicates that such a study might add a great deal to our knowledge of the electoral process in Texas. San Antonio's conservative tendencies, for example, have been nourished in no small measure by the conservatism of the adjacent German counties. Only recently have such pressures been offset partially by the growing influence of moderate-to-liberal Latin Americans on the central city's west side. A stronger case of mutual attraction is that found in the Midland area. The rural counties serviced by Midland are dominated by oil and gas production, cattle ranching, and large-scale farming; while Midland itself contains a high percentage of high-income, professional-managerial-technical, white-collar elements. The result is that city and countryside reinforce each other's ideological outlook to the point that this region of the state is a center of rock-ribbed conservatism.

This process is not one that benefits only the conservatives. Voting in McLennan (Waco) County has almost certainly been edged toward the liberal side by virtue of its setting in the midst of a farm area that has a heritage of Populism. A similar though somewhat weaker reinforcing relationship exists between labor in Wichita Falls and rural liberals from nearby North Texas counties. Where the connections involve commuters the possibilities are even more intriguing. Political organizers of the Texas AFL-CIO insist, for example, that the true

TABLE 17

Urban-Rural Differences and Ideological Position in the Texas House of Representatives: 1957 and 1959 Sessions

	1957 Session						1959 Session								
	All Issues[d]			Labor Issues			All Issues[d]			Labor Issues			Tax Issues		
	C[a]	M[b]	L[c]	C	M	L	C	M	L	C	M	L	C	M	L
Metropolitan Counties															
Harris	2	5	1	2	0	6	0	0	8	0	0	8	0	0	8
Dallas	6	1	0	5	2	0	7	0	0	6	1	0	7	0	0
Tarrant	5	1	1	6	0	1	3	0	4	1	2	4	3	0	4
Bexar	5	2	0	5	2	0	6	0	1	6	0	1	6	0	1
El Paso	1	3	0	2	1	1	2	0	2	3	0	1	2	0	2
Jefferson	1	0	3	1	0	3	0	1	3	0	0	4	1	0	3
Nueces	2	1	0	2	0	1	1	0	2	1	0	2	2	0	1
TOTAL	22	13	5	23	5	12	19	1	20	17	3	20	21	0	19
Rural Districts[k]															
Panhandle[e]	3	0	0	3	0	0	2	0	1	3	0	0	2	0	1
West Central[f]	1	2	2	1	0	4	3	1	1	3	0	2	2	0	3
South-Southwest[g]	1	0	2	1	0	2	1	0	2	1	0	2	1	0	2
Central-South Central[h]	2	1	3	4	0	2	4	0	2	4	1	1	3	0	3
Gulf Coast[i]	2	1	0	2	0	1	2	0	1	1	1	1	1	0	2
East Texas[j]	3	3	5	4	1	6	5	1	5	6	1	4	4	0	7
TOTAL	12	7	12	15	1	15	17	2	12	18	3	10	13	0	18

[a] Classified as "conservative" (C) if rated "bad" on 60 per cent or more roll-call votes according to AFL-CIO scoreboard.
[b] Classified as "moderate" (M) if rated "good" on 41–59 per cent of roll-call votes according to AFL-CIO scoreboard.
[c] Classified as "liberal" (L) if rated "good" on 60 per cent or more of roll-call votes according to AFL-CIO scoreboard.
[d] 1957 "All Issues" includes "Labor Issues." 1959 "All Issues" includes "Tax Issues" and "Labor Issues."
[e] Districts 88, 89, 96.
[f] Districts 71, 76, 83, 85, 90.
[g] Districts 69, 70, 78.
[h] Districts 45, 46, 47, 57, 74, 77.
[i] Districts 30, 31, 34.
[j] Districts 2, 3, 5, 6, 7, 11, 12, 26, 27, 43, 55, 56.

measure of the strength of Dallas labor unions is to be found not in Dallas proper but in the election returns from surrounding cities and counties where union members who work in the larger city have taken up residence.

Whether or not new regional alignments based on mutual and largely economic ties between cities and surrounding rural counties will emerge is not yet clear. This much, however, is already apparent—the future outcome of Texas' political warfare will be determined largely in the metropolitan areas. For instance, Texas' 12 most urban counties accounted for no less than 42.5 per cent of the total vote in the 1956 Democratic gubernatorial primary; and in the 1957 Senate contest their share rose to approximately 51 per cent.

Because they contain such a large and increasing share of the state's electors, Texas cities have become the scene of close and intense ideological battles. The closeness of the struggle is illustrated by the fact that from 1952 to 1958 only 4 of the state's 12 most populous counties could be definitely classified as either conservative or liberal. Dallas ranked as "consistently conservative" while McLennan, Nueces, and Wichita Counties were "usually liberal," which is defined as follows:

Usually Liberal Democrat

Liberal majority or plurality in 1957 Senate race and majority for the liberal Democrat in three of four other races (1952, 1954, and 1956 gubernatorial primaries and 1958 United States Senate election); never below second quartile of liberal Democratic vote in at least four of the five above designated elections.

The remaining 8 (Bexar, El Paso, Harris, Jefferson, Lubbock, Potter, Tarrant, and Travis) were either so evenly divided or so prone to fluctuate that they could not be placed in either camp. The ideological intensity of urban battles is borne out by the fact that the forces at the two extremes of the political spectrum—conservative Republicans and liberal Democrats—have both made sizable gains in metropolitan areas. (The achievements of the former have been described in Chapter II; those of the latter will be revealed in the chapter to follow.)

Throughout the 1950's, particularly from 1952 to 1956, the conservative Democrats held the edge in the expanding cities. In the 1954 gubernatorial primary, conservative Democrat Allan Shivers carried 14 (82 per cent) of the 17 counties with cities of 50,000 or more population (see Table 18). At the same time, he won in 39 (64 per cent) of the 61 counties whose largest cities were in the 10,000 to 49,999 range, and only 104 (59 per cent) of the 176 counties without a city of 10,000

TABLE 18

Conservative Democratic Voting in 1954 According to Size of City

County Category According to Size of Largest City (1957 Estimate)	Percentage of Category Giving Indicated Share of Vote to Conservative Democrat Allan Shivers			
	Under 40%	40– 49.9%	50– 59.9%	60% and Over
50,000 and over (17 counties)				
Number of counties	0	3	11	3
Percentage	0%	17.6%	64.8%	17.6%
10,000 to 49,999 (61)				
Number of counties	4	18	24	15
Percentage	6.5%	29.5%	39.4%	24.6%
Below 10,000 (176)				
Number of counties	21	50	51	54
Percentage	11.9%	28.5%	28.9%	30.7%

or over. In 1956 52.5 per cent of the voters in the 12 most urban areas favored moderately conservative Democrat Price Daniel for governor, while only 45 per cent of the electors in the most rural counties did likewise. All of this conclusively demonstrates that at least in the mid-1950's conservative Democrats controlled the cities and, as a matter of fact, fared better in the more urban than in the more rural areas.

The reasons for this conservative advantage in Texas' metropolitan centers were touched upon in Chapter II, but are well worth repeating and clarifying. First, in comparison with their Northern counterparts, Texas cities are oriented more toward commerce than manufacturing. For example, in Dallas, Houston, and San Antonio from 11 per cent (San Antonio) to 20 per cent (Houston and Dallas) of the working force is employed in manufacturing establishments while the figures for cities like Cleveland, Chicago, Detroit, and Philadelphia range from 33 per cent (Chicago and Philadelphia) to 41 per cent (Cleveland). Similarly, at a smaller level, liberally inclined cities like Evansville, South Bend, and Toledo have ratios of 30.6, 39.4, and 34.4 per cent respectively while conservative-minded Texas cities like Amarillo, Lubbock, and Midland have percentages of 11.9, 10.6, and 4.5 per cent respectively.[4]

[4] For greater detail on percentages of manufacturing employment in Texas and Northern cities see Chapter II. It should also be recalled that these percentages and those on white-collar employment are for the central cities and do not include fringe areas.

Second, even when some manufacturing is present in Texas cities the plants are smaller and a larger percentage of the labor force is professional, managerial, or technical. For instance, with the exception of Port Arthur, where the manufacturing employment ratio is the largest in the state (36.9 per cent), in 1960 the proportions of white-collar workers in Texas' larger cities were between 45.5 per cent (San Antonio, Houston, Corpus Christi, and Fort Worth had percentages of 45.5, 47, 47.1, and 47.3 per cent respectively) and 54 per cent (Austin, Wichita Falls, Dallas, and Lubbock had figures of 54, 50.5, 50.3, and 50 per cent respectively. In smaller but rapidly expanding Midland the white-collar ratio was 54.8 per cent). In contrast, the white-collar percentages for cities like Cleveland, Chicago, Detroit, Evansville, Philadelphia, South Bend, and Toledo ranged from 32.9 (Cleveland) to 42.9 per cent (Evansville) with most of them clustering around the 40 per cent mark. Moreover, within the general white-collar classification, the percentages for such subcategories as "professional, technical, and kindred workers" and "managers, officers, and proprietors" as against those for plain "clerical and kindred workers" are markedly higher in the Texas than in the Northern metropolitan centers.[5]

Third, despite improvement of working conditions and despite labor's growing influence in Texas politics (particularly in the Legislature), unionization is not yet far along in many areas. According to recent estimates by the state AFL-CIO headquarters, Texas ranks thirty-eighth in degree of union organization. Of course, a white-collar, managerial city like Dallas resists unionization for somewhat different reasons than would San Antonio with its large, poverty-stricken minority and its surplus labor supply. Whatever the causes, however, the weakness of the liberal-oriented labor movement unquestionably improves the relative power of the conservatives.[6]

Closely related to labor's problems is the failure of liberal elements to capitalize on the potential power of the minorities, which in Northern cities often provide the mainstay of liberal forces. Racial and ethnic minorities are not particularly large in several Texas cities, but even when they do represent sizable portions of a city's population their potential is never realized. One problem, of course, is lack of leader-

[5] U.S. Bureau of the Census, *Summary of Social and Economic Characteristics of the United States: 1960.*

[6] One leading union official in Dallas has been quoted as saying that labor there is so weak and intimidated that only one of some 100 union officials was serving as a precinct chairman; by contrast, one of the major oil companies had sixteen employees who were listed as precinct chairmen, all apparently representing the conservative Democratic faction (*Texas Observer,* October 17, 1958).

ship and organization within the liberally inclined minority groups. In addition to this handicap the *actions,* or lack thereof, of Anglo-white liberals have sometimes failed to appeal emotionally to such status-starved minorities.

Also significant is the impact of community power structures. With the growing closeness of urban ideological battles, the interrelationship between a city's socio-economic leadership and its politics is likely to have an even greater bearing upon the outcome of future elections. This possibility is well illustrated by the following statement from one student of Rio Grande Valley politics:

Do you know that you can take two counties, side by side, with the same background, mores, and beliefs, and have one county with a big civic leader taking an active part for the liberals and the other county with the local leadership for the conservatives, and the liberals will carry one county and the conservatives the other? Local leadership is that important. Counties, quite similar, will take diametrically opposed voting positions, solely because of the local leadership.[7]

More often than not this community leadership leans toward the conservative camp because in many Texas cities it is comprised of a fairly close-knit business and professional oligarchy.

Once again, the classic example of such high-powered conservative organization is Dallas, where civic leadership is in the hands of a Citizens Council composed of some 175 business and professional leaders who informally, efficiently, and—so it seems—sensibly make the important decisions affecting the city and its future.[8] This is not necessarily to condemn such a situation or even to imply that it is undesirable; such judgments are matters for each individual to decide. In fact, it seems clear that in many cities such groups have provided effective and honest city administration, and that members of the oligarchy earn their positions of community leadership by devoting much of their time to worthwhile civic projects. Rather, this reference to busi-

---

[7] *Texas Observer,* November 14, 1958.

[8] See, for example, such divergent sources as "The Dynamic Men of Dallas," *Fortune,* February, 1949, and George Feurmann, *Reluctant Empire,* pp. 128–131. The Dallas Citizens Council (which has absolutely no connection with White Citizens Councils) received its greatest publicity in 1961 when it took the lead and performed ably in preparing Dallas for integration of its public schools.

Of course, Dallas conservatives are never perfectly united. In the 1958 congressional election, moderate-liberal Democrat "Barefoot" Sanders was supported by some of the more progressive businessmen who were beginning to tire of the "doctrinaire" conservatism espoused by Republican incumbent Bruce Alger. The group included a number of downtown businessmen, bankers, and property owners who wanted urban renewal and development of the Trinity River, with national government funds if necessary.

ness oligarchies merely reflects the truism that urban businessmen in Texas provide heavy support for conservative politicians on a relatively united basis, that they exert more than normal influence over the communications and educational systems, and that they possess a reservoir of power and prestige that more or less automatically and effortlessly provides extra political influence.

Conservative community elites are not always as cohesive as they are in Dallas. Harris County (Houston) politics in 1956 and 1958 provides an example of what can happen when businessmen bicker among themselves over leadership, tend to be too doctrinaire, and assume that elections can be won without grass-roots organization if enough money is made available. In these two elections liberals took advantage of such failures on the part of the opposition and managed to improve their own political position considerably. However, when in 1960 the Houston business community closed ranks, organized at the precinct level, and moderated its stand, it was able to unseat five of the county's liberal legislators and to replace them with staunch conservatives.[9]

Despite victories in the mid-1950's, conservative control of Texas cities—especially that of the conservative Democrats—is by no means firm. Even in 1954 urban voters tended to be more evenly divided than their rural counterparts (see Table 19). Of the 17 counties with cities of 50,000 or over, 11 counties (64.8 per cent) were clustered together in the 50–59.9 per cent for-Shivers category. Only 3 (17.6 per cent) gave him more than 60 per cent support, and the remaining 3 were all found in the 40–49.9 per cent bracket. In contrast, among the counties with no city of 10,000 almost exactly the same number of counties are found in each of the three categories ranging from 40 per cent and above, thereby indicating that the rural counties were more likely than urban areas to have pronounced preferences for either the conservatives or liberals, as the case may be.

The figures for the 1957 and 1958 Senate contests more clearly demonstrate the decline in stability of conservative Democratic hegem-

---

[9] This paragraph is based on information derived from interviews with key Houston newsmen, leaders of the Texas Manufacturers Association, and union officials active in the area, conducted for the most part in the summer of 1959. Officials of TMA particularly emphasized the need for conservative precinct organization. That steps in that direction were taken is indicated by the *Houston Post* story (recounted in the *Texas Observer*, May 6, 1960). In the 1960 Democratic primary at least twelve of the conservative candidates for precinct chairman were management employees of Sheffield Steel, another nine of Humble Oil, and several others from Gulf Oil, the Texas Company, A. O. Smith Corporation, Tennessee Gas, Sohio Petroleum, and Brown and Root. Many of these business-affiliated conservatives were successful in their bid for party office.

TABLE 19

Conservative Democratic Voting in 1957 According to Size of City

County Category According to Size of Largest City (1957 Estimate)	Percentage of Category Giving Indicated Share of Vote to Conservative Democrat Martin Dies			
	Under 20%	20–29.9%	30–39.9%	40% and Over
50,000 and over (17 counties)				
Number of counties	1	7	8	1
Percentage	5.9	41.1	47.1	5.9
10,000 to 49,999 (61)				
Number of counties	1	22	18	20
Percentage	1.6	36.1	29.5	32.8
Below 10,000 (176)				
Number of counties	13	52	69	42
Percentage	7.4	29.5	39.2	23.9

ony in the cities. In the three-cornered 1957 election 88 per cent of the counties having cities of 50,000 and above fell within the two intermediate percentage groupings. Actually, all but 6 of these 17 counties gave liberal Democrat Ralph Yarborough winning pluralities ranging from 34 to 52 per cent. (Exceptions were Bexar, Dallas, Smith, Tarrant, Tom Green, and Webb Counties.) And in the 1958 Senate race Yarborough swept to victory in no less than 15 of the 17. (In this case Dallas and Taylor Counties were the exceptions.) One should not, however, leap to the unjustified conclusion that these figures represent resounding renunciations of the conservative creed. If one adds together the totals of both the conservative Democrat and the conservative Republican in the 1957 election, it is apparent that conservatives received majorities in all but 2 of the 17 most urban counties (the 2 exceptions were McLennan and Wichita Counties). One might well attribute Yarborough's 1958 success to his being the incumbent; his performance in Congress had allayed some of the exaggerated fears about his "radicalism"; and, above all, his personality image was more appealing to the voters than that of his opponent.

PERSPECTIVE FOR THE FUTURE

We are inclined to conclude that, though conservatism is still a virile force in Texas politics, the conservative Democrats per se are likely to find the going increasingly rough in Texas cities. In part, this judgment is derived from the expectation that the Republican Party will continue to siphon off conservative Democratic votes. It is based equally on the assumption that the liberal Democratic potential will be better realized in the future. More specifically, though we do not anticipate any outstanding growth in union membership and support, we assume that the liberally inclined minority groups will become better organized and that liberal politicians will learn to make more convincing appeals to such groups. At the very least, the conservative Democrats will have to think more seriously about making changes if they are to avoid being crushed in the gradually tightening nutcracker formed by the Republicans and the liberal Democrats.

IV

THE LIBERAL DEMOCRATS BEFORE 1962

Texas conservatism is deeply implanted in Texas history and is being continuously fertilized by favorable economic and social factors. But one must not forget the radical heritage of the state. Liberals and reformists have been attacking the traditional conservative hegemony from the time of the Civil War. Today they not only are challenging the conservatives with increasing fervor, but are approaching a rightful place of their own in the political structure of Texas. Just what motivates and characterizes the liberal loyalists, how many voters have responded favorably to their call for liberal policies, and what groups may respond to it in the future—these are matters of great moment in the Texas political scene.

HISTORICAL PERSPECTIVE

From the end of Reconstruction (1876) until World War I the controlling conservative Democrats were constantly harassed by a number of protest movements. In the late 1870's and early 1880's the Granger and Greenback Movements expressed rural dissatisfaction and frustration. Though largely unsuccessful, they in turn provided the nucleus for the Farmers' Alliance and the People's Party (Populists) of the late 1880's and early 1890's.[1] The Populists polled 44 per cent of the vote in the 1896 gubernatorial campaign on a platform calling for government ownership of railroad and telegraph lines, restrictions on corporate land ownership, an eight-hour day, and more public education; hence, it is understandable why we refer to a significant liberal strain in Texas history.[2] Because the Populists failed to win any major

[1] The best single treatment of protest politics in Texas from Reconstruction through the Populist era is Roscoe Martin, *The People's Party in Texas: A Study of Third-Party Politics.* See also Rupert H. Richardson's, *Texas: The Lone Star State,* pp. 352 ff.

[2] The various platforms of the Populists (including that of 1896) are found in E. W. Winkler, *Platforms of Political Parties in Texas.*

offices the movement soon collapsed; but for a decade they pushed the Democratic Party into a posture quite different from that of the preceding post-Reconstruction days. Indeed, one could say that the Populist demise was in part the work of a reforming Democrat, Jim Hogg, who took away much of the appeal of the Populists by espousing certain aspects of their program—particularly antitrust and railroad regulation. As a result it was difficult for his Democratic successors to turn their backs completely upon reformist pleas.

After the Populist Movement, spent by 1898, there was a brief respite from liberal attacks. Then, in the decade just before World War I another outbreak came in the form of the Progressive Movement. Although the courts eventually nullified part of the Progressive accomplishments, legislation passed on behalf of labor unions, plus tax reforms that increased the levies on business, clearly indicated a brief revival of liberalism.[3]

From the First World War until the New Deal the tone of Texas politics was predominantly conservative. Nevertheless, some deviation appeared in the form of "Fergusonism." First elected governor in 1914, "Farmer Jim" Ferguson was impeached and removed from office in 1917. Blocked from office himself, he thereafter campaigned for his wife on the platform of "two governors for the price of one." (Mrs. Ferguson served as governor during 1925–1927 and again during 1933–1935.) Whatever their personal faults, the Fergusons consistently preached for the poor farmer,[4] opposed prohibition, and attacked the Ku Klux Klan. In many ways their pleas smacked of rural demagoguery, but to V. O. Key they were also in some degree deserving of the "liberal" label.[5]

For all its passions, Fergusonism could not force a reorientation of state politics and policies. The Depression and the New Deal did. Under Governor James Allred, who was first elected on a conservative platform but who gradually became the state's most liberal chief executive of modern times, Texas began its slow transition to the welfare state. The results were predictable. Organized labor grew in strength, minority groups became restless, and farmers once again turned to politics. The threat to the old business hegemony soon became ap-

[3] On the Progressive period see James Tinsley, "The Progressive Movement in Texas" (unpublished Ph.D. dissertation).

[4] As governor, Jim Ferguson pushed through a law limiting farm tenancy (later declared unconstitutional) and worked for rural education.

[5] V. O. Key, Jr., describes the Fergusons as the liberals of Texas politics at a time when clear-cut economic issues were lacking. See *Southern Politics in State and Nation*, pp. 263 ff. The Ferguson era is also summarized in Richardson's *Texas: The Lone Star State*, pp. 289–295.

parent, and counterattacks were launched challenging sharply the philosophy and the programs associated with the New Deal. Industrialization, wartime growth, and reviving prosperity only heightened the tensions by reinforcing both camps. By the mid-1940's it was becoming apparent that Texas had a "politics of economics."[6]

In the late 1940's and early 1950's the liberal-conservative split was further intensified by the commanding presence of Allan Shivers. He first came to high office from the lieutenant governor's chair upon the death of Governor Beauford H. Jester in 1949 and subsequently was re-elected for three full terms—an unprecedented accomplishment at that time. Other governors of Texas have been more conservative in their convictions (e.g., Coke Stevenson or W. Lee O'Daniel), but none matched Shivers in his frankly ideological appeal and his capacity to organize and lead the right-of-center forces.

In 1956 Lyndon Johnson and a moderate-liberal coalition defeated Shivers in the battle for control of the Democratic Party's state convention. Thereafter, during the late 1950's, signs of a definite drift away from conservatism were apparent.[7] Despite his espousal of the conservative cause, Price Daniel, Shivers' successor as governor, was not afraid to attack proposals for a general sales tax and to denounce gas and banking interests for opposing his own tax program. In 1957 liberal Ralph Yarborough won the special election to fill an unexpired United States Senate term, and in 1958 he nailed down the victory by winning a full term by a sizable margin of 58.7 per cent. After an extended session of the 1959 Legislature the liberals also beat back a determined bid to pass a general sales tax.

The elections of 1960 appeared to continue this trend. In the gubernatorial primary Price Daniel—who by then was under attack by many conservatives—soundly defeated the more conservative Jack Cox. Similarly, in the November presidential election, the liberal-moderate Democratic ticket carried the state, albeit by a small margin.

Recently, however, the liberals have suffered several defeats. In the 1961 Senate race both of the liberal hopefuls, Maverick and Gonzalez, failed to make even the runoff. Of course, the first stage of the 1961 contest was by no means a complete reversal of the Kennedy-Johnson triumph in 1960. Among the initial top six contenders the two liberals and the two moderates (Wilson and Wright) together had a vote percentage almost equal to the combined vote garnered by the two avowed

---

[6] Key, *Southern Politics*, pp. 254 ff.

[7] This behavior pattern is by no means peculiar to Texas politics. For example, see H. J. Doherty, "Liberal and Conservative Voting Patterns in Florida," *Journal of Politics*, 14 (1952), 403–417.

conservatives (Blakley and Tower).[8] Then during the 1961 session of the State Legislature the conservatives finally pushed through a general-sales-tax measure. And in 1962, liberal Don Yarborough fell short in his bid to win the Democratic nomination for governor.

Despite recent setbacks it is evident from the foregoing survey that Texas is not always as monolithically conservative as often pictured. In the late 1950's, at least, some persons even referred to a trend toward liberalism. The extent and nature of this change is more clearly revealed by the following examination of the location and the socio-economic nature of the liberal counties in Texas.

LOCATION AND SIGNIFICANCE OF MOST LIBERAL COUNTIES

The starting point for an inquiry into the liberal vote is the special Senate election of 1957. This race, it will be recalled, pitted a clearly identified liberal Democrat (Ralph Yarborough) against a strong Republican (Thad Hutcheson) and a prominent conservative Democrat (Martin Dies). Under such conditions pro-Yarborough counties generally can be regarded as the "hard core" of liberal strength.

Most of the first-quartile Yarborough counties are certainly worthy of the liberal label. Despite the three-cornered nature of the 1957 race, within these counties Yarborough received winning majorities of 53.5 per cent and above. Furthermore, as demonstrated in Table 20, they were consistently in the top two quartiles of the liberal vote in preceding gubernatorial and presidential contests.[9] Fifty-four of these 62 counties were in the upper half of the Yarborough gubernatorial vote in 1954; no fewer than 44 of them were in the top half of the Democratic tally in the 1948 and 1952 presidential elections; and in the 1956 presidential sweepstakes 59 of them were so ranked. Indeed, in the four elections just cited, never more than 5 of the 62 fell into the last quarter of the liberal vote.

Geographically, the most liberal counties are somewhat scattered throughout the central and the west central regions of the state, with a

---

[8] See *Texas Observer*, April 8, 1961.

[9] For the full list of counties in the top quartile of the vote for Yarborough in the 1957 election, see Appendix B. This section at various points makes use of the Democratic vote in presidential elections as an indication of liberal voting. In spite of limitations this procedure may be justified on two grounds: the liberal program in Texas heavily emphasizes loyalty to the national Democratic Party, and both the liberals in Texas and the national Party generally stand for similar social and economic policies. For the policy positions of a large sample of national Democratic Party leaders, see Herbert McClosky *et al.*, "Issue Conflict and Consensus Among Party Leaders and Followers," *American Political Science Review* (*APSR*), LIV (1960), 406–427.

TABLE 20

Previous Voting Patterns of Counties in the First Quartile
of Yarborough's 1957 Vote

Elections	Number of Yarborough Counties Falling into Indicated Category (Total: 62)
a1948 presidential election vote	
for Democrat	
Top half	44
Lower half	11
1952 presidential election vote	
for Democrat	
Top half	44
Lower half	18
1954 gubernatorial primary vote	
for Liberal	
Top half	54
Lower half	8
1956 presidential election vote	
for Democrat	
Top half	59
Lower half	3

a Only 55 counties are involved here because some counties failed to make official election returns.

few in East Texas proper and in the Gulf Coast arc from Brownsville to Galveston Bay. The most significant clusters are in the Rolling Plains area of West Central Texas and in Central-East Central Texas (see Figure C). A sizable group of counties in and slightly below the Panhandle also endorsed Yarborough, but in many such counties the pro-Yarborough vote resulted from a reaction to temporary drought conditions rather than from true liberal convictions.

As in the case of the most conservative Democratic counties, the 62 most liberal counties do not provide the bulk of the liberal vote. Specifically, in the 1952 gubernatorial primary these counties contributed but 17.1 per cent of Yarborough's total tally (see Table 21). By 1958, when Yarborough carried the state by slightly over 58 per cent, the share he received from these 62 liberal counties had declined to 11.6 per cent.

Although their bulk is not impressive, the consistency of the most liberal counties is significant. According to their records for Yarborough's four contests in 1952, 1956, 1957, and 1958, these 62 counties were quite regular in their contributions to Yarborough's vote. The same stability appears in comparisons of state and presidential elec-

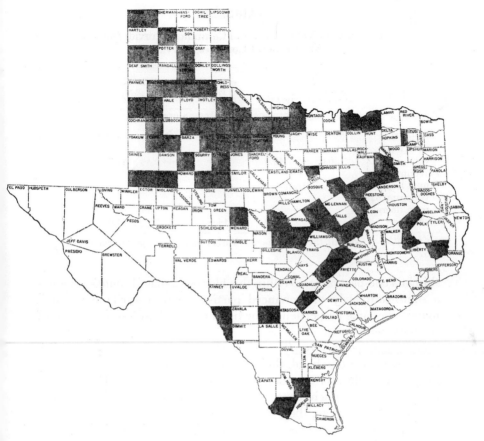

Figure C. Texas counties in first quartile of the 1957
vote for Ralph Yarborough.

tions in 1952 and 1956. In 1952 these 62 liberal counties provided 13.9
per cent of Stevenson's vote and 17.1 per cent of Yarborough's total; in
1956 the same group yielded percentages of 13.8 and 14.4 respectively
for Stevenson and Yarborough (see Table 21).

More remarkably, the figures remain quite similar *despite differences in voter turnout*. The greatest discrepancy in turnout is that
between the 1952 presidential election, in which more than two million
votes were recorded, and the 1957 special Senate election, when less
than 900,000 ballots were cast for the three major contestants. Despite
such a wide gap, each time these counties yielded almost exactly the
same share of the vote garnered by the liberal candidates.

All this suggests an unusual structuring of the electorate's partisan-

TABLE 21

Percentage of Vote for Liberal Candidates Provided by the Most Liberal Counties in Texas

	1952 Gub. 1st Primary (3 Candidates)	1952 Pres.	1956 Gub. 2nd Primary (2 Candidates)	1956 Pres.	1957 Senate Special (3 Major Cand. Only)	1958 Senate Primary
Total vote	1,356,392	2,072,106	1,576,798	1,955,528	874,999	1,296,993
Liberal vote	488,345	969,228	694,830	859,958	364,605	761,511
% of total vote	36.0	46.8	49.9	44.0	41.7	58.7
Percentage of total liberal vote from 62 most liberal counties[a]	17.1	13.9	14.4	13.8	14.6	11.6

[a] Counties ranked in the first-quarter Yarborough vote, special Senate election, 1957.

ship in a one-party state. Within this bloc of 62 liberal counties there is a significant body of convinced partisans who contribute approximately the same proportion of the liberal vote regardless of the type of race or voter turnout.

In broader perspective, Texas liberals draw support from two political streams. On one hand, there is a not too large but stable group of supporters in the aforementioned 62 most liberal counties. On the other hand, there is a much larger but more unstable coalition of liberally inclined voters among the industrial workers and among the increasingly politically conscious ethnic and racial minorities. Each of these sources of liberal votes will now be examined in greater detail.

ECONOMIC CHARACTERISTICS OF MOST LIBERAL COUNTIES

Though the increasing significance of urbanization and racial-ethnic background in the state as a whole cannot be denied, such factors have little to do with the liberalism of the first-quartile Yarborough counties. As of 1960 no county with a city of 100,000-plus population was among these 62 most liberal counties; in fact, 59 of them had county populations of less than 25,000. In 1950 only 9 such counties had 20 per cent or more Negro residents and but 7 had a Latin population of 20 per cent and above. The latter figures represented 14.5 and 11.3 per cent of the first-quartile Yarborough counties—considerably below the statewide percentage of counties with like characteristics. (A slightly higher percentage of the second-quartile Yarborough counties were urbanized, but not significantly so, and they contained 20 per cent or more Negroes or Latins.)

Economic factors appear to have a more direct bearing upon the liberal tendencies of the pro-Yarborough counties. The 62 most liberal counties are predominantly engaged in agricultural pursuits and are more agriculturally oriented than the most conservative Democratic counties. As indicated in Table 22, only 10 (16.1 per cent) of the most liberal counties had 10 per cent or more of their labor force employed in manufacturing establishments in 1950, while the figure for all counties in the state was 64 (25.2 per cent). By contrast, 11 (19 per cent) of the most conservative Democratic counties had 10 per cent or more manufacturing employment. Furthermore, in no more than 4 (6.5 per cent) of the most liberal counties was the annual value added by manufacturing $10 million or more, whereas there were 40 (15.8 per cent) such counties throughout the state. And, in none of the 4 did

TABLE 22

Economic Characteristics of Liberal Counties in Texas, 1950–1958

	Most Liberal Counties (62)		All Counties (254)	
	No.	%	No.	%
Per Cent of labor force employed in manufacturing (1950)				
10% or more	10	16.1	64	25.2
Value added by manufacturing (1958)				
Above $50 million annually	0	0.0	10	3.9
Below $10 million annually	58	93.5	214	84.2
Pattern of agricultural operations (1954)				
Mostly small farms	14	22.6	118	42.5
Predominantly crop farming[a]	35	56.4	88	34.6
Median family income (1949)[b]				
$3,000 and over	9	15.5	45	18.8
Below $2,000	20	34.5	96	40.0
Percentage of families earning $5,000 or more annually (1949)[b]				
20% and over	15	25.9	55	22.9
10% or less	22	37.7	90	37.5

Sources: The statistics on value added by manufacturing were taken from U.S. Bureau of the Census, *Census of Maufactures: 1958.* All other data were derived from the U.S. Bureau of the Census, *County and City Data Book: 1956.*

[a] The term "predominantly crop farming" means that 60 per cent or more of a county's total agricultural income was derived from the sale of crops.

[b] The base number for all counties is 240 because income statistics were not available for 14 counties, including 4 of the most liberal.

the value of manufacturing exceed $50 million. In comparison, among the 58 most conservative Democratic counties 8 (13.8 per cent) counties had $10 million or more value added by manufacturing and in one of these the amount exceeded $50 million.

More specifically, crop farming is the dominant agricultural pursuit in 35 of the 62 first-quartile liberal counties. Data on the size of farm sales are also enlightening. Category A includes all counties in which farms selling more than $25,000 worth of products accounted for at least 20 per cent of county sales, and farms selling less than $2,500 annually provided less than 40 per cent of the total. Category B contains all counties wherein farms selling in excess of $25,000 were less than 10 per cent while farms having sales of less than $2,500 contributed more than 40 per cent of the countywide figure. Among the 62 first-quartile Yarborough counties in 1957, approximately 16 per cent were in Category A; for the state as a whole some 21 per cent were so classified. On the other end of the scale, some 39 per cent of these most liberal counties were in Category B, while the statewide figure was 47 per cent. In substance, therefore, the liberal counties seldom contain many farms of high value, and to a slight degree they tend to have farms with a small sales value.

The most liberal counties appear to have neither the highest nor the lowest income. As of 1949 20 of 58 such counties (4 could not be classified) or approximately 34.5 per cent had median family incomes of less than $2,000; some 40 per cent of 240 counties in the state (14 could not be classified) were below that mark. Altogether 55 per cent of the most liberal counties had median family incomes of less than $2,500, while 60 per cent of the counties throughout the state fell below this figure. The opposite extreme is avoided equally well. In the entire state 7 counties in 1949 had 30 per cent or more of their population earning over $5,000 annually; only one of these was among the 62 most liberal counties. (Within the 64 counties in Yarborough's second quartile—moderately liberal counties—there seems to be somewhat greater economic polarization and a lower economic level. Specifically, as compared to all the counties in the state, a greater proportion of these counties falls into the lower-income categories while about the same ratio shows up in the $3,000-and-above family-income category.)

The economic data for the first-quarter liberal counties reveal only a slight inclination toward smaller farms and lower incomes. Perhaps the failure of the data to illustrate a stronger correlation between liberalism and small farms and low income is due, in part, to the rough character of the statistics themselves (based as they are on county figures). But the weak correlation may indicate also the possibility that other factors—especially historical traditions—may be playing a significant role.

HISTORICAL TRADITION OF LIBERAL DEMOCRATIC COUNTIES

There is good reason to believe that the liberalism of the 62 most liberal counties is related to their past association with Populism and to their strong traditional identification with the national Democratic Party.

In our effort to test the influences of Populism upon today's liberal counties, we first eliminated from consideration all those first-quarter liberal counties which experienced significant increases in population, urbanization, and industrialization (19), on the assumption that a half-century-old viewpoint could not survive in such counties, and then eliminated 23 most liberal counties from West and West Central Texas on the grounds that they were only beginning to be settled in the 1890's when Populism was flourishing. Of the remaining 20 first-quarter liberal counties, 15 were carried at least once by the Populists in the four gubernatorial elections from 1892–1898.[10] Seven of these are located in a strip running from a point east of Dallas to a point just east of Austin, and two are in the vicinity of San Antonio (see Figure D).

An examination of the historical characteristics of the 64 counties in Yarborough's second quarter in 1957 also supports this thesis: 18 of these liberal counties in Central-East Central Texas have a history of Populism.

Thus, while one cannot say with certainty that the Populist tradition is still of paramount importance in all counties where it once thrived, it is fair to say that such sentiments contribute to liberal majorities or strong minorities within several of the agricultural counties of present-day Texas.

Simultaneously, many of the most liberal counties in East, Central, and West Central Texas have long been noted for containing high numbers of "brass-collar" Democrats. Since liberal Democratic candidates have usually been the staunchest advocates of loyalty to the national Democratic Party, it is not surprising to find many counties in these regions in the liberal Democratic column.

[10] See Roscoe Martin's map of counties carried by the Populists during the 1890's in his *The People's Party in Texas*, p. 60.

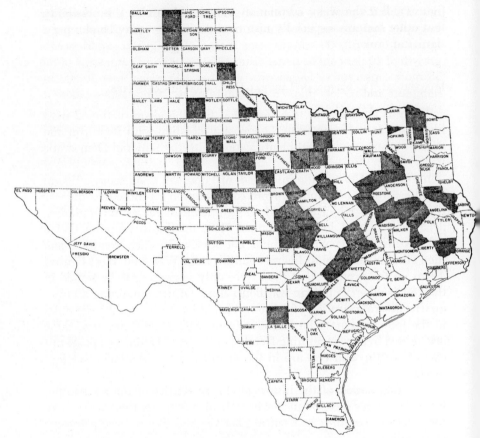

Figure D. Present-day liberal counties in Texas which were
carried by Populists in the 1890's.

LIBERALISM AND THE METROPOLITAN COUNTIES[11]

Dedicated as some of them may be, the counties in the first quartile
of Yarborough's 1957 vote cannot produce majorities for liberal candidates. If liberals are to win with any degree of regularity, they must
find other sizable sources of support, namely, among the industrial
workers and the middle-of-the-road swing voters within the rapidly
expanding cities and among the slowly organizing minorities.

The data presented in Chapter II demonstrated that the liberals have
been confronted with an uphill battle in the state's metropolitan coun-

[11] For comparable studies of urbanization and voting see Leon D. Epstein, *Politics in Wisconsin*, Chap. 4, and Nicholas A. Masters and Deil S. Wright, "Trends
and Variations in the Two-Party Vote: The Case of Michigan," *APSR*, LII (1958),
1078–1090.

ties. Table 23 provides additional evidence of this fact. It shows, for example, that among the 62 most liberal counties only 2 had a population of over 50,000 and no more than 8 of the group experienced a growth of 20 per cent or better from 1950 to 1960; in contrast, 7 of the 58 most conservative Democratic counties had more than 50,000 inhabitants and no less than 18 of them grew by 20 per cent or more in the decade of the 1950's.

However, liberal candidates can appeal to the industrial workers and even to a considerable number of "middle-of-the-road" swing voters within the cities.[12] This is demonstrated by the increase in Yarborough backers from 1952 to 1957. According to Table 24, Yarborough's greatest percentage gain was in the metropolitan category (counties that were 70 per cent or more urban in 1950 and contained a city of 100,000 or more by 1957). This change stands out all the more because voter turnout in the metropolitan counties was about the same in 1952 and 1957. Hence, Yarborough's increased portion of the vote must have been due, in part at least, to an actual shift of sentiments within the urban electorate.

In order to uncover the particular metropolitan centers that are most receptive to liberal overtures, an overall average of the percentages cast for liberal candidates in nine recent elections—including four

TABLE 23

Comparison of Population Patterns in Most Liberal and Most Conservative Democratic Counties in Texas

Population	Most Conservative Democratic Counties (58)		Most Liberal Democratic Counties (62)		All Counties (254)	
	No.	%	No.	%	No.	%
In 1960						
Above 50,000	7	11.8	2	3.3	27	10.6
Below 25,000	45	76.3	59	95.1	197	77.6
Growth from 1950 to 1960						
20% or more increase	18	30.5	8	12.9	60	23.6
Static (less than 10% increase) or declining	34	57.6	49	79.0	156	61.4

Source: Statistics on population patterns are taken from U.S. Census Bureau, *General Population Characteristics, Texas.*

[12] O. Douglas Weeks comments on the role of the middle-of-the-road element in his *Texas One-Party Politics in 1956*, p. 1. See also his "Republicanism and Conservatism in the South," *Southwestern Social Science Quarterly*, 36 (1955), 248–256. Weeks argues that the Southern Democrats are composed of three main elements: liberals and two kinds of conservatives—the new rich and the rural traditional.

TABLE 24

Liberal Voting Shifts from 1952 to 1957 According to
Population and Urban-Rural Divisions[a]

Urban-Rural Scale	Per cent of Total State Population		% Increase (Decrease) From 1950 to 1957	Vote (and Percentage of Total) for Yarborough in Each Category		% Increase (Decrease) From 1952 to 1957
	1950	1957[b]		1952[c]	1957[d]	
I: Metropolitan (12)	44.1	52.6	+8.5	169,766 34.8	168,270 46.1	+11.3
II: Large Urban (17)	14.3	13.8	—0.5	63,446 13.1	42,836 11.7	— 1.4
III: Intermediate Urban (22)	5.6	4.7	—0.9	27,760 5.8	15,938 4.3	— 1.5
IV: Small Urban (7)	2.8	2.6	—0.2	13,061 3.8	11,493 3.1	+ 0.3
V: Agri.-Urban (20)	8.1	6.5	—1.6	46,116 9.5	29,027 7.9	— 1.6
VI: Nonfarm Rural-urban (27)	3.0	2.8	—0.2	17,043 3.6	10,517 2.9	— 0.7
VII: Nonfarm Rural (65)	8.5	7.7	—0.8	66,076 12.9	38,976 10.8	— 2.1
VIII: Farm Rural (84)	13.6	9.3	—4.3	85,077 17.5	47,548 13.2	— 4.3
Total (254)	100.0	100.0		488,345 100.0%	364,605 100.0%	

[a] Data were compiled from the *Texas Almanac*, 1958–1959, pp. 450–452, 457–458, and 522 ff. The urban-rural categories applied here are defined in Chapter II and listed in Appendix E.

[b] Derived by interpolation using 1950 and 1960 Census data.

[c] Democratic gubernatorial primary.

[d] Special Senate election.

presidential, three gubernatorial, and two United States senatorial races from 1948 to 1960—was calculated for each of the state's 12 most urbanized counties. Once these averages were computed, the counties were then ranked according to the average per cent given to the liberal candidate, with those providing the highest liberal averages grouped at the top and those yielding the lowest bunched at the bottom of the scale. (All the state elections involved the candidacy of Ralph Yarborough. Hence, by consolidating the averages for both state and national elections, variations due to the personal appeal of Yarborough or the effectiveness of his campaigning were reduced.) For purposes of more intense comparison the averages for the presidential and state races separately were also calculated. All of this material is presented in Table 25.

The figures in Table 25 indicate that, during the 1948–1960 period, Nueces (Corpus Christi), McLennan (Waco), Wichita (Wichita Falls), and Jefferson (Port Arthur-Beaumont) Counties were the most liberally inclined. To a slight extent, particularly in presidential elections, Travis (Austin), El Paso, and Lubbock Counties were receptive to moderate appeals. (Lubbock's average of above 50 per cent for Democrats in presidential elections is due solely to Truman's high percentage in 1948; its Democratic percentage in the other three national elections fell below 50 per cent.) In contrast, Tarrant (Fort Worth), Potter (Amarillo), Harris (Houston), Bexar (San Antonio), and Dallas Counties responded more favorably to conservative candidates.

More important than the names of the liberally inclined cities and counties are the reasons for their drift to the left. Table 25 discloses a rather consistent pattern which suggests that, in part at least, an ideological factor is at work. It is noteworthy, for example, that the

TABLE 25

Distribution of Vote for Liberal Democrats in
Metropolitan Counties

Counties Ranked According to Support for Liberal Democratic Candidates	Average Democratic Vote in 4 Pres. Elections[a]		Average Vote Cast for Liberal Candidate in 5 State Races[b]	Combined Average (Col. 1 and 2)
	%	%	%	%
More liberal counties				
Nueces (Corpus Christi)	58.3	(71)[c]	52.2	56.9
McLennan (Waco)	60.5	(80)	53.4	56.4
Wichita (Wichita Falls)	58.8	(77)	51.4	54.7
Jefferson (Port Arthur-Beaumont)	56.0	(67)	50.2	52.8
Moderate counties				
Travis (Austin)	55.5	(73)	46.8	50.7
El Paso (El Paso)	53.5	(72)	44.6	49.1
Lubbock (Lubbock)	51.3	(73)	44.2	47.3
More conservative counties				
Tarrant (Fort Worth)	46.8	(60)	45.2	45.9
Potter (Amarillo)	46.8	(68)	44.6	45.4
Bexar (San Antonio)	48.5	(55)	42.8	45.3
Harris (Houston)	43.8	(48)	46.2	44.4
Dallas (Dallas)	40.0	(51)	38.2	39.0

Source: Election returns were compiled from the relevant issues of the *Texas Almanac.*

[a] Presidential elections of 1948, 1952, 1956, and 1960.

[b] Yarborough's vote in gubernatorial contests in 1952, 1954, and 1956 and his Senate races in 1957 and 1958.

[c] Figures in parentheses indicate percentage of vote for Truman in 1948.

ranking of the 12 most urban counties according to the average of *all* nine elections gives a scale that runs from the more liberal to the more conservative in much the same rank order as that yielded when the averages for both presidential and state elections are viewed separately. Though not exact, the similarities are sufficient to indicate more than a chance order. This does not signify, of course, that other factors such as party loyalty, the personality of the candidate, the degree of organization, and local events are not also important. Moreover, some of these counties show signs of shifting from one political orientation to another (Bexar County is shifting in the liberal direction, Lubbock more in the conservative direction), a point that will be probed in a subsequent analysis. Nevertheless, on the basis of the figures in Table 25, one would seem justified in predicting that in future elections the counties at the top of the list will more often than not lean toward the Democratic Party in general and toward moderate-to-liberal candidates in particular, while those at the other end will frequently side with conservatives—either from the Democratic or Republican Parties.

The specific data on income levels (Table 26) also lend support to an ideological thesis. On both scales of income—median family income and the percentage of population earning over $5,000 annually—the 4 counties in the "more liberal" category are generally at lower levels than the 5 counties classified as "more conservative."

On the basis of such general statistics one might be tempted to conclude that the gradual upswing in liberal fortunes is due largely to increased urbanization and industrialization in general and to accelerated efforts by organized labor and by lower-income groups in particular. Such generalizations, however, involve far too much oversimplification and, at best, must be carefully qualified.

The 4 more liberal counties are small to medium-sized urban centers. As indicated in Table 27 the larger metropolitan counties have a slight conservative tendency. Furthermore, none of the more liberal counties show anything like the population increases of the more conservative counties. With the exception of Jefferson County the more liberal counties do not display any unusual degree of manufacturing activity. As a matter of fact, the cities in which the value added by manufacturing is greatest are generally found on the conservative end of the political spectrum (see Table 26).

Finally, Table 26 reveals that the preceding generalization about the relationship between liberal voting and income must be modified. On one hand, Bexar County, the metropolitan area with the third lowest median family income in 1949, is classified among the more conservative counties; this county's low-income level, however, is probably due

TABLE 26

Economic Characteristics of Metropolitan Counties in Texas, 1950, 1958

| Name and Political Complexion of County | 1950 Family Income | | Per Cent of Labor Force Employed in Manufacturing (1950) | Value Added by Manufacturing (1958) (Millions of Dollars) |
	Median (in dollars)	Per Cent Earning $5,000 or More Annually		
More liberal counties				
Nueces	2,119	21.4	11.4	118
McLennan	2,553	14.6	14.6	91
Wichita	3,173	19.0	9.0	29
Jefferson	3,624	22.4	31.5	259
Moderate counties				
Travis	2,993	19.8	6.6	33
El Paso	3,048	21.8	11.5	91
Lubbock	3,283	25.3	7.3	44
More conservative counties				
Tarrant	3,256	20.6	25.2	514
Potter	3,518	24.1	10.5	36
Bexar	2,724	16.9	11.4	156
Harris	3,476	25.2	22.3	1,154
Dallas	3,433	26.1	18.6	810

to its large Latin population. On the other hand, the urban county with the highest income figure—Jefferson County, a wealthy Gulf Coast county with much industrial and shipping activity—is in the more liberal category. It has also what is for Texas a high degree of unionization, which, apart from the county's overall wealth, may help to explain its higher wage scales. In addition, the county has a politically active minority population of just over 25 per cent. Thus, unionization and the minority element in this relatively wealthy county are determinants of liberal support.

Although discrepancies between the actual voting record and the logically expected vote can therefore be explained in part, at least, they nevertheless raise some doubts about rigidly applying any economically oriented ideological thesis. Specifically, they suggest that when liberals do win in the cities, their victories are more often produced by broad coalitions between organized labor and other groups than by doctrinaire appeals to working-class interests. To be sure, organized labor contributes much to the liberal movement in Texas.[13] For ex-

[13] The issues of the *Texas State AFL-CIO News* for the fall of 1960 and the spring of 1961, particularly the lead stories, illustrate labor's political interest well.

TABLE 27

Social Characteristics of Metropolitan Counties in Texas, 1950–1960

Name and Political Complexion of County	Total Population (1950)	Total Population (1960)	Per Cent Increase in Population (1950–1960)	1950 Minority Population %		
				Negro	Latin	Both
More liberal						
Nueces	165,471	221,573	33.9	4.8	38.1	42.9
McLennan	130,194	150,091	15.3	17.1	4.2	21.3
Wichita	98,493	129,638	23.1	6.3	1.7	8.0
Jefferson	195,083	306,016	29.9	22.6	3.9	26.5
Moderate						
Travis	160,980	212,136	31.8	13.9	13.5	27.4
El Paso	294,968	314,070	61.1	2.1	48.7	50.8
Lubbock	101,048	156,271	54.7	7.8	4.4	12.2
More conservative						
Tarrant	361,253	573,215	46.0	10.9	3.1	14.0
Potter	87,140	149,493	71.6	4.8	3.0	7.8
Bexar	500,460	687,151	37.3	6.5	38.8	45.3
Harris	806,701	1,243,158	54.1	18.5	6.6	25.1
Dallas	614,799	1,083,601	45.7	13.4	3.5	26.9

ample, AFL-CIO strongly urges all its members to participate in politics and vote. Since the labor laws in Texas are so stringent—probably the most restrictive of any state in the Union—labor is keenly conscious that its own freedom and success depend importantly on political victories that can be translated into legislation more favorable to unions and to workers as a group. Money, skilled leaders, leg work, election surveys, and precinct organization—all this and more is part of labor's year-round efforts to influence the course of state politics.

But it must be remembered that other factors hinder union labor's political efforts in Texas more than in most Northern metropolitan areas. In general, most Texas cities are more preoccupied with commerce, trade, and finance than with industry per se; Texas has no single industrial center comparable to Detroit; and when industrial establishments are present, they tend to be smaller in scale and to employ relatively high percentages of white-collar as opposed to blue-collar workers. Organized labor is relatively scattered and its organizational drives are handicapped by stringent labor laws, native suspicions concerning unionization, and a prevailing atmosphere of bustling free enterprise with free wheeling individualism. Consequently, union officials in Texas have been quick to realize—perhaps more so than some of the nonacademic, independent liberals—that the political success of the liberal movement is dependent upon labor's ability to form broad alliances with several other groups.

In Jefferson and Nueces Counties, for example, the liberal edge has resulted from the teaming up of organized labor with racial-ethnic minorities. In Jefferson County, though union labor is probably the stronger partner, a labor-Negro coalition has formed the core of the liberal movement. In Nueces County the liberal alliance consists largely of rather evenly balanced trade-union and Latin American elements.

Labor and intellectual liberals have also benefited from a loose alliance with a number of Democratic Party loyalists. This type of arrangement goes a long way toward explaining why McLennan (Waco) and Wichita Counties are more often than not found in the liberal Democratic column—though in McLennan County the presence of a substantial Negro element has also helped.

Such coalitions, however, are more effective during national than state races. As demonstrated in Table 25, the voters in the metropolitan counties were more willing to vote for the Democratic nominee in presidential elections than they were for the liberal against the conservative Democrat in state contests. Houston, with its reputation as a center of conservatism and considerable Republican activity, was the only exception.

In the future the liberals will be less able to rely on the support of Party loyalists—at least in the cities. Middle-class elements in urban areas are fast becoming less attached to party labels. Certainly they are not as party-oriented as their rural brethren.[14] Graphic proof of this fact is again offered in Table 25, which shows that in every case, including Houston, the percentage received by Truman in 1948 (found in parentheses to the right of averages for the four presidential elections) was greater than that given any other Democratic candidate in subsequent presidential races.

In essence, if liberals want to win in the future they must make greater appeals to the gradually organizing minorities and to the growing number of middle-class "swing voters." When and if they do so they have a good chance of increasing their strength in cities like Austin (Travis County), San Antonio (Bexar), and El Paso. Austin contains a sizable group of Party loyalists and Populist-inclined rural migrants; several small bands of sympathetic—though understandably timid—government employees and university teachers; a substantial minority of Latins and Negroes amounting to slightly over 25 per cent

[14] See Donald Strong, *Urban Republicanism in the South*, p. 3.

of the population; and the numerically weak but organizationally active state headquarters of the AFL-CIO. This extremely diverse coalition has not yet jelled enough to produce liberal majorities in state races, but it has come close on several occasions. As the Latin population develops politically, Bexar County also is showing signs of a shift away from the conservative camp. In 1960 a coalition of the large Latin group, organized labor, and moderates carried the county for the Kennedy-Johnson ticket; and in 1961 the two liberals, Maury Maverick and Henry Gonzalez, received 52.1 per cent of the county vote. (The ideological import of the results in the 1961 special Senate election are clouded, however, by the fact that both Gonzalez and Maverick are natives of San Antonio.) To a lesser degree the organizational growth of the large Latin element in El Paso is diverting it from its former conservative course. Like the voters in Bexar County, those in El Paso endorsed the Kennedy-Johnson ticket in 1960. Although the Maverick and Gonzalez forces were able to garner only 30.4 per cent of the ballots in 1961, the combined El Paso total for these two liberals plus that for moderates Will Wilson and Jim Wright was greater than the combined vote for conservatives Blakley and Tower.

The success or failure of the liberals in these three cities—and in Texas as a whole—will depend a great deal on their ability to maintain close ties with both the Negroes and the Latin Americans. Today racial and ethnic minorities are recognized not only as a source of potential strength for the liberals but also as a growing force in state politics—and consequently the importance of their vote should not be underestimated.

RACIAL-ETHNIC MINORITIES AND LIBERALISM

The following analysis of the Negroes and the Latin Americans in Texas—covering their voting patterns, their psychological motivations in politics, and social and economic factors influencing them—presents evidence of some strong tendencies toward liberalism. Yet the discussion brings forth some equally important obstacles confronting the liberals in their efforts to capitalize on this reservoir of potential liberal power.

The Negro Voter in Texas

The preference of the Northern Negroes for liberal Democratic candidates has been widely reported and analyzed.[15] Whether the Negro in

[15] One of the recent reports emphasizing Negro bloc voting is that by James Q. Wilson in *The Reporter*, No. 22 (March 31, 1960).

Texas shares these preferences in his voting—and for that matter, whether he votes at all—is a question of obvious importance. The Negro has been a main cause of the South's one-party system, and changes in his position can have a powerful effect on the Southern potential for a two-party system.[16]

The ratio of Negro to white population (12.7 per cent of the 1950 total of 7,711,194, and 12.4 per cent of the 1960 population of 9,522,677 were Negroes) is lower in Texas than in any other state of the old Confederacy. Furthermore, from 1940 to 1950 the Negro population grew only 5.7 per cent while the white population grew 22.7 per cent.[17] Negroes have been steadily emigrating from Texas, particularly the more energetic and enterprising of them,[18] but this movement has been partially offset by a high birth rate and by the influx from other Southern states of Negroes seeking better economic and social conditions. Thus, although the Negro population has not quite maintained its relative position, it did increase absolutely from 977,000 in 1950 to 1,187,125 in 1960.

Despite the fact that Negroes now comprise only about one-eighth of the state's population, the "Negro question" still has transcendent importance in certain areas and among certain groups. In 4 counties Negroes represented in 1950 more than 50 per cent of the population, and in another 18 they comprised over 30 per cent. In the same year another 61 counties had a Negro population equal to 10–30 per cent of the whole. By and large, the counties with the highest Negro to white

[16] Alexander Heard, *A Two-Party South?*, p. 247. Donald S. Strong ("The Presidential Election in the South," *Journal of Politics*, 17 [1955], 343–388) is cautious in suggesting the rise of any two-party system, but does claim that the Democrats need the Negro vote to balance defections to the Republicans among upper-income suburbanites (p. 388). Samuel Lubell writes (*The Future of American Politics*, p. 125), "Probably the crucial factor which will determine how quickly or slowly a two-party system develops is the changing status of the Negro, who has always been the basis of the one-party South." Other valuable sources on the Negro in Southern politics are the following: V. O. Key, Jr., *Southern Politics*; Hugh D. Price, *The Negro and Southern Politics*; and Donald S. Strong, "The Rise of Negro Voting in Texas," *APSR*, XLII (1948), 510–522. Margaret Price is author of two pamphlets published by the Southern Regional Council in Atlanta: *The Negro Voter in the South* (1957) and *The Negro and the Ballot in the South* (1959). *The American Voter* by Campbell, Converse, Miller, and Stokes, contains some references to Southern Negro voters. For a fuller account of Negro voting in Texas itself, see Harry Holloway, "The Negro and the Vote: The Case of Texas," *Journal of Politics*, 23 (August, 1961), 522–556. A major part of the discussion of the Negro vote in Texas in this chapter comes from Holloway's article.

[17] *Texas Almanac*, 1958–1959, p. 95.

[18] The young generation, especially, is leaving. One Austin leader formed a group of forty veterans interested in political activity after World War II. Now, he says, only one is left in town. The graduates of the local Negro college, Huston-Tillotson, are reported to be departing also.

ratios are concentrated in East and Southeast Texas—areas which were settled and adapted to a slave-plantation economy prior to the Civil War—as well as in the Blackland Prairie counties of Central and East Central Texas where—at a later date—King Cotton came to rule supreme (see Figure E).[19]

Economically, socially, and physically, this region of Negro concentration today is highly diverse. It encompasses several metropolitan areas, including the state's two largest cities (Houston and Dallas), as well as some of the state's most rural counties. Light and heavy manu-

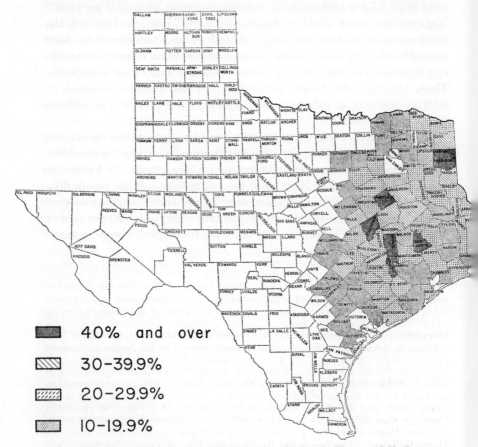

40% and over

30–39.9%

20–29.9%

10–19.9%

Figure E. Distribution of Negro population in Texas, 1950 (by per cent of total).

[19] The figures on Negro-white ratios and the socio-economic characteristics of Negro areas are from the *Texas Almanac*, 1958–1959, pp. 522 ff. One odd exception to this regional concentration is Foard County in West Texas, with a Negro population of 10.1 per cent.

facturing (including a steel mill) is scattered throughout the region. Considerable small-scale agriculture, including share cropping, also is a means of livelihood. The nation's single greatest oil field is within the region; so are some of the state's most poverty-stricken counties. Of 53 counties having a Negro population of 20 per cent or more, fully three-fourths had static or declining population. Most of these, of course, are rural counties, with no city of 10,000 or more, and with economies based mostly on crops, livestock, and timber. In the total group of 83 counties with a Negro population of 10 per cent or more, one-third had median family incomes in 1950 of less than $1,500; another one-third were in the $1,500–$2,000 bracket. One can conclude, therefore, that much of the eastern third of the state shares many of the features typical of the so-called "Black-Belt" areas, but, aside from deep East Texas, in a less concentrated and more varied form.

The *Civil Rights Report* estimated that the number of eligible Texas Negro voters in 1958—the only year for which a fairly complete survey is available—was 226,495.[20] This total represented 38.8 per cent of the nonwhite population over 21. White registration in the 1956–1958 period was estimated at 49.0 per cent. These figures, however, are estimates because of exemptions from paying the poll tax; generally it is estimated that since 1955 the actual number of qualified voters is about 25 per cent above the number of paid poll taxes.[21] So far as these figures are comparable, they indicate that total Negro registration is sizable and, overall, only about 10 per cent below that of the whites. Thus, in 180 of the state's 254 counties 25 per cent or more of the Negro population registered. And the 14 counties with no nonwhite registrants contained negligible numbers of nonwhites.[22]

As these figures indicate, the resistance to Negro voting in Texas has been slight. Some incidents followed the Supreme Court's 1944 decision that Negroes could not be barred from the Democratic primary, but, on the whole, Texas experienced a quiet and orderly transition. By 1956 Margaret Price concluded:

Intimidation as a means of limiting Negro voting in Texas was found to be relatively rare. . . . There have been occasional reports of local discrimination against

[20] The survey contained in the *Report of the U.S. Commission on Civil Rights, 1959*, included a count of 165 of the state's 254 counties and various kinds of estimates for the remaining counties (see p. 586).

[21] See the *Texas Almanac*, 1958–1959, p. 453.

[22] *Report of the U.S. Commission on Civil Rights*, p. 586. The figures are for nonwhites but Negroes are more than 99 per cent of the nonwhite population. Texas has by far the largest number of Negroes registered, but its percentage of 38.8 is exceeded slightly by Florida's 39.5.

potential Negro voters. . . . But, by and large, the poll tax remains the only obvious deterrent.[23]

And today it is widely accepted that the poll tax probably reduces the vote among low-income whites as much as it does the Negro vote.[24]

Granted that the Negro does register and vote in considerable numbers, how does he use this vote? Is the kind of bloc voting characteristic of the Northern cities appearing also in Texas? And is it a liberal, socially conscious vote which could be an important element in an emerging two-party system?

Partial answers to these questions are found in an analysis of voting behavior from 1956 to 1958 in four major cities—Austin, Dallas, Houston, and San Antonio. The Negro voters in these four metropolitan centers situated in the eastern third of the state constituted approximately 33 per cent of the total number of registered Negro voters in 1958.

To this group can be added a few other cities included by Donald Strong in his study of the 1952 presidential election.[25] The Negro voters in Strong's additional cities behaved much like those in our four metropolitan areas and, for analytical purposes, there is no reason to believe that their behavior in the more recent elections covered in Table 28 would differ significantly. Together, the total for both groups of cities amounts to 44 per cent of all eligible Negro electors in 1958.

The returns in Table 28 show a decisive and, in some instances, an overwhelming majority sentiment for the Democrat and the liberal. In the 1956 presidential election liberal Democrat Adlai Stevenson received a respectable 57–64 per cent of the vote in the Negro precincts of Austin, Dallas, Houston, and San Antonio. Stevenson's 1956 margin, however, was considerably less than that which he received in 1952 when his civil rights' position was considered to be much stronger. For

[23] Margaret Price, *The Negro Voter in the South*, p. 18. This same survey cites resistance to Negro registration in Dallas in 1956. However, her figure on 1956 registration is far below vote tallies from Negro precincts that year and is even further from the registration figure in the *Civil Rights Report* for 1958. In all likelihood there was resistance but less than she indicates.

[24] A recent study of the effect of the poll tax explains that the tax discourages minority groups, but chiefly because of its economic impact on all low-income groups. And today low-income whites may well have less incentive to vote than Negroes. See Frederic D. Ogden, *The Poll Tax in the South*, pp. 175–177.

[25] His complete list of cities includes: Austin, Corpus Christi, Dallas, Fort Worth, Houston, Port Arthur-Beaumont, San Antonio, Waco, and Wichita Falls. See Strong's article, "The Presidential Election in the South," *Journal of Politics*, 17 (1955), 373–377.

example, in 1952 Austin and Dallas Negro precincts gave him a whopping 92 per cent of their vote.[26]

Negro preference for liberal Democrats carries over into state politics, as shown by the returns for 1956, 1957, and 1958 elections. In the 1956 gubernatorial primary contest between Ralph Yarborough and moderately conservative Democrat Price Daniel, the liberal-minded Yarborough carried the Negro precincts by margins of approximately 9 to 1. To a lesser degree, these Negro precincts continued their preferences for Yarborough in the 1957 special Senate election. This time, among the three major candidates who received the bulk of the votes Yarborough received from 64 to 84 per cent of the Negro vote. (Specifically, his percentages were less in Dallas and San Antonio—two cities with a conservative reputation—thereby demonstrating that Negro voters are to some extent influenced by the prevailing atmosphere in urban communities.)

TABLE 28

Per Cent of Total Vote Cast for Democrats and/or Liberal Candidates
in Predominantly Negro Precincts of Four Texas Cities

Election	Candidates	Austin 4 Precincts %	Dallas 14 Precincts %	Houston 36 Precincts %	San Antonio* 3 Precincts %
1956 presidential	Stevenson (D)	63	57	64	64
	Eisenhower (R)	37	43	36	36
1956 gubernatorial: 2nd primary	Daniel (D)	7	12	9	11
	Yarborough (D)	93	88	91	89
1956 gubernatorial: general	Daniel (D)	70	66	73	73
	Bryant (R)	30	34	27	27
1957 special senatorial: 3 highest candidates only	Dies (D)	2	11	3	12
	Hutcheson (R)	14	25	16	24
	Yarborough (D)	84	64	81	64
1958 gubernatorial: primary	Daniel (D)	7	13	6	11
	Gonzalez (D)	90	80	88	83
	O'Daniel (D)	3	7	6	6

* Here, as elsewhere, the writers are indebted to Mitchell Grossman's paper for all data on San Antonio precincts. The selection of precincts in other cities was made after consultation with local officials and political leaders. Bexar County (San Antonio) is the only one of these three in which the ratio of Negro to white population was less than 10 per cent (6.5 per cent). The returns are from records of these counties or from records kept by county chairmen of the Democratic Party.

[26] For an extended analysis of the Dallas returns in 1952 see Strong's article, "The Presidential Election in the South," *Journal of Politics*, pp. 373–375.

Equally if not more impressive than the Negro vote for Yarborough was that given to Latin American Henry Gonzalez in the 1958 gubernatorial primary—a contest in which incumbent Price Daniel won much more handily than he did in 1956. In the Negro precincts of Austin, Dallas, Houston, and San Antonio, Mr. Gonzalez, who is well known as one of the state's leading liberals and who campaigned on an equal-rights platform, heavily defeated Daniel and rural conservative Pappy Lee O'Daniel[27] by margins of 8 and 9 to 1.

It is clear, therefore, that city Negroes in Texas have a tendency to vote Democratic and liberal. However, there are signs of some minority sympathy for Republicanism. Whether the vote for Eisenhower in 1956 signifies much, that for Republican candidates in state races does. William R. Bryant, the Republican candidate for governor in 1956, received from 27 to 34 per cent of the Negro vote in the precincts covered by Table 28. This was in a campaign that is normally a race in name only. This same type of behavior manifested itself in the 1957 special Senate election. Republican Hutcheson's Negro vote of from 14 to 25 per cent in his contest with two strong Democrats—one of whom was a liberal—can only be interpreted as an indication that a considerable Republican *minority* exists among the state's urban Negroes.

The question arises of whether the Negro vote for liberal Democratic candidates is based on adherence to liberalism as a whole or "race consciousness" in particular. The sizable decline in Stevenson's vote when he diluted his civil rights' stand in 1956 and the high percentages given to Henry Gonzalez—a clear-cut defender of equal rights for Negroes and Latin Americans alike—would certainly indicate the presence of a considerable amount of race consciousness or at least a deep concern about civil rights' issues. On more than one occasion Negro leaders present at statewide meetings of the liberal Democratic Coalition have refused to endorse otherwise liberal nominees who failed to take an unequivocal stand for Negro rights. Thus, racial considerations strongly influence their political decisions whether in general elections or in intraparty, intrafactional meetings. However, the unusually strong Negro preference for Yarborough, a man who has spoken out for Negro rights but who is not as well known for this as Congressman Gonzalez, signifies that a strain of general liberalism is also present among some Negro voters in the cities.

A more direct test of race consciousness is, of course, the vote for

---

[27] V. O. Key analyzes O'Daniel's earlier political career in his *Southern Politics*, pp. 265–327. He describes O'Daniel as "more Republican than most Republicans." In the lore of Texas politics, O'Daniel is famous as the man who campaigned on the Bible, a hillbilly band, and hot biscuits.

Negro candidates. Studies of other states demonstrate that Negro candidates can normally count on heavy support in Negro areas but not uniformly so.[28] A sampling of city elections in Texas yields similar results. In the 1951 Austin election Arthur Dewitty, a Negro, ran eighth in the field and was not far from the fifth place of the lowest winner of a Council seat. As indicated in Table 29, Dewitty polled 28 per cent of the vote in the predominantly Negro precincts. By way of contrast, a spot check of precincts singled out by local politicos as representative of white groups in all income brackets showed Dewitty's percentages running from 2 to 7 per cent, far below his figure in Negro precincts.[29] More convincing is the vote received by John D. Walker, the colored candidate, in the 1959 San Antonio City Council election. Walker gathered 58 per cent of the vote in San Antonio's Negro precincts, while in a selected sample of white precincts[30] his totals ran from 3 to 4 per cent. (Interestingly, the Latin precincts showed much less enthusiasm for Walker in 1959 than the Negro precincts did for Gonzalez in 1958.)

Although the candidacies of Harry Lott, Arthur Dewitty, and John D. Walker (see Table 29) were unsuccessful, at least three Negroes have been elected to office in postwar Texas. In 1958 Mrs. Charles H. White won a seat on the Houston School Board. In the spring of 1960 a Negro minister, supported by a coalition of Negroes and Latin Americans, was elected as city commissioner in the small Panhandle city of Slaton.[31] Finally, in 1961 a Negro gained a position on the Galveston City Council.

The fact that three Negroes have won elections and that several others have been candidates for elective offices in Texas is evidence of the increasing Negro political interest in general and of their desire to have true rather than vicarious representation in particular. The percentages for Negro candidates in city elections, however, are neither as high nor as stable as those recorded for their Northern brethren.

Further analysis also reveals that the Negro voters frequently do not agree with the views of their leaders, with the result that leaders cannot deliver "bloc" votes at will. That is, they cannot, without great risk

[28] Margaret Price, *The Negro Voter*, p. 46; Hugh Price, *The Negro and Southern Politics*, p. 79.

[29] The procedure used was to ask leaders identified with various factions in Austin politics and experienced in local affairs to select several precincts in each of three main income brackets. An official of the Chamber of Commerce also was asked to give such a selection. The returns for those precincts on which there was substantial agreement were checked.

[30] These white precincts were selected on the basis of census data and consultations with local politicians.

[31] See "Negro Surprise Victor," *New York Times*, April 8, 1960.

TABLE 29

Per Cent of Total Vote Cast for Negro Candidate in Predominantly
Negro Precincts of Two Texas Cities

Election	Negro Candidate	Per Cent of Total Vote Cast for Negro Candidate Only	
		In Predominantly Negro Precincts	In Predominantly Latin Precincts
1949 Austin City Council, 17 candidates; 5 highest candidates win	Harry Lott	17	6
1951 Austin City Council, 14 candidates; 5 highest candidates win	Arthur Dewitty	28	6
1959 San Antonio City Council, Place 2; 4 candidates	John D. Walker	58	10

to themselves, ignore some fairly consistent voting propensities of their
Negro followers. Hugh Price reached this conclusion on the basis of his
study in Florida[32] and there is no reason to think that Texas Negroes
are different. For example, a long-standing Negro leader in Austin
admitted privately that he cannot swing even his own precinct's vote
if he takes the "wrong" position, and that his people will go the way
they want to regardless of his endorsement if the candidates and their
positions are well known to them.

Of course, the leaders' area of discretion may be enlarged when the
endorsement applies to candidates about whom the ordinary voters
have little or no knowledge. Of late, however, there have been signs
that Texas' urban Negroes are discontented with some of the old-time
leaders and are searching for new leaders—but they have not yet
found them. Until new leadership emerges, Negro voters may be temporarily inclined to reject suggestions in elections involving lesser-
known candidates and, accordingly, may refrain from voting.

In any event, it should be stressed that urban Negroes—leader and
led alike—will not blindly follow the liberal and/or Democratic candidate, particularly if they suspect a weakening of his civil rights'
position. This Negro vote has a mind of its own on issues of foremost
concern to the group.

What has been stated thus far applies to city Negroes. A slightly

[32] Referring to Negro political leagues, Price writes: "League endorsement of a
wrong candidate in a contest where a clear difference in attitude toward the Negro
exists does not sway many Negro voters; rather it raises the question, Who sold
out?" (*The Negro and Southern Politics*, p. 72).

larger element still remains to be analyzed, namely, the rural Negroes of East Texas. Unfortunately, this latter group is not as easy to investigate as the urban Negro. The East Texas region is large and mostly rural; although agriculture predominates, there are considerable variations in economic activity; and the county-by-county percentages of Negro population vary from as little as 10 per cent to over 50. Southern customs and attitudes prevail here more than elsewhere in the state, thereby making inquiry about the race question a touchy matter. Nevertheless, it is possible to discern a pattern of behavior—a pattern in which the rural Negro is in large part a "controlled" voter who behaves quite differently from his urban counterpart. For the most part, this white influence operates peacefully and noncoercively and is based upon a psychology of acceptance by the Negro.

Some significant evidence as to the distinctive behavior of the rural Negro comes from the registration figures given in the *Civil Rights Report*. In Dallas, Austin, and San Antonio Negro registration in 1958 fell in the 30–40 per cent bracket.[33] In the total of the 6 most urban counties with a Negro population from 10 to 30 per cent the average registration was 38.8 per cent. On the other hand, the 7 relatively nonurban counties with Negro population as high as 40 per cent or above have a median registration of 46.1 per cent. In general, of the 83 counties with 10 per cent or more Negro population, 44, or a little more than half, have Negro registration of 40 per cent or more. And 36 of these same 44 counties have no city of 10,000 or larger. On the other hand, among those counties with a Negro registration under 40 per cent, more than half have a city of 10,000 or more people. Individually, there are some astonishing cases. Waller County is listed by the *Civil Rights Report* as having over 50 per cent Negro population and more than 40 per cent of the eligible Negroes registered. And, according to estimates, Marion County next to the Louisiana border has more qualified Negro voters than white. In sum, urban counties with low ratios of Negro to white population have registration medians somewhat lower than those in rural counties with relatively high ratios of Negro to white population.

To understand the real implications of these registration figures, one must set alongside them the actual election results. Alexander Heard in his *Two-Party South* points out that the bulk of the anti-Negro Dixiecrat vote in 1948 came from the same East Texas region where Negroes are most numerous.[34] More recently, in the 1958 gubernatorial

---

[33] Houston is an exception with 47 per cent registered. The figures are from the *Civil Rights Report*, pp. 581–586.

[34] Heard, *A Two-Party South?* pp. 253–261.

election Henry Gonzalez, who received from 80 to 90 per cent of the Negro vote in the cities, fared badly in rural East Texas. As a matter of fact, his vote in the area correlated negatively with the size of the Negro population. Of the 53 counties with 20 per cent or more Negroes, 51 gave him less than 20 per cent of their vote and 21 of these 53 counties gave him less than 10 per cent. (The exceptions were the metropolitan Gulf Coast counties containing Galveston, Port Arthur, and Beaumont, where the vote was above 20 per cent but below 30.) All the counties with a Negro population of as much as 30 per cent or more gave Gonzalez less than 20 per cent support.

In view of the foregoing data on registration and election returns, it is quite obvious that the rural Negro from East Texas acts quite differently from his city brother. Specifically, these figures and explanations offered by persons familiar with East Texas politics all point to the fact that, with some exceptions and variations, the rural Negro is politically manipulated.[35] As one liberal East Texas lawyer described the situation, a system of "white paternalism" prevails, based on the extension of the caste system of racial relations to politics.[36]

Briefly, white paternalism means that the white community encourages Negroes to register and to vote in the normally well-founded belief that the vote will be a friendly one. Much of the Negro vote is an adjunct to the white vote, not the independent self-willed vote of the city Negro. In the words of an elderly East Texas Negro: "Where a colored man lives on a white man's place, he's influenced by the white man but there is no force or intimidation felt." As these words reveal, the striking feature is that the Negro accepts his role "with no force

[35] Most of the information presented on East Texas Negroes came from Dr. Harry Holloway's correspondence with about two dozen informants—both local Negro and white leaders. The medium was questionnaires and interviews. The best informants, most of whom asked that their names not be used, turned out to be a number of lawyers living in small East Texas urban centers. W. Astor Kirk (cited below) expressed cautious disagreement with this conclusion of political manipulation and felt that changes had occurred in the last few years, though he admitted to having knowledge of only a small part of East Texas. Those interviewed in Austin included: Arthur Dewitty, secretary of the Travis County Voters League; Dr. Everett Givens, a Negro leader long active in state and local politics; O. H. Elliott, financial secretary of the Masonic Temple and active in League work; Kenneth R. Lamkin, a lawyer and organizer and participant in the League; Stuart Long, a newsman whose news service conducted the 1958 survey for the *Civil Rights Report*; W. Astor Kirk, member of the Political Science Department of Huston-Tillotson College and president of the Austin Commission on Human Relations; Trueman O'Quinn, Travis County chairman, Democratic Party. Carter Wesley of Houston, editor of the state's leading Negro paper, was contacted by mail.

[36] Gunnar Myrdal's *An American Dilemma* is still the most exhaustive examination of the racial caste system in American life, whether North or South.

or intimidation felt." The relationship is not typically coercive. The caste system has been extended to politics and continues much of the control exercised before the Negroes gained the legal right to participate in the white primary.[37]

In the first step of political manipulation the white man solicits the Negro vote by encouraging him to pay his poll tax, possibly lending him the money to do so. Negro voting leagues manipulated by the whites may also cooperate in this task. Apparently the relationship is usually on a small scale, with one white man "influencing" perhaps ten or a dozen Negroes whom he knows personally and with whom he has dealings. Economics plays a powerful role in this system, but it is certainly not the only factor. The Negro dependent on a white man for his job may accept political advice in voting as a part of the normal course of affairs. Or the Negro may accept the white man's leadership simply because he considers him a friend who asks a favor. In actual voting, variations appear too. If a "machine" works in the area, the leader may pass the word to the Negro organization en masse. Or the Negro leader working with the whites may pass on this information in a night meeting the day before the election to avoid giving the other candidate a chance to raise a hue about Negro bloc voting. As another alternative, the whites may solicit support among the small circle of Negro voters they can influence.

The older generation, in particular, is often the target of special solicitation. Elderly Negroes are more amenable to influence than the younger generation and thus the easiest group to solicit; and, because of the departure of many young people from the declining rural counties, elderly Negroes constitute a large proportion of the rural Negro population. In addition, they need not go through any form of registration if the county is small. Specifically, those over sixty years old are exempt from poll-tax payment, and in counties of under 10,000 population they need not even register as exempt. At times the absentee ballot is used as a device for "making sure" that these elder Negroes vote "correctly." Technically the absentee ballot should be used only by those not able to get to the polls on election day because of illness, business, or other matters that take them away from the area, but certification of these exemptions is so loose that the privilege can easily be abused.

The outlook of many rural Negroes caught in this system of influence is aptly illustrated by the remarks of two Negro witnesses

---

[37] According to C. Vann Woodward and others the present system of segregation and the relegation of the Negro to a secondary role did not fully evolve until the 1890's. See Woodward's *The Strange Career of Jim Crow*, p. 7.

during a recent trial in deep East Texas.[38] This trial concerned a hotly disputed local election in which evenly balanced white factions had solicited Negro votes. One elderly Negro called upon to explain his vote stated,

I said all of those people down there, I live with them, and they all I got, and I knowed I couldn't vote but one way; knowed if I voted for one, would have to go against the other one, and I have to go to all of them for everything, and I didn't want to fall out with none of them; I had rather went to the field to plow.

And he repeated in answer to a further question, "Rather went to the field to plow than voted at all." Later on, emphasizing his desire to live peacefully with all elements of the white community he said, "You see, I don't want to run, I can't run, have already tried it."

Another witness explained his reaction when white men came to solicit his vote:

. . . and I told this white fellow, I don't want you all to feel that I have got smart and trying to take over you all's business, because I have lived with you all all of my life, and my parents, they were good to them, and they have gone out, and I have come this far and everything has been very peaceful, and as I have said, I have always got along all right, and I want to go out that way, and I said I wouldn't care to sign any more or say any more about it.

Like the other witness, he preferred not to vote at all, especially if it meant possible retaliation. And so far as he did use the ballot he used it to try to please the white man. Through much of the 1950's this type of sentiment was apparently strong among rural Negroes. Small wonder that one East Texas correspondent explains, "Bear in mind that the average adult Negro in East Texas has not the advantage of a normal education or environment." It is not surprising, in view of these attitudes, that the white community can use the Negro vote for its own purposes, with "no force or intimidation felt."

If the usual means of manipulation fail, activity which is either illegal or close to the line of legality opens further possibilities. The role of corruption in controlling the Negro vote is difficult to establish; but rumor circulates constantly and some amazing reports come to light. Both Key and Strong cite the story of the San Antonio Negro leader of earlier years who, according to local tradition, had 3,000 poll taxes that he kept in his safe to be distributed on election day to "trustworthy" voters. When interviewed recently, two Austin Negro

---

[38] The remarks that follow are from copies of the court record sent by a correspondent. The testimony was given on August 4, 1958, in the District Court in Harrison County.

leaders have described with scorn the system of control, extant some years back, by which city-hall politicians used the Negro leader of that day to deliver votes. A Houston Democratic leader, respected for his knowledge of the Negro vote, has said that much money was spent buying up small groups of Negro voters in the 1960 primary. A liberal lawyer in an East Texas county reports the existence of a sheriff-controlled machine by which the liquor interests support the sheriff who keeps the county wet; and the sheriff in turn controls the bloc of Negro voters that gives him and his policies consistent majorities. It is also said that in order to avoid control and even the actual changing of ballots in this same county Negroes vote the absentee ballot by as many as 600 votes in a total of about 5,000. Such stories can be multiplied and are undoubtedly subject to exaggeration and distortion. But these and other reports are sufficiently frequent and widespread to leave an impression that vote-buying and manipulation are by no means uncommon. Margaret Price's reference to vote-buying—"By and large, this manipulation of Negroes has ended but it has not disappeared altogether"—seems optimistic when applied to Texas.[39]

Another possibility is reprisal from the white voters when they fear that a bloc Negro vote will work against their interests. Racial violence occurs but little in Texas, and the main form of "retaliation" seems to be heightened electoral activity by the white community or the tinkering with electoral districts. Of one rural community it is reported that pre-election rumors of sharply increased Negro voting brought an enormous turnout among the white voters, even though the Negro vote remained about the same as usual. In another county it is said that control of the Negro bloc vote by a corrupt local official is causing rising resentment among the white community and is gradually increasing the white vote. The city fathers may also change election districts to split the Negro vote, especially if the candidacy of a Negro shows signs of success. Austin's electoral system was changed after Dewitty's race in 1951, whether because of Dewitty's good showing or for other reasons. An abortive effort to change Slaton's electoral system followed a Negro's victory in the race for city commissioner there in 1960, but the same coalition that put him in office successfully beat back this proposal.

It is apparent that white paternalism rooted in the caste system is a complex relationship. The main element is the Negro's acceptance of his dependent, submissive role, supplemented by such corruption as exists. And the ever-present possibility of reprisal, though largely nonviolent, helps to maintain the system.

[39] Margaret Price, *The Negro Voter*, p. 50.

There are, however, some significant variations and exceptions to this general pattern. It was consistently reported by local observers that the Negroes do normally vote their own interests on the offices of sheriff and county commissioner.[40] The sheriff is all-important to the enforcement of justice in these predominantly rural counties. And the county commissioner has much to say about the county roads. For these two offices, therefore, the Negroes as a rule make their own decisions and may revolt and refuse to accept "recommendations" they think contrary to their own interests. The swaggering sheriff with a reputation for rough treatment of Negroes is a declining or almost defunct breed today; and in this respect, particularly, the rural Negro has learned the value of the ballot and uses it effectively. For other offices and issues the interest of the Negro electorate as a whole is not great and many ballots will be only partially marked. For this reason, too, voting turnout may be low, especially in the general elections. Understandably enough, the request of a white friend to vote a certain way on offices with which the Negro is not concerned may be accepted with no "feeling of force or intimidation."

Less frequent exceptions also exist. Not all Negroes are amenable to white pressures, although their percentage does not seem to be great. The president of the Texas NAACP, N. Y. Nixon, has had some effect on his county. In another county a correspondent reports that members of the union working for a steel mill in the area are required by that union to register and to vote. A few white liberals of some standing (especially lawyers) can discreetly exert influence among the Negroes.

Also some Negroes, especially teachers, who are natural leaders, could lead them away from this manipulation, but as yet they have not assumed this role to any marked degree.[41] In one county the older Negroes are said to be more militant than the younger ones because they reflect the spirit of the preachers, whereas the youth are influenced by the timidity of their teachers. And even the preachers,

---

[40] Hugh Price in his Florida study found a similar concentration on these offices, plus a tendency to leave the rest of the ballot unmarked (*The Negro and Southern Politics*, p. 73).

[41] Margaret Price reports teachers are becoming more civic conscious and active, but says that they have usually been aloof and timid throughout the South (see her *Negro Voter*, p. 39). One East Texas lawyer with a low opinion of Negro teachers claims many literally bought their academic job qualifications (degrees) and had no real training. He added that if he told local Negro teachers of his reform work in the Negro community they would "inform" on him to their white superintendent. At the Dallas NAACP meeting in the spring of 1960 one speaker, formerly of Texas, said "our teachers are our greatest enemies to social rights." Others present "excitedly" agreed (see "Negroes Militant," *Texas Observer*, March 11, 1960).

typically a powerful influence in Negro life, do not take the lead as much as they could in racial and political campaigns.[42]

Finally, where the Negroes are less dependent economically on the white community they may use the vote less amenably. A white liberal familiar with East Texas explained that the markedly lower registration in the county containing Marshall in contrast to that in nearby counties with little urbanism was due to the relative independence of Negroes in Marshall's economy. So far as these Negroes could afford independence the whites did not want to encourage their vote. Another experienced informant who traveled through East Texas during 1960 cited two other towns as possible exceptions to the pattern of white control—Tyler in Smith County and Longview in Gregg County. In the case of Smith County the percentage of eligible Negroes registered was decidedly lower than that in adjoining counties, thereby lending support to the observation that Negroes in Tyler are not manipulated. But it is doubtful that Gregg County, with about 60 per cent of eligible Negroes registered, would record such a high percentage if the Negroes from Longview were completely independent. These examples illustrate the variations and countertrends which must occur in varying degrees all over the East Texas region in spite of the normally dominant influence of the whites.

Probably the best summary of the situation prevailing in many counties of this East Texas area is provided by the following words of an informed correspondent.

We have a substantial number who evidence no interest in voting and have never qualified to vote or voted. . . . The broad base of the Negro population here votes about 40% of its potential strength of which I hazard a guess that 50% is subject to white suggestion—perhaps as much as 80% in some races. In such as the county commissioner and sheriff's races, they usually have personal acquaintance and in substantial part make an independent selection, being subject only to the usual campaign soft talk and a little coercive pressure from the "ins" who are in position to favor or frown.

. . . barely 10 to 20% of the local colored care to vote on any office outside the county—a statewide office that is—and many ballots are incomplete as to all offices other than county offices. Voting in the general election is light

---

[42] Myrdal described the role of the Negro church some years ago as,

". . . on the whole, passive in the field of intercaste power relations. It generally provides meeting halls and encourages church members to attend when other organizations want to influence the Negroes. But viewed as an instrument of collective action to improve the Negroes' position in American Society, the church has been relatively inefficient and uninfluential" (*An American Dilemma*, p. 873).

This statement would not apply as fully today as when written in the early 1940's but Texas has yet to develop a Martin Luther King.

and the number voting will probably not exceed 30% of the number in the primary election.

Why do the Negroes accept this white influence? Margaret Price in her analysis of the Southern Negro's present political consciousness attributes this behavior to a compound of factors: namely, the Negro's heritage and the effect it has upon his sense of civic responsibility, his low economic status and lack of education, his apathy and indifference, and his own fears rooted in a past that he cannot forget.[43] Added to such influences is the corruption, among some white and Negro leaders, that prevents the Negro from using the ballot in his own interests. Finally, the possibility of reprisals, even if they do take a comparatively mild form in Texas, is another factor influencing the voting behavior of the Negro.

From the preceding examination of both urban and rural Negroes, it is possible to draw some conclusions about their characteristics as voters and their impact upon party politics as a whole.

Like their Northern counterparts, city Negroes in Texas are already a "politically embattled solidary ethnic group."[44] The term may be cumbersome but it conveys the notion of their common political consciousness expressed in a liberal and racially sensitive bloc vote. Ordinarily, these urban Negroes will vote for the liberal Democratic candidate by large majorities and overwhelmingly so if he takes a decisive pro-civil-rights position. Their vote is strongly colored by ethnic or racial considerations. In the main, it will go to a Latin American candidate as well, but—other things being equal—above all for a Negro. Yet, city Negroes in Texas do not vote blindly for liberals, Negroes, or ethnics; nor do they follow the leader's endorsement regardless of the candidate's known positions. The leader must lead where his people want to go.

Negro organizations in Texas cities give the impression that they are uneven but occasionally capable of surprising efforts. Such organizations have neither drawn in all potential voters nor stabilized those that are mobilized. Their difficulties stem not only from low educational and economic levels, but from the voting habits of many urban Negroes who have only just arrived from rural areas where they are not accustomed to voting regularly or freely. Also, many of the more energetic city Negroes have departed for "greener" pastures in the North. And always present are the stultifying effects of segregation

---

[43] Margaret Price, *The Negro Voter*, pp. 30–35. See also Abram Kardiner and Lionel Ovesey, *The Mark of Oppression*, Chaps. 12, 13, and Robert E. Lane, *Political Life*, pp. 251–253.

[44] The phrase is Lane's. See *Political Life*, pp. 251–253.

throughout the nonpublic sector. Still, amidst these limitations, Texas' city Negroes have made great progress, and increasingly they are taking advantage of their political assets.

The interests of urban Negroes in Texas are for the most part similar to those of Northern Negroes. Urban Negroes in Texas apparently participate in politics a little less than do Negroes in the North, and the Texas group contains a slightly larger minority of pro-Republicans;[45] such differences are, however, matters of degree. Otherwise, Texas Negroes bear a close resemblance to their liberal, racially conscious, and bloc-voting brethren in the North.

Because of the problems involved in gathering and interpreting evidence, generalizations about the rural East Texas Negroes, who comprise about one-half of the state's registered Negro voters, must be treated cautiously. Yet, these rural Negroes obviously behave quite differently from city Negroes. On occasion, they may exert some "independent" influence upon the choice of sheriff or county commissioner, and they do have a few effective organizations or individuals who do yeoman's work. But, for the most part, the rural Negroes from East Texas are apathetic and quite vulnerable to the white man's "suggestion" and, at times, they are susceptible to corruption and fear of reprisal. And, as illustrated by several recent elections, they more often than not vote against rather than for the liberal Democrat or, at best, do not vote at all in such cases.

In many ways the South—especially states such as Florida and Texas—is changing and becoming more like the North. It is tempting, therefore, to say that the plight of the rural Negroes in Texas will also change. But, it is also possible that the countryside will be left far behind the cities.[46] The heritage of the past hangs heavily on these rural Negroes; their sense of inferiority and their submissiveness are deeply ingrained. The rural areas have the lowest education and income levels

[45] Comparing Northern and Southern Negroes as a whole, Angus Campbell and his associates cite as significant differences the degree of Republicanism and the extent of political participation—with Northern Negroes being more active and more heavily Democratic. See Campbell *et al.*, *The American Voter*, pp. 452–453.

[46] In the evolution of the Southern racial problem a special report of the Southern Regional Council on school desegregation (as of August, 1959) is of note. The report's conclusion (pp. 43 ff.) argues that an isolation of the "hard core," the rural Black Belt extending across the South, is taking place. The large cities of the South are integrating, albeit with stress and strain, and the authors point to the likelihood of integration in Texas cities, in New Orleans, and Atlanta. Since this prediction was written integration has come or soon will come in the areas cited. The interesting implication is that the rural Black Belt is left behind in continuing total resistance to integration. The "hard core" may be reduced in influence but it is difficult to predict when and how rapidly it will itself change, as presumably it must.

and the least mobile population. These communities, too, are the most insular in outlook and the most resistant to change. To these factors must be added the loss of much of the young population as it moves to the city and from there out of the state. Here also the fears of reprisal, even if exaggerated, are not altogether unfounded. The problems of the rural Negro are ultimately isolating him from his urban counterparts in both the South and the North. In essence, one is reminded of Key's comparison between Southern political problems and those of under-developed nations in the world: "The suffrage problems of the South can claim a closer kinship with those of India, South Africa, or the Dutch East Indies than with those of, say Minnesota."[47] Perhaps, as in the case of many African nations, Negro urban elites will eventually instill an awareness of race and politics in their rural brethren. As of today, however, urban-based leaders of Negro organizations seem content to concentrate almost all of their efforts on the city Negro. In fact, Negro organizations like the Texas Council of Voters are considerably less prone to enter rural politics than is their Latin American counterpart—PASO—which in conjunction with the Teamster's union elected in 1962 the first all-Latin town government in Crystal City (Zavala County).

Thus, at least half of the state's Negro voters are substantially less effective than Northern Negroes. Despite gradual changes and improvements it is unlikely that rural East Texas Negroes will become a "politically embattled solidary ethnic group" in the near future. Nevertheless, city Negroes have, for all intents and purposes, already attained this status and, with the increasing closeness of Texas political battles, their votes are significant enough to tip the scales from time to time.

The Latin American Voter in Texas

Numerically and organizationally, Latin American voters loom even larger on the Texas political horizon. It was estimated in 1955 that 1,500,000 Latins were in the state, a figure that included legal, transient workers.[48] As of 1962, Latin organizations calculated that at least 900,000 of these were potential voters. And, according to the *Congressional Quarterly Weekly* of June 23, 1961, leaders of the newly formed PASO (Political Action for Spanish-Speaking Organizations), contended that about 500,000 Spanish-speaking voters were actually reg-

---

[47] Key, *Southern Politics*, p. 661.
[48] *Texas Almanac*, 1958–1959, p. 112.

istered.[49] In comparison, the Texas Council of Voters estimated in 1962 that from 265,000 to 300,000 Negroes were registered in the state. (The number of potential Negro voters may be as high as 850,000.) Even when an allowance is made for some inflation of the number of Latin American voters and, particularly, for discrepancies arising from the problem of defining the term "Latin voter," these statistics certainly suggest that in Texas the Latin Americans are more numerous and slightly better organized than the Negroes.

The heaviest concentrations of Latin Americans are in the border region stretching from El Paso on the west to Cameron County at the southeastern tip of the state (see Figure F), although recently a considerable number of Latins have moved to other areas—particularly South Central Texas. Approximately 55 per cent of the state's Latin population resided in the counties of Bexar, Hidalgo, El Paso, Cameron, Nueces, and Webb.[50]

It is difficult to generalize about the political preferences of the Latin counties shown in Figure F. Within several of these counties the ratio of organized Latin voters to Anglo voters fluctuates considerably and the interpersonal relations between Latin and Anglo leaders also vary from time to time. With these changes the counties often shift from one ideological position to another. Likewise, the degree of Latin organization differs significantly from county to county. Latin Americans in El Paso, for example, are generally less aggressive and less united than their compadres in San Antonio.[51] And in some regions, particularly the so-called "machine counties" in South Texas,[52] the Latins are subject to the control of bosses who change their positions from one side of the ideological fence to the other, depending on their chances for personal advantage. In any case, whatever the reason or combination of reasons, over the years there have been frequent fluctuations in party and factional preferences among and within the Latin counties.

In party preference, the Latin counties have generally sided with the winning Democrats. However, on occasion, some indications of substantial Republican sentiment and activity have appeared. In the presidential elections of 1952 and 1956 the Latin counties, particularly those in the Rio Grande Valley, seemed to have definite Republican leanings. Among the 27 counties with 50 per cent or more Latin Amer-

[49] Congressional Quarterly Weekly, June 23, 1961, p. 1042.

[50] Texas Almanac, 1958–1959, p. 97.

[51] Texas Observer, June 1, 1962.

[52] Among the counties generally considered within that group are Duval, Jim Wells, Starr, and Webb.

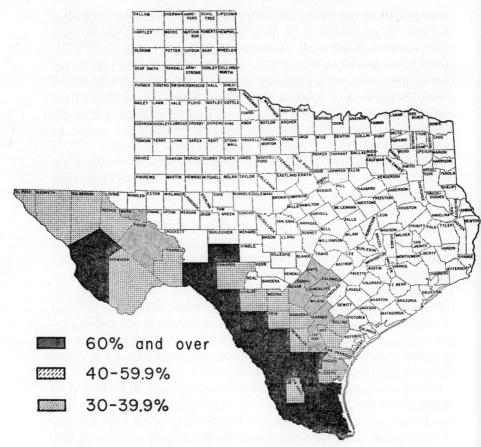

60% and over

40-59.9%

30-39.9%

Figure F. Distribution of Latin American population in Texas, 1950
(by per cent of total).

ican population (1950 estimate), 14 gave majorities to Eisenhower in
both elections, 4 did so in one of the two races, and only 9 solidly
backed Stevenson. But by 1960 the vast majority of the Latin counties
switched back to the Democratic Party. Of the 27 counties just cited
the Kennedy-Johnson ticket carried all except 2 in 1960, and even
these 2 were lost by less than 5 per cent of the vote. In part this Democratic revival may have been due to collaboration between liberal
Democrats and moderate-conservative supporters of Johnson, who has
long had close personal ties with a number of the "old-guard" South
Texas politicos. Some observers credited the shift to Kennedy's Cath-
olicism, since Latin Americans are overwhelmingly of that faith.[53]

[53] The *Texas Observer* of November 11, 1960, pointed out that of 39 Texas coun-

Latin leaders of the "Viva-Kennedy" movement, however, contended that the victory resulted from their organizational efforts among their own people—a thesis made plausible by the heavier than usual turn-out of Latin American voters. They claimed, for example, that 90 per cent of the Latin poll-tax holders in Nueces County and that 89 per cent in Bexar County voted in 1960. These leaders of the "Viva-Kennedy" movement, in turn, were motivated not by religion, but by the belief that a Democratic administration in Washington would be more sympathetic to their appeals for equal treatment.

A somewhat better measure of the depth of Republican feeling within the Latin counties is provided by the results of the 1957 and 1961 special Senate elections. In the 1957 contest Republican Thad Hutcheson was able to obtain a plurality in only 3 (Medina, Sutton, and Terrell) of the 27 counties having 50 per cent or more population with that ethnic background. In 10 of the 27 he finished in second place, and in 14 he placed third. In the first of the two 1961 elections contests, Republican John Tower obtained a plurality in 10 of the 27 counties, and finished in second place in another 13. The second run-off contest a few weeks later indicated that Tower's showing in these counties did not depend altogether upon the division of the vote among the numerous Democrats. In this runoff Tower won a majority in 10 of the 27 counties; with two exceptions these were the same 10 that he had carried by a plurality earlier.[54]

Rather interestingly, the Republican second-place strength in both 1957 and 1961 was more likely to be found in liberal than conservative Democratic counties. Thus, in 1957 Republican Thad Hutcheson finished second behind liberal Ralph Yarborough in 9 counties; second behind conservative Democratic Dies in only one county. In the first 1961 contest Tower finished second behind liberal Gonzalez in 9 counties, and second behind conservative Democrat William Blakley in only one. These figures suggest, of course, that the Republican Party in such counties is sometimes regarded as providing a better base from which to challenge the liberal Democrats than is offered by the conservative Democratic faction. Within a few counties like Duval and Webb the nucleus of the small but growing GOP organization is formed by anti-machine elements—that is, persons who find it dif-

---

ties with Catholic majorities 35 went for Kennedy in 1960. Previously, 27 of them had supported Eisenhower in 1952, and 28 in 1956.

[54] The eight counties which supported Tower in both the first heat and the runoff were Brewster, Cameron, Hidalgo, Jeff Davis, Kinney, Medina, Sutton, and Val Verde.

ficult to work for reform within the county's boss-dominated Democratic organization.[55]

A fundamental question, of course, is whether the Republican sentiments within the Latin counties are generated more by the Anglos or the Latins. There is good reason to believe that the Anglo, and not the Latin, element is most responsible for whatever Republican leanings that occur. This supposition is based on the fact that almost all of the 14 Republican-minded counties—as measured by Eisenhower majorities—were located in the Southwest-West and lower Rio Grande Valley areas, where considerable Republican activity among the Anglo elements has been present for some time.

Even more convincing evidence is brought out by an examination of voting in clearly Latin American precincts in urban San Antonio and surrounding rural areas. In 1956 Bexar County as a whole gave Eisenhower a majority of 65,700 to 46,694, but in the 16 precincts with 70 per cent or more Latin Americans, Stevenson won better than two to one (8,689 to 3,116).[56] Similarly, in the 1957 Senate election Republican Thad Hutcheson gathered a plurality in Bexar County as a whole but was soundly trounced by Yarborough in the Latin American precincts, 3,200 votes to 461 for Hutcheson. There was a shift in degree but not in kind in the nearby rural towns of Pearsall and Encinal. In the three precincts with 80 per cent or more Latin Americans (Precincts 2 and 14 in Pearsall and Precinct 5 in Encinal) Stevenson defeated Eisenhower 183 to 132, while in 1957 Yarborough triumphed over Hutcheson 96 to 47. By way of comparison, the vote in Anglo precincts (1 and 15 in Pearsall) went to Eisenhower by 374 to 331 for Stevenson in 1956, while Hutcheson in 1957 received 111, Dies 105, and Yarborough only 83 votes.

It seems doubtful, therefore, that the Republican Party in Texas as presently constituted will be able to win over Latin American voters in large numbers. An attractive candidate may be able to make some inroads into their normal Democratic voting, but even Eisenhower's ability to cut down the Democratic majorities of Latin Americans was in good part due to the inability of Stevenson to arouse the personal feeling and sense of involvement especially important with Latin Americans. When the Latin vote is well led and well organized, as it was in 1960, then it endorses the Democratic ticket.

[55] *Texas Observer*, July 20, 1962.

[56] Bexar County precincts 1, 2, 8, 12–15, 17–21, 23–25, and 119. These and other precinct figures are from an unpublished study by Mitchell Grossman, "Multi-Factional Politics in San Antonio and Bexar County, Texas" (unpublished typescript, 1959).

Republican chances of winning over greater numbers of Latin Americans in the future depend on two factors. First, if the national Democratic administration fails to give the Latin Americans the recognition and rewards they expect, some may be tempted to register a protest by voting for a suitable Republican candidate, or simply by "going fishing" on election day. Second, Texas Republicans could undoubtedly gain strength among Latin Americans by making some effort to meet their demands for betterment of their social, economic, and political status. To date, however, there has been little evidence to indicate that the Texas GOP is aware of this possibility, or at least that it is willing to act upon it.[57] So long as this is true, one is forced to conclude that the Latin American vote will be heavily Democratic.

The Latin counties, although for all purposes a Democratic stronghold, have had some difficulty deciding which side to back in intraparty factional fights. Until recently they seemed to prefer the conservative Democrats. This historical affinity for conservative candidates is demonstrated by the figures on the 1954 gubernatorial primary. As indicated in Table 30, liberal Ralph Yarborough's conservative Democratic opponent, Allan Shivers, captured over 60 per cent of the votes in 58 per cent of the most heavily Latin American counties, as contrasted with similar margins in but 20 per cent of the counties with the least Latin population. Yarborough himself obtained simple majority support in only 10.5 per cent of the most heavily Latin counties. Much the same pattern emerges from a study of the 1956 gubernatorial primary in which these same Latin American counties heavily favored moderate conservative Price Daniel. As late as the special Senate election in 1957, Yarborough, despite considerable improvement, received a smaller percentage of the votes in heavily Latin as compared with non-Latin units.

Since 1958, however, a significant change has been taking place. Of the 36 counties with 40 per cent or more Latin American population, only 5 had given Yarborough a majority or better in 1954. In 1958 he won majorities in 30 of the same counties. To be sure, Yarborough had improved his showing in the non-Latin counties as well, but less impressively so. In some ways the showing of Henry Gonzalez in the 1958 gubernatorial primary is even more significant, despite his having trailed Yarborough in the number of counties carried. For such a little-known candidate to carry 9 of the 36 counties with 40 per cent or more Latin population was clearly an indication of things to come.

[57] The extent of neglect can be judged from the fact that in 1958 the usually well-organized Republicans in San Antonio failed to hold a single precinct convention in Latin American areas of the city (Grossman, "Multi-Factional Politics").

TABLE 30

Voting Trends in Latin American Counties in 1954 and 1958

Percentage of Vote for Liberal Candidate in Democratic Primaries

Population in 1950 (Number of Counties in Parentheses)	1954 Gubernatorial[a]				1958 Senatorial[a]				1958 Gubernatorial[b]			
	60% and Over	50–59.9%	40–49.9%	Under 40%	60% and Over	50–59.9%	40–49.9%	Under 40%	60% and Over	50–59.9%	40–49.9%	Under 40%
60% or more Latin (19)												
Number	2	0	6	11	10	5	3	1	5	3	2	9
Percentage	10.5	.....	31.6	57.9	52.6	26.3	15.8	5.3	26.3	15.8	10.5	47.4
40–59.9% Latin (17)												
Number	0	3	3	11	10	5	1	1	1	0	2	14
Percentage	.....	17.6	17.6	64.8	58.8	29.4	5.9	5.9	5.9	.....	11.6	82.5
20–39.9% Latin (23)												
Number	0	3	10	10	8	11	4	0	0	0	0	23
Percentage	.....	13.0	43.5	43.5	34.8	47.8	17.4	.....	.....	.....	.....	100.0
Less than 20% Latin (195)												
Number	23	65	68	39	113	59	19	4	1	0	0	194
Percentage	11.8	33.3	34.9	20.0	57.9	30.3	9.7	2.1	0.5	.....	.....	99.5

Source: Latin American percentages were calculated by the authors from figures in the *Texas Almanac, 1956–1957.*
[a] Vote for Ralph Yarborough.
[b] Vote for Henry Gonzalez.

Although Gonzalez was supported probably because of his ethnic origin rather than his liberalism, it seems clear nevertheless that he had perceived and was tapping some new moods in the Latin American community. This new mood carried over to the 1960 presidential election in which, as already noted, all but a few Latin counties endorsed the Kennedy-Johnson ticket.

Geographically, the Latin counties with the most pronounced liberal tendencies are scattered throughout South Central Texas and the Gulf Coast region in and around Corpus Christi. Analysis of election returns from 1952 to 1958 reveals specifically that among the counties with 35 per cent or more Latin population, Caldwell, Frio, and Atascosa in South Central Texas, and Nueces, Kleberg, and Brooks in the Corpus Christi area most frequently voted for the liberal nominee. On the other hand, the most conservatively inclined Latin counties are generally situated in West-Southwest Texas and in the southernmost tip of the state. During the same 1952–1958 period, for example, 7 of the 9 counties west of the Pecos River (El Paso and Terrell were the exceptions) and the adjacent counties of Edwards, Sutton, and Val Verde in Southwest Texas were generally conservative. Cameron, Willacy, and Kenedy Counties along the southernmost Gulf Coast edge of the state displayed similar tendencies. Of course, as the returns for the 1958 Senate race demonstrate, the lumping together of election results from 1952 to 1958 underestimates the exact degree of proliberal sentiment. But, from a relative standpoint, it does show which Latin areas and counties are most or least susceptible to liberal appeals.

The figures in Table 31 suggest that urban Latin Americans are more liberal than their rural brothers. For example, they show that, despite the liberal tendencies of both groups, voters in San Antonio precincts with 80 per cent or more Latin American population were more disposed to endorse liberal candidates than those from like precincts in the nearby rural counties of Frio and La Salle.

More important than their existence are the reasons for regional and urban-rural differentials in Latin American voting habits. The truth is that they are due more to organizational than to ideological factors. Latin American leaders generally agree that they have been most successful in mobilizing the vote in urban centers such as Corpus Christi and San Antonio, and in the belt of Gulf Coast and South Central counties, running from Corpus Christi on the east to Del Rio on the west. Since 1960, PASO leaders have also mobilized large numbers of Latin voters in the heavily urbanized lower Rio Grande Valley, though in terms of percentages the degree of organization is not quite

TABLE 31

Latin American Voting for Liberal Democrats in
Selected Urban and Rural Precincts[a]

Precinct	1956 Gubernatorial Primary[b]	1957 Special Senate Election[b]	1958 Senate Primary[b]	1958 Gubernatorial Primary[c]
	%	%	%	%
16 San Antonio precincts	66.9	78.5	84.3	89.9
4 precincts in rural La Salle and Frio Counties	68.3	60.0	76.2	74.9

[a] The selection of San Antonio precincts with 80 per cent and over Latin population was based on school census data gathered in 1955 and 1956, while in Frio and La Salle Counties the determination was made on the basis of information supplied by local political leaders.
[b] Vote for Ralph Yarborough.
[c] Vote for Henry Gonzalez.

as high as that in San Antonio or Corpus Christi. They readily admit, however, that they find it difficult to organize the Latin Americans in rural counties of West and Southwest Texas. Simultaneously, they insist that the ideological predispositions of the two groups do not differ, and that the organizational problem among members of the rural group stems from their physical and psychological isolation.

In South Texas counties like Duval, Starr, and Webb the lingering presence of the traditional boss system of political organization also makes ideological classification hazardous if not impossible. Of late, however, the bosses in such areas have found it necessary to collaborate a little more with "outside" Latin organizations and, in the case of the Gonzalez candidacy in 1958, they were compelled to yield to a ground swell of popular sentiment on his behalf.

In the final analysis then, *when they are organized and free to express their true beliefs,* Latin American voters *tend to endorse liberal candidates.*

It would be a mistake, however, for liberal leaders to assume that more and more Latins will automatically and wholeheartedly adopt the liberal creed. Whether the liberals can capitalize on this growing Latin potential will depend upon how well they adjust their programs to certain underlying characteristics of the Latin American psychology.

First, liberal politicians must realize that Latin Americans are concerned more about civil rights in the liberal program than about its economic aspects. A significant example is the complaint by liberal leaders of the "Viva-Kennedy" movement that after the 1960 election the Kennedy Administration failed to provide Spanish-speaking people in general and their group in particular with a fair share of federal appointments. In fact, this discontent over patronage is reputed to be one of the main reasons why these Latin leaders decided in 1961 to forego their usual emphasis on indirect voter education and to form PASO for the purpose of engaging in direct political action.[58] More specifically, when interviewed in 1960, Dr. Hector Garcia, a founder of the American GI Forum and the national president of PASO, stressed that he was not concerned with ideological stands but, rather, with making certain that Spanish-speaking Americans receive long overdue recognition for their contributions to American culture and defense and that they are given an equitable number of federal appointments.

Along this same line, the Latin Americans, like the Boston Irish, the Cleveland Poles, and the Wisconsin Germans, prefer (other things being equal) a candidate with a surname indicating that he is a member of the group. For example, in San Antonio both the conservative and the liberal factions have found it convenient to include at least one person with a Spanish name on their respective slates of candidates. And, as we have already noted, conservative leaders in some normally conservative communities were unable to restrain the enthusiasm for the liberal Gonzalez. Nevertheless, the Latin Americans have not yet reached the point where they are voting along strictly ethnic lines, nor are they likely to do so soon. If this were the case, then Gonzalez would have swept more counties and would have run a generally stronger race than he did. When interviewed, many Latin leaders were quick to insist (even before the question was raised directly) that if a man had integrity and a sound position on issues his ethnic background became immaterial; in a number of instances, they pointed out, a "good" Anglo had been backed against a "bad" Latin.

Though they may fail to act accordingly, most Anglo liberals are aware of the ethnic coloration of the Latin American vote. They are not, however, as conscious of the fact that a good many leaders of the Spanish-speaking people are unimpressed by the economic doctrines associated with present-day liberalism. A sizable number of the "old-line" Latin American leaders—probably more than in the case of the Negro community—are engaged in running business enterprises. Such individuals often share the Anglo businessman's skepticism of government economic controls and welfare spending. At the very

[58] For a complete description of PASO's origins and objectives see *Congressional Quarterly Weekly*, June 23, 1961, pp. 1042–43.

least, they are likely to behave so as not to antagonize predominantly conservative civic leaders who oppose the welfare state.

Some liberals are inclined to dismiss such behavior as representative of old and fading leaders of the Latin American community, but the following words by a new champion of Latin rights, Henry Gonzalez, should cause them to pause and ponder:

There is no mystery to me why Barry Goldwater's philosophical mouthings have become such a siren song. . . . People are concerned about their "right" not to be interfered with. . . .
    . . . There is an eternal war between individuals and the laws of government and I think the so called liberals are slow to recognize it and expound on it. . . . I believe we liberals must search hard for ways to simplify government, to reduce government to its nearest essentials.[59]

Of course, it would be absurd to suggest that Congressman Gonzalez is attracted by Goldwater conservatism. He has consistently ranked high on the AFL-CIO legislative scorecard. But such remarks indicate that he prefers to emphasize the individualistic rather than the collectivist side of the liberal philosophy and, accordingly, frowns upon the inclination of liberals to turn consistently to government—particularly the national government—for economic aid and controls.

In a sense, there is also a tendency for some liberals as well as some ultraconservatives to underestimate the importance of Latin American voters. This minimizing probably results from their recognition of the obstacles confronting the Latin Americans in their political drives. In the past many of them have voted more from "fear and friendship" than from personal conviction.[60] They were, that is, easy targets for political bosses who capitalized on their economic distress and on their psychological tendency to follow the leadership of the *patrons* (landlords) and *jefes* (political chiefs who often had economic power as well). Fortunately, this pattern is changing. Even before World War II, young Latin Americans in the cities began to think for themselves. One expression of this was the League of United Latin American Citizens (LULAC), founded in 1927 for the purpose of providing civic education and legal assistance in fights for equal rights for their people.[61] Most significantly, after World War II the many Latin Americans who had served in the armed services returned imbued with a new determination to run their own affairs. As a result of their or-

---

[59] *Texas Observer*, April 6, 1963.
[60] See O. Douglas Weeks, "The Texas-Mexican and the Politics of South Texas," *APSR*, XXIV (1930), 625.
[61] O. Douglas Weeks, "The League of United Latin American Citizens: A Texas-Mexican Civic Organization," *Southwestern Political and Social Science Quarterly*, 10 (1927), 257–278.

ganizational efforts (as in the GI Forum), and as a result too of economic and social changes related to their status as veterans (e.g., the educational opportunities opened up by the GI Bill of Rights), the old-style Latin American politics has been slowly fading. Rank-and-file Latin Americans still tend to rely upon the advice of their leaders with whom they have strong personal ties. But at the very least control by a single boss has been giving way to multiboss competition. In Webb County, for example, the political dynasty of the Martin family (Independent Club) is now faced with stiff challenges from at least two other groups—the Kazen family and the Reform Party element.[62] (The Reform Party disbanded in 1961 and formed the core of the county's Republican movement.)

As could only be expected, these changes have been most marked in the areas of ferment, particularly the growing cities and towns.[63] In some of the isolated rural communities old fears and the lack of self-confidence still operate to limit Latin American political efficacy. A number of rural Latin leaders express fear of economic reprisals "if we become openly vigorous." They point to the need for better educational opportunities, and yet bemoan the fact that "many young people with education are leaving the community to seek fortunes in the city." Nevertheless, there is considerably less evidence of psychological subservience to Anglos in rural Latin than in rural Negro areas.

According to leaders among the Latin Americans, the really big problems facing them are the poll tax and the recruitment of leadership. There can be little doubt that the poll tax cuts down their political participation, not only because of the money involved but also because of the method and timing of administration. Also significant, however, is the tendency of Latin American professional people either to identify with existing Anglo leadership or to refrain from political activity altogether. In either case, in some areas the Latin American community is thus deprived of the leadership of its more able and educated middle-class citizens.

Despite these problems, the strong and rapidly expanding organizational activities of Latin American groups are producing results. The

[62] Ramon Garces, "Laredo Report" in the July 11, 1958, issue of the *Texas Observer*.

[63] James R. Soukup's interviews in 1959 and 1960 with then State Senator (now United States Representative) Henry Gonzalez; Hector Garcia, founder of the GI Forum; and a number of local Latin American leaders in South Central Texas provided much of the information on the organizationl problems and successes of Latin American citizen groups. Mitchell Grossman of the faculty of San Antonio College provided statistical data on San Antonio precincts and further information he gained from his interviews with San Antonio politicos including PASO chairman Albert Pena.

number of poll taxes paid by Latin Americans has increased appreciably—a change especially noticeable prior to the 1960 presidential and the 1961 special Senate campaigns. In Bexar County the number of poll taxes paid by Latins in 1961 remained about the same as in 1960 while that paid by Anglos declined by about 20,000.

Among the statewide Latin groups most active in mobilizing voters are the aforementioned LULAC and the GI Forum. The former tends to be content with indirect civic education and legal action to guarantee equal rights, and—in Texas at least—focuses more on local than on national objectives. The GI Forum, although cautious at times, has been somewhat more inclined to pressure directly and to align itself with one political faction or another. Furthermore, that organization tends to be interested in the national as well as the local scene. The most avowedly political of the Latin American groups is the recently formed PASO and, while it is still too early to attempt a judgment on its prospects, all the signs indicate that it is vigorous, well led, and determined in its political moves. It may, therefore, emerge as the best known and politically most important of the Latin American organizations.

Because of the stepped-up efforts of such organizations and the slowly growing self-confidence of their members, the Spanish-speaking vote will become increasingly important in Texas politics—probably more so than many Texans realize. In fact, as will be demonstrated in the ensuing discussion of the 1962 election, it has already begun to play a key role in the outcome of close political campaigns.

LIBERAL STRENGTHS AND WEAKNESSES: A SUMMING UP

On the eve of the 1962 elections conservatives still held the edge within the Democratic Party. However, the liberals were slowly narrowing the power gap between the controlling conservatives and themselves. Indeed, there were several reasons for liberals to view the future with optimism—albeit cautious optimism.

Liberal candidates could count on consistent majorities in many counties of West Central and East Central Texas and, with the assistance of droughts and organization to mobilize worried farmers, they could hope to win occasionally in some West Texas and Panhandle counties. More significantly, by 1961 Republican efforts to woo conservatives within the Democratic Party were beginning to cut deeply into the votes for conservative Democrats. Conservative candidates still fared better than liberal nominees in Dallas, Fort Worth, Houston, and San Antonio, but, with increasing industrialization and the accompanying growth of industrial labor, the liberal share of this big-city vote appeared to be rising slowly. And in medium-sized cities like Corpus Christi, Beaumont-Port Arthur, Waco, and Wichita Falls liberal coalitions were able to garner a majority of the votes. Simultaneously, urban Negroes and Latin Americans—especially the latter—were rapidly expanding their political organizations. Moreover, voting statistics showed that both of these minority groups had a definite tendency to cast their ballots for liberal candidates.

Amidst such signs of progress, however, there were also indications of weakness. Lower-income groups were not as proportionally liberal as the higher-income groups were conservative. Rural Negroes and, to a smaller extent, rural Latins were still subject to white-Anglo suggestion and manipulation. Most important, it was obvious that the success of liberals depended heavily upon their ability to pull together a coalition composed of organized workers, small farmers, Negroes, Latin Americans, and intellectuals. This task is by no means an easy one. On one hand, small farmers and industrial workers are primarily attracted by the economic programs of the liberals; on the other hand, Negroes and Latins are primarily concerned about their civil-rights platforms, and many Negro and Latin leaders—more than economic liberals would like to admit—are actually repelled by liberal economic doctrines. Furthermore, top leaders of the AFL-CIO, despite their general sympathy with the cause of minority rights, have a difficult time convincing rank-and-file workers to support the fight for civil rights, for many of them come from racially prejudiced East Texas. In addition to such differences of opinion over ideology are disagreements over tactics and leadership. Symptomatic of the latter problem were the apparent divisions among Texas liberals over the questions of whether to oppose Lyndon Johnson in his bid for the Presidency in 1960 and of whom they should endorse in the 1961 Senate race.

Thus 1962 promised to be a year of both opportunity and problems. Whether the liberals could capitalize on their opportunities depended upon their ability to handle their chief problem—that is, to mobilize and to unite diverse elements into a strong coalition. The liberal handling of this organizational challenge is a significant part of the following story of the 1962 elections.

V

THE 1962 ELECTIONS: RESULTS AND IMPLICATIONS

As the 1962 political season got underway the pundits generally agreed that Texas politics was in a state of fluidity unseen since 1946, when returning veterans roiled the political waters both as voters and as candidates. Republicans in 1962 were priming themselves for serious contention in a number of races, an effort in nonpresidential election years as unusual as it was unpredictable. The element of uncertainty introduced by Republican plans was compounded by the relative anarchy that suddenly emerged in the Democratic Party. Six contenders entered the race for the Democratic gubernatorial nomination, each of them with a background and an orientation that made prediction a hazardous matter. Furthermore, the Democratic incumbents in the office of attorney general and of lieutenant governor were not seeking re-election to their respective posts, and there was no heir apparent for either. Thus, in the Democratic primary a wild scramble for the three top elective offices in state government developed—the outcome of which could only be guessed. Observers sensed as well changes in the mood of voters, and in the issues that interested them.

Hindsight enables us to say that the preliminary assessment was too cautious. The year 1962 seems likely to be a watershed in Texas politics, marking the point of departure on a new course. The validity of that proposition and the nature of the new patterns taking shape are indicated in various ways.

The First Democratic Primary

The first Democratic primary for the gubernatorial nomination was held on May 5, 1962; it was a slam-bang contest, with few holds barred.

Governor Price Daniel, veteran of a quarter-century of Texas politics, emphasized the unfinished business of his administration in seeking an unprecedented fourth full term. In contrast with his orientation in the 1950's toward the conservative camp, Daniel's approach in 1962 was essentially moderate.

Attorney General Will Wilson, who had won his previous berth on the State Supreme Court and his third term as attorney general with relative ease, was known as a moderate conservative, but his general tendency was to play down the ideological issues and to dwell upon individual abilities and personalities. Most of his fire was centered upon Governor Daniel, although he belatedly brought John Connally within his sights as well.

Connally was making his first public plunge into Texas politics, but his many years as an aide and associate of Lyndon Johnson meant that he was far from inexperienced as a politician. Although associated with the Kennedy Administration by virtue of his one year (1961) as Secretary of the Navy, Connally did not campaign as a New Frontiersman, but took instead a somewhat conservative tack.

The New Frontier had its exponent, however, in the liberal candidate, Don Yarborough. A Houston lawyer, whose only previous exposure had come in connection with an unsuccessful but surprisingly strong bid for the lieutenant governorship in the 1960 Democratic primary, Yarborough keyed his remarks to the need for improvement in the state's social services and economic policies.

A person who openly courted the conservative Democrats was Marshall Formby, whose previous service in state government and politics was confined almost entirely to an appointed term as chairman of the Highway Commission. However, for various reasons Formby was unable to mobilize conservative Democrats behind his candidacy, and was regarded primarily as a regional (West Texas Plains) candidate.

The sixth and most controversial person in the race was former General Edwin Walker, whose difficulties with the Army due to troop indoctrination and ties with the John Birch Society had gained him considerable notoriety.

Thus the list of candidates presented a varied assortment: two seasoned veterans (Daniel and Wilson); two newcomers (Connally and Yarborough), who nevertheless could be expected to mobilize considerable factional support; and two newcomers (Formby and Walker), whose chances were considered poor but who might greatly affect the prospects of others for making the runoff. The results probably surprised the candidates as much as the voters, for the two candidates who were best known before the primaries got under way faltered badly, Daniel winning only 17.2 per cent of the vote and Wilson only 11.9 per cent. Close behind Wilson was Formby with 9.6 per cent and Walker with 9.5 per cent of the total vote. Connally had a sizable plurality of 29.8 per cent, with Don Yarborough in second place on the basis of his 22.0 per cent of the total.

Two of the central figures in Texas politics for the preceding period were thus retired by the voters, and two unsuccessful newcomers were supported individually by a small, but almost equal number of voters. Although these four contenders were only also-rans in the first Democratic primary of 1962, their fate in this election provides important clues to the new dimensions of Texas politics.

The relatively poor showing of Governor Daniel was undoubtedly the most unexpected of the primary results. The fourth-term issue no doubt hurt him, as did the bitter tax fight, which ended in 1961 with the passage of a general sales tax he had pledged to prevent. His campaign was not a fast-paced and aggressive one, in part because he is not that kind of campaigner, and partly because he was holding back in anticipation of a hard runoff campaign. Still, there is reason to believe that what really cost him a place on the second primary ballot was his failure to line up in the ideological and factional warfare, or more exactly, his failure to hold to the same line. Known in the 1950's as a conservative, Daniel as governor pursued a middle-of-the-road course, so much so that in 1960 his challenge came from the conservative Democrats, and his support from the liberals. But in 1962 other candidates were more attractive to both factions, and Governor Daniel was forced to rely on friendship, patronage, and moderation.

The absence of organized group and factional support was even more deadly for Attorney General Will Wilson. Part of Wilson's success in politics in the 1950's appears to have been due to his skill in side-stepping the ideological issues, remaining a candidate who would not get anyone terribly excited for or against him. While this may very well remain a successful formula for offices below a certain level, the really big prizes increasingly require organized support. Wilson had entered the 1961 special Senate election but had fared poorly, and for much the same reason that he faltered in 1962: too heavy a reliance on personal ties and personal organization, and the consequent lack of strong factional support.

The vote for Walker provides additional support for the emphasis on the importance of organized backing. The former general proved to be a very erratic, unpredictable, and sometimes inarticulate campaigner who knew little and cared less about the issues of Texas politics, preferring to use the platform merely as a vehicle for airing ultraconservative views on national and international affairs. Yet with the backing of the John Birch Society, its front organizations, and various other ultraconservative groups, Walker did unexpectedly well.

True, he finished last, but Formby's fifth-place total of 139,094 barely exceeded Walker's 138,387, and Wilson received only 171,617 votes in finishing fourth. Significantly, in the 12 most metropolitan counties in Texas, where organizational needs are most important, Walker received 58,546 votes to Wilson's 59,065 (out of a total of 612,872 votes cast in those counties). Although Formby made a pitch for the conservative Democratic vote, he was unable to capture it, and hence he too suffered from the lack of organized group and factional support. Of course, the fact that he led the other candidates in virtually all of the counties of the Panhandle and South Plains area from which he comes indicates that regionalism is by no means gone as an influence on voters, although its relative impact has greatly diminished.

The fate of these four also-rans indicates the necessity of organized factional support. Of the two others, Connally was the most successful in his effort to rally this support, while Yarborough was successful to a smaller degree.

John Connally demonstrated conclusively, in amassing his first-place total of 431,498 votes, that the years spent behind the scenes in Texas politics had not been wasted. One of the first candidates in the race, he campaigned strenuously and effectively. His approach generally had conservative overtones, but he was careful to avoid any head-on ideological conflicts. Conservative leaders sensitive to strategic considerations and uncomfortably aware of their increasingly precarious position in the Democratic Party soon swung into line behind Connally, who, however, took care to seek support from liberal-moderate forces as well. His multifactional appeal, his vague identification with the Kennedy Administration, and his personable appearance added further to his potential. His campaign was well organized and well financed.

The strategy paid off. Connally held much of the conservative vote, and yet managed to cut into the liberal vote, notably in the rural and small-town areas of North and Central Texas, in Negro areas, and among Latin Americans. The latter group was especially strong in its enthusiasm for Connally, partly because his past associations with Johnson and with the Kennedy Administration brought many of the old and some of the new Latin American leaders to his camp. Connally's appeals for party unity and moderation apparently won over a number of party loyalists and moderates, as indicated by the pluralities obtained in counties that normally vacillate or even lean heavily toward the liberal side.

Specifically, Connally led the other five candidates in a broad band of counties down the center of the state from the Red River to the Rio

Grande. His supremacy was virtually absolute in North and North Central Texas, and in South, South Central, and Southwest Texas, including most of the Rio Grande Valley. Connally also captured pluralities in Far West Texas, and even in a few counties of East Central Texas that are normally liberally inclined. His most significant victories, however, were in three key metropolitan counties. Since Connally had for many years called Fort Worth "home," his 41 per cent of the Tarrant County vote was not particularly surprising, but the 53 per cent registered in Bexar County and the 35.6 per cent gained in Dallas County were higher than expected. In the 12 most metropolitan counties of the state as a whole, Connally bettered his statewide mark, winning 199,874 or 32.6 per cent of their total of 612,872 votes.

Liberal Don Yarborough showed some strength in West Central and Far West Texas and in the Panhandle and South Plains areas, gaining a plurality in a few instances and finishing second behind the regional favorite Marshall Formby in a great many other counties. However, his best geographical showing was in East Texas and the Gulf Coast areas, where he acquired large pluralities.

Although an avowedly liberal candidate, Yarborough had trouble pulling together the elements normally constituting the liberal vote. He received considerable support from organized labor, but a division which saw some leaders supporting Connally and others backing Daniel reduced the help normally forthcoming from that quarter. Yarborough had even more difficulty with the minority vote. The Texas Council of Voters, composed of Negro leaders throughout the state, was unable to agree between Yarborough and Wilson, and ended up making no endorsement in the first primary.[1] Worse still, Connally's earlier entry into the race had given him a headstart in lining up local Negro leadership, so that the Negro votes were more divided than usual. Some individual Latin American leaders were committed to Connally, and key officers of the most ambitious of the Latin organizations, PASO, announced for Daniel after the governor intimated that he might do something about getting Latin Americans their fair share of state jobs.[2] Hence, although Yarborough got some support from the Latin Americans, it was far less than liberals were accustomed to getting. The moderate and loyalist vote, particularly in North and Central Texas, likewise showed support for Connally. The impact of all these factors on the Yarborough vote is most clearly seen in the returns from the metropolitan counties. Yarborough won 36.2 per cent of the vote in Harris County, his home, but in the other eleven metropolitan counties

[1] *Austin American-Statesman*, March 4, 1962.
[2] *Austin Statesman*, April 12, 1962, and *Texas Observer*, April 28, 1962.

he had only 19.7 per cent of the aggregate vote, well below his state-wide average of 22.0 per cent.

Despite the fact that the normal liberal vote did not materialize for him and despite too the perennial financial problems of liberal candidates, Don Yarborough made an exceptionally strong first-primary race. A hard and persistent campaigner, he proved particularly effective in reaching the grass-roots voters. In this he was perhaps aided by his lack of previous identification with the liberal faction—to many voters, he was an earnest, fresh, and engaging personality who compared quite favorably with the older candidates scarred by previous political warfare.

Thus, both Connally and Yarborough reached the runoff in part because of their effectiveness as campaigners. Since both of them also benefited greatly from organized group and factional support, our earlier remarks about the importance of organization are not contradicted. Nevertheless, their records in the 1962 first Democratic primary serve as a reminder that other factors are sometimes involved as well.

The Democratic Runoff

In the runoff primary the big question was where the 697,622 votes polled by Daniel, Wilson, Formby, and Walker would go. If one makes the not unreasonable assumption that most of those who voted for Connally the first time and turned out to vote in the second primary continued to support him, it appears that he gained only a small part of the released votes, since his total increased from 431,498 to 565,174, a net gain of only 133,676. By contrast, Yarborough showed a net gain of 220,938, increasing his total from 317,986 to 538,924. However, a majority of those who supported losers in the first primary probably did not vote in the second one, for total turnout in June was only 76.29 per cent of what it had been in May, a drop from 1,477,115 to 1,104,098. Connally's margin was only 26,250 votes, giving him 51.2 per cent and Yarborough 48.8 per cent of the total.

The geographical picture shows Yarborough consolidating and expanding his sphere of influence in East, East Central, and Southeast Texas. His support was somewhat weaker in Northeast Texas, and even more so in Smith, Gregg, Harrison, Marion, and Panola Counties. He held on to his Gulf Coast support and improved his showing in the Rio Grande Valley. Yarborough managed to drive a thin wedge (consisting particularly of Travis, Bastrop, Llano, and Mason Counties) between the Connally strongholds in South and Southwest Texas on the one hand and Central and North Texas on the other; but not until one reaches the West Texas Plains and Panhandle areas do his counties again form a significant cluster. Generally, Yarborough exceeded Connally in the number of South Plains and Rolling Plains counties carried, while Connally won a majority of the Panhandle counties.

In North and Central Texas Connally was almost without exception the leader, even in counties that had been identified for years as liberal. His most impressive showing was undoubtedly in South and Southwest Texas, where a single, entirely contiguous block of 32 counties each gave Connally 58 per cent or more of the vote. Bounded by Val Verde and Sutton on the west; Kimble and Gillespie on the north; Karnes, Gonzales, and Lavaca on the east; and Duval and Starr on the south, this group includes one of the 4 most populous counties (Bexar) and several of the most sparsely populated ones. Some of them have been previously identified as traditionally conservative counties, but additional cement binding them all together in this case appears to have been provided by the Latin American population.

In the crucial urban areas the two candidates battled almost to a draw. Each one continued to carry his home county, but interestingly enough neither picked up very many of the votes cast for candidates defeated in the first primary. Thus in Harris County Yarborough gained less than 20 per cent of his first primary total, while Connally's vote increased by upwards of 80 per cent; in Tarrant County Connally's vote increased by about 15 per cent while Yarborough's climbed by around 90 per cent. Outside their home counties the results were mixed. Yarborough won Lubbock, McLennan, Nueces, and Travis Counties, but only by a whisker; he carried Jefferson by a heavy majority and El Paso by a respectable one. Connally had smashing majorities in Bexar and Dallas Counties, and respectable ones in Potter and Wichita. The results show that Connally won 53 per cent of the aggregate vote of 480,676 in these 12 metropolitan counties. The turnout, it might be added, varied tremendously within the group, El Paso being the highest with 94 per cent of the first primary vote, and Dallas the lowest with 69.5 per cent of its first primary total.

Even before the second primary was held, there was speculation—based on personal contact and political gossip, as well as on the obvious GOP enthusiasm at the prospect of facing a liberal Democratic nominee—that staunch conservatives would throw their weight behind Don Yarborough in the interest of long-range strategy. One analyst concluded after the runoff that something of the sort had in fact taken place:

Connally was caught in the middle. Many conservatives evidently voted for Yarborough in a campaign aimed at nominating a liberal with the idea of making it easier for Republican Governor nominee Jack Cox in November. And there were conservatives who voted against him just because they didn't like his longtime political buddy, Vice-President Lyndon Johnson. On the other side were the liberals who hate Johnson and turned out in militant numbers to support Yarborough.[3]

This explanation has gained considerable currency, particularly since the county returns revealed that a number of counties in generally conservative territory seemed to reverse their field between June and November. To be exact, 17 of the 114 counties that favored Yarborough in the second Democratic primary turned around and cast their lot with Republican Jack Cox in the general election. This included 2 counties in the Panhandle; Lubbock and 3 other counties of the South Plains; 5 counties in the Midland-Odessa area, including Ector; 3 counties in the San Angelo area, and Harris County itself. (The remaining counties were Rusk in East Texas and Terrell in Far West Texas.)

Unfortunately, data are not at hand to test rigorously this proposition that Yarborough's strength was in good part derived from conservatives. The figures just cited probably bear out the theory, but it is also possible to argue that they show exactly opposite results, i.e., that the switching voters in those areas were liberals who were so bitter over Connally's primary victory that they refused to support him in the general election. One can get somewhat closer to the truth by scrutiny of certain precinct returns.

This detailed inquiry involved 18 of the most conservative precincts in Harris County, each of which gave Republican Cox 70 per cent or more of the vote in the general election. In the group as a whole Yarborough was able to gain only 952 votes over his first-primary tally; Connally picked up an additional 2,648. Thus 26.44 per cent of the gain went to the liberal; 73.56 per cent to the conservative-backed candidate. Since both Will Wilson and Governor Daniel had shown considerable strength in these precincts, and since both of them directed their appeal particularly to the unaffiliated and moderate voters, it seems likely that Yarborough's very modest gains represented support from the same quarter. Although the figures do not prove it, the supposition might well be that the more conservative voters continued to support the more conservative candidate (Connally) and the less conservative ones swung to Yarborough. Certainly the percentages for

[3] *Dallas Morning News*, June 10, 1962.

the two candidates in the second primary did not depart greatly either way from the tendency established in other elections and in the general election itself, except in 2 and possibly 3 of the 18 precincts.

In Harris County Precinct 112, Yarborough increased his vote by 54 while Connally gained only 19, a result giving Yarborough 66⅔ per cent of the total. In the general election Cox carried the precinct with 75.4 per cent of the total vote. In Precinct 119, Yarborough gained 110 votes, and Connally only 73, giving Yarborough 49.7 per cent of the precinct vote. Cox carried the precinct in the general election with 76 per cent of the vote. In only these 2 of the 18 precincts did Yarborough outgain Connally, but in Precinct 233 Connally gained only 58 to Yarborough's 47 votes. In all the other precincts the Connally increase was overwhelming as compared to Yarborough's.

Additional insight into what took place can be had in the case of the first two precincts (112 and 119) by going back to their first-primary results. The leader in 112 was ultraconservative Walker, who received 76 of the precinct total of 166 votes cast. Wilson, Daniel, and Formby together received a total of 43 votes. Since Yarborough's second-primary total increased by 54 votes, he must have received some of his support from Walker backers. In Precinct 119 Walker led the field with 111 of the precinct total of 349 votes cast. While the Wilson-Daniel-Formby vote (131 total) was large enough to prevent one from saying that a part of Yarborough's gain of 110 votes *had* to come from Walker supporters, this is almost certainly what happened. Thus some conservatives, particularly the ultras, voted for the liberal candidate, but the vast majority seemingly continued to support the more conservative candidate.

The second Democratic primary of 1962 saw an inexperienced, generally unknown and avowedly liberal candidate come within a hair of winning the Democratic gubernatorial nomination. The conservative-backed opponent seemed to have all the necessary elements of a smashing victory—ample campaign funds, looks, personality, political expertise, and connections. What are the more significant implications of this close race? One of the most obvious is the nature of the political squeeze facing conservative Democrats. Victory for candidates they endorse necessitates help from moderates and middle-of-the-roaders, but moves to pick up that support carry the risk that the more conservative element will be alienated and will turn to the Republican Party.

Figures for 15 of the 18 conservative Houston precincts previously mentioned testify graphically to this erosion of the conservative Democratic base. The 15 precincts in 1962 had a grand total of 20,648 qualified voters, i.e., persons who had paid their poll tax or obtained exemption certificates. Only 8,375, or 40.6 per cent of them voted in the first Democratic primary; another 3,242 or 15.7 per cent voted in the Republican primary. In the general election, however, a total of 15,000 or 72.6 per cent of the qualified voters cast ballots for gubernatorial candidates. Thus some 3,383 actual voters in those 15 precincts sat out both primaries, and another 3,242 preferred the Republican primary—a total of 6,625 votes missing from the Democratic primary, the bulk of them lost to conservative Democrats.

Conservative Democrats are not the only ones who find the 1962 primary results unsettling. Although Don Yarborough did an exceptionally good job in cutting into the moderate and even the conservative vote, his opponent located what is perhaps the Achilles heel of Texas liberalism—the minority vote. Connally's tremendous showing with the Latin American voters was well publicized and was previously mentioned in this analysis, but this important development should be re-emphasized. Not as immediately obvious but equally impressive was Connally's improved showing with Negroes. In 51 predominantly Negro precincts in Harris County—the single largest bloc of Negro votes in the state—Connally in the second primary emerged with 34.7 per cent of the total. Although this figure might normally be regarded as a relatively poor showing, compared with the top-heavy majorities that liberal candidates in other elections had registered there, it was a Connally victory.

The reasons for this drop in Negro support of the liberal Democrat are readily apparent. Yarborough chose to stress the economic appeals of the liberal creed; he said little—at least in a concrete way—about a liberal civil-rights program. As a matter of fact, after the election a group of Negro business and professional people formed another state-wide political organization—the United Political Organization—most of whose leaders supported Connally in 1962 and are liberally inclined on racial issues but basically conservative on economic questions.

In a word, then, the 1962 primaries saw conservative Democrats pushed to the limits of their strength, with liberals showing unexpected power. Still, an obituary for the conservatives would be premature, for they gave every indication of a determination to continue the fight in the Democracy, albeit with some shift in strategy and techniques. And the liberals experienced difficulty in holding together their coalition—particularly minority elements.

THE GENERAL ELECTION

Without question the Republican effort in the 1962 general election was the strongest since Reconstruction days. The Texas GOP fielded candidates in races for 8 statewide offices, 18 of 23 United States congressional seats, 13 of 31 state Senate posts, 84 of 150 state House seats, and some 150 local offices. A postelection tally by the Party credited Republicans with 2 United States representatives, 8 state representatives, 3 county judges, 4 justices of the peace, 8 county commissioners, 2 constables, one county superintendent of schools, 2 county attorneys, one district attorney, and a judge of the Dallas County Court at Law. Almost all of the local offices filled by Republicans were won in 1962.

The gubernatorial contest was by all odds the most bitterly contested one. The final tally showed a turnout of 1,569,181, of which 715,025 votes or 45.8 per cent were taken by Republican nominee Jack Cox, and 847,036, or 54.2 per cent by John Connally.[4] Cox won majorities in 56 counties, with 11 of them concentrated in the Panhandle; another 11 grouped in the Edwards Plateau-German area around San Antonio; a group of 8 counties east and west of the Midland-Odessa core; and a 4-county oasis in East Texas composed of Gregg, Rusk, Smith, and Harrison Counties.

As expected, the lion's share of Cox's votes came from the metropolitan counties, with 54 per cent of the ballots recorded for him cast in the 12 most metropolitan counties of the state. The "big four" of Harris, Dallas, Bexar, and Tarrant Counties alone provided no less than 40 per cent of the total Cox tally, although the percentage in each varied greatly, from a low of 40.8 per cent in Bexar County to a high of 57.7 per cent in Dallas County. Of the remaining 8 counties in the metropolitan category, Cox carried 2 (Lubbock and Potter) but did not win in the remainder; in several instances his vote level fell just below or just above the 40 per cent mark. However, in several of the counties having slightly smaller cities, such as Ector, Midland, Smith, Taylor, and Tom Green, Cox picked up majorities.

It is instructive to compare the Cox vote over the state with our earlier findings on the most conservative Democratic counties, 1952–1958 (see Figure B), and with the results of the Connally-Yarborough runoff. No less than 21 of the 63 counties in the first quarter of the Connally vote in that runoff ended up by giving Cox a majority of their votes in November, as did 27 of the 58 counties previously identified

4 The Constitution Party candidate, Jack Carswell, received an insignificant 7,120 votes—not even one-tenth of one per cent. Therefore, all county percentages for Cox and Connally were calculated as a per cent of the total Cox-Connally vote.

as the most conservative Democratic counties (the two groups are not mutually exclusive). A look at returns from some of the middle- and upper-class precincts in the large cities makes even clearer that conservative Democrats preferred the Republican nominee. Thus, in the 18 Houston precincts discussed in connection with the Connally-Yarborough runoff, Connally margins of 60–70 per cent and better in the June primary were converted in November to Cox majorities, averaging 76 per cent of the total votes cast in those precincts.

Of the two candidates, Connally clearly was in the more delicate situation. Liberals had demonstrated in the 1961 runoff between Tower and Blakley that they would just as soon stay home as choose between a conservative Democrat and a conservative Republican, even if failure to vote insured Republican victory. Hence it would not do to repeat Blakley's mistake of holding out absolutely nothing to interest liberal voters. On the other hand, any significant overtures to liberals might very well speed the shift of conservatives to the Republican Party. Connally walked this figurative tightrope throughout the campaign, and the consensus was that he performed admirably. The most severe test was the state convention, when liberals pushed hard for some public commitments from Connally for at least some liberal objectives. Although he subsequently made some private commitments to liberal groups, Connally refused to declare himself openly for major liberal objectives. At the same time, he avoided taking extreme conservative positions sure to inflame liberal feelings. Reluctantly, liberals had to recognize that Connally was almost certainly the less conservative of the two candidates, and as this recognition spread, it became difficult for them to justify opposing him. Efforts at organizing liberal support for Cox were the results of reasoning that a Cox victory would contribute still more to the conservative exodus from the Democratic to the Republican Party, but by and large liberal voters refused to be persuaded that a vote for Cox was a vote for liberalism in the long run.

Connally was thus successful in putting together a very fragile and uneasy conservative-moderate-liberal coalition, particularly so in the Gulf Coast areas. Losses in the traditionally Democratic counties of East, Central, and West Central Texas were held down, and he continued to enjoy strong support from South and Southwest Texas. Perhaps the greatest danger Connally faced was a low-voter turnout, for Republicans were confident that anything less than a 1,200,000 turnout would bring them easy victory. The actual recorded total of 1,569,181 meant that the Democratic nominee had successfully skirted the danger, but one set of figures does provide some insight into the precariousness of Connally's position. In 233 of the state's 254 counties the total vote cast for the two gubernatorial nominees was 37,519 less than the total vote cast for the parties' nominees for the office of lieutenant governor. Only by virtue of the fact that the remaining 21 counties, including some of the most populous ones, tallied 49,635 more votes for both gubernatorial nominees than for the two candidates for lieutenant governor was it possible for the state total in the governorship race to exceed that for the lieutenant governorship by 12,116 votes.

For the top office on the ballot—the one getting most of the attention and campaign effort—to barely outpull an office less important and less strenuously contested runs contrary to the observed pattern of Texas voters for many years; the record invariably shows a higher vote for the more important offices when they are seriously contested. The 1962 results suggest that a number of persons who took the trouble to go to the polls on election day could not or would not make a choice in the gubernatorial contest. One can only speculate as to whether this resulted from conflicts in loyalty that made decision impossible, or from a deliberate abstention by voters, possibly those of liberal persuasion; but had Connally inadvertently acted to swell perceptibly this small number of abstainers, the outcome of the election might well have been different.

What conclusions can one draw about the future of the Republican Party in Texas as a result of the 1962 elections? Certain types of evidence point in the direction of continued growth. The Republican primary in 1962 attracted some 117,000 voters despite the lure of an exciting slugfest in the Democratic gubernatorial primary. As previously pointed out, the GOP fielded a record number of candidates and for its efforts elected a record number of officials. Even the defeat of Cox for the governorship does not dim the lustre of his accomplishment in polling 45.8 per cent of the total vote, thereby setting a twentieth-century record for his party.[5] Furthermore, the other unsuccessful candidates on the Republican ticket made impressive showings. Desmond Barry, who campaigned vigorously for the post of congressman-at-large received 43.9 per cent of the total vote, and the Republican nominee for the post of lieutenant governor secured 39.5 per cent. In addition to winning two congressional seats, the GOP managed to poll more than 45 per cent of the vote in two other districts, 41.2 per cent in a third one, 39.4 and 36.7 per cent in another two, and from 30 to 35 per cent in another five districts. In the other five House races contested, Republicans won from 25 to 30 per cent in

[5] The previous percentages were 41.1 per cent in 1924, 37.5 per cent in 1932, and 27.2 per cent in 1960.

two, from 20 to 25 per cent in another two, and 12 per cent in the fifth. The Republican Party won 38.7 per cent of all votes cast in congressional district elections where Democratic nominees faced Republican opposition. In the less important and less seriously contested races for the state Senate, the thirteen Republican candidates polled more than 40 per cent of the vote in three districts, from 30 to 39 per cent of the vote in four districts, from 25 to 29 per cent in four districts, and from 20 to 24 per cent in two.

The evidence concerning Republican support in congressional and state senatorial races is particularly relevant to the issue of just how strong the Party now is. Some surveys of individual voter preference have reported the absence of a general shift in the South and in Texas toward identification with the Republican Party. This was the conclusion of researchers at the Michigan Survey Research Center after a study of surveys of Southern voters made in connection with the 1960 general election. A survey released by a veteran pollster in Texas, known as the Belden Poll, reported similar findings after the 1962 elections. Specifically, the Belden Poll reported that when people were asked the question "As of now do you consider yourself a Democrat, Republican, or an Independent?" the results obtained in November of 1962 differed little from those obtained when the identical question was asked in 1952.

TABLE 32

Party Identification of Texas Voters, 1952 and 1962

Identification	1952	November 1962
	%	%
Republican	7	9
Democrat	59	59
Independent	24	27
Undecided	10	5

Source: Belden Poll, as reported in the *Houston Post*, December 23, 1962, Section 1.

That is, the Democratic identifiers remained constant at 59 per cent, with a Republican increase in the ten-year period from 7 to 9 per cent, with an increase in independent ranks from 24 per cent in 1952 to 27 per cent in 1962, and with the undecided group trimmed from 10 to 5 per cent.

Although questions might be raised about the design and conduct of this survey, one possible explanation for the low Republican percentage given is compatible with the impression derived from the election returns. The Belden Poll *may* have sampled the opinions of all *potential* voters, of which Texas has in the neighborhood of 5,000,000. If one applies 9 per cent to this base, then a finding of around 450,000 confirmed Republicans in Texas is not inconsistent with the election returns, particularly since these voters by virtue of their socio-economic status turn out to vote in much higher percentages than do other voters. Unfortunately, the director of the poll did not specify whether he meant 9 per cent of all potential voters or 9 per cent of all holders of poll tax and exemption certificates, or 9 per cent of the voters who actually went to the polls.

Actually, the most troublesome aspect of the survey reports is that portion indicating very little increase in the percentage expressing a preference for the Republican Party. One might explain this in part by noting that some who identified with the GOP in 1952, particularly Negroes, probably shifted to the Democratic Party. However, it is hard to believe that such countermoves would be almost enough to offset what appears to have been steady growth of the GOP's popularity with middle-class and upper-class Anglo-Saxons in Texas. One suspects that the question put to the respondents is not suitable for bringing out all Republican sentiment, a suspicion reinforced by Belden's admission that "the independent group is composed of voters who, in some respects, are more akin to Texas Republicans than to Texas Democrats." It seems, in fact, that a more realistic appraisal of Republican strength in Texas would include most of the 27 per cent identified as independents. Thus, one might estimate that the GOP has a fairly certain 30–35 per cent of the vote at an intermediate level of turnout, a figure which seems consistent with what has just been reported concerning the lesser candidates on the Republican ticket.

Although the estimate just made of dependable Republican strength does not take into consideration the additional support that may be obtained by successful exploitation of divisions within the Democratic Party, or of resentment directed against the national Democratic Party, or by the appeal of an unusual Republican candidate, it does indicate that the Republican Party in Texas is still not in a securely competitive position. The weakness pointed to in Chapter II—too narrow an appeal—was further dramatized by the 1962 election. No statewide figures on Negro voting are available as yet, but it seems likely that the story in Houston's precincts is not unusual for the state. Overall, predominantly Negro boxes in Houston gave Connally around 95 per cent of their total vote, with some of them hitting the 97–98 per cent mark.[6] By contrast, in the unexciting 1958 gubernatorial

[6] One indication that the Houston figures are representative of urban Negro

election a Republican candidate who hardly campaigned at all won from 10 to 15 per cent of the vote in most of the same Negro precincts, and in a number of them he obtained 15–20 per cent of the total. In part, of course, the stronger Democratic showing in 1962 simply reflected a much better turnout in Negro precincts, but the ability to obtain that turnout is itself a measure of Democratic strength that cannot be ignored.

Republican lack of success with Latin Americans is equally noteworthy. On occasion, the Texas GOP has made some efforts to appeal to voters in that ethnic group, especially in El Paso and in the Rio Grande Valley. While it is doubtful that the strongest possible drive would ever produce Republican majorities among Latin electors, the Republicans with greater recognition of their importance and with appropriate adjustment of policy might be able to win over a minority sizable enough to make the difference in some elections. The failure of GOP leaders to recognize these factors and the price they pay are clearly illustrated by what happened in the 1962 gubernatorial election, when South and Southwest Texas counties racked up heavy Connally majorities. Connally margins in Bexar, El Paso, Cameron, and Hidalgo Counties must have been particularly disappointing to the GOP, for much effort had gone into their bids in those counties, and past voting records augured well for the Republican candidates. That the crucial factor continued to be the Latin Americans is indicated by the returns from San Antonio. In the fourteen precincts with the highest percentage of Latin poll-tax holders (80 per cent and above) Connally amassed 94.8 per cent of the ballots cast while in 15 high-income Anglo precincts 56.7 per cent of the voters supported Cox.

In summary, it appears that the Texas GOP is gaining steadily in experience, organization, and confidence. Work in the metropolitan areas is progressing, precinct and county organizations are being improved, state headquarters is furnishing more and more assistance. It seems true too that the party is finding increasing favor with the voters, except with certain elements whose votes are crucial, particularly the minority groups. If Tower's election to the Senate in 1961 was correctly described by Allen Duckworth as establishing a "Republican beachhead," it seems fair to say after 1962 that the beachhead has been expanded into a major front—in fact two fronts, one involving statewide races for national offices, and the other, statewide contests

---

voting behavior is the fact that in the five San Antonio precincts with the highest percentages of Negro poll-tax holders (74 per cent and above in 1961) approximately 94.6 per cent of the voters backed Connally.

for the top state offices. However, before the Republicans can win the war as well as isolated battles it will be necessary to mobilize still more.

THE 1962 ELECTIONS IN CONTEXT

Except in a very general way, no effort has been made thus far in this chapter to relate results of the 1962 primaries and elections to our findings concerning the previous decade or so of Texas politics. It might be well at this point to explore briefly that relationship. By focusing on those two groups at opposite ends of the political continuum in Texas—the first-quarter Republican voters and the first-quarter liberal Democratic voters in key elections from 1957 through 1962—we may be able to get a better idea of how far the process of political polarization had gone. It should be emphasized that we have no intention of implying thereby that the conservative Democrats have already or shortly will become extinct. Our analysis of the 1962 primaries should be enough to indicate otherwise.

Because of the great importance of socio-economic characteristics as influences on voter behavior, it also seems worthwhile to re-examine the political complexion of Texas counties in the light of data provided by the 1960 Census. It was both necessary and desirable to utilize 1950 Census materials in the analyses conducted in the preceding chapters of this study, as well as data obtained by more specialized censuses, such as the *Census of Manufactures* in 1958. Nevertheless, results obtained by holding socio-economic factors constant and making electoral behavior the variable are never entirely satisfactory, particularly in a system changing as rapidly as this one. Accordingly, the more recent electoral patterns will be reviewed from the standpoint of certain 1960 socio-economic characteristics for the counties involved.

Geographic Patterns of Republican and Liberal Democratic Counties

A careful comparison of the results in the general election of 1962 with those of the special Senate elections of 1957 and 1961 (first) leaves little doubt of the continuity of Republican appeal. As Figure G indicates, 30 of the 63 counties comprising the first quarter of the Republican vote in 1962 (48.4 per cent and over) appeared in the first quarter of the Republican vote in the two Senate elections; another 14 appeared in the first quarter of the Republican vote in 1961, with all except one of the 14 ranking in the second Republican quarter in 1957; and 2 other counties ranked in the Republican first quarter in 1957 as well as in 1962. Thus, 46 of the 63 first-quarter Republican counties

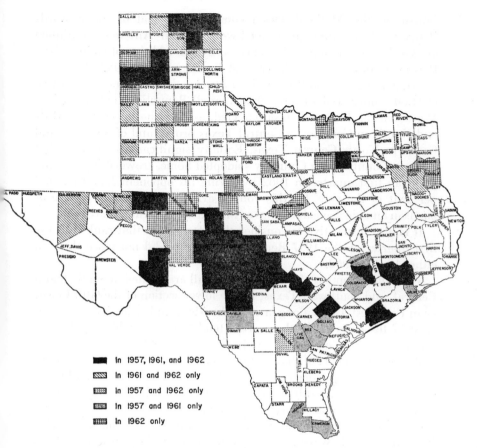

Figure G. First-quartile Republican counties in Texas: 1957 and 1961 senatorial and 1962 gubernatorial elections.

in 1962 had already been conspicuous by their relatively high Republican percentages.

Several particularly revealing comparisons can be made between the 1962 first-quarter counties and the others. Of greatest interest are the 17 counties that ranked in the first quarter of the Republican vote in 1962 for the first time in any of the three elections. The oasis in East Texas first formed in 1961 when Rusk and Smith Counties ranked in the first Republican quarter was expanded in 1962 by the addition of three adjacent counties: Gregg, Harrison, and Panola. The move of Upton, Reagan, Glasscock, and Sterling Counties into the Republican first quarter in 1962 filled in a conspicuous gap between the Republicanism of the Midland-Odessa complex and that of the Edwards Plateau-Hill Country area northwest of San Antonio. Continued growth in the Panhandle is indicated by the addition of Oldham and Parmer Counties to the Republican first quarter in 1962. A similar ranking of Taylor and Runnels Counties for the first time in the three elections considered suggests that a small Republican extension into West Central Texas has been effected, as does the presence of Mills and Hamilton Counties in Central Texas proper and of Stephens and Cooke in North Central Texas. Equally significant is the fact that Tarrant County, John Connally's adopted home, crowded into the Republican first quarter in 1962 by giving his opponent Jack Cox 49.7 per cent of the vote, for this vote is striking proof of the growth of partisan and ideological feelings as influences on voting behavior.

It is also instructive to consider the 21 counties that ranked in the first quarter of the 1957 Republican vote but did not place there in either 1961 or 1962.[7]

With the exception of Parker County, all are located in South, South Central, and Southwest Texas; in the lower section of the Gulf Coast; or in Far West Texas along or near the Mexican border. The fact that most of the counties in these areas tend to have sizable numbers of Latin Americans suggests strongly that the GOP has been lagging in winning the support of that ethnic group. Since the 1961 results were affected by the presence of Henry Gonzalez on the ballot as a Democrat, and the 1962 results by the fact that Connally grew up in South Texas, it may be that this failure of the Republicans to hold their relative position in South and Southwest Texas is a passing thing. The indications are, however, that Republican failure to grow as rapidly in those areas as elsewhere is more deeply rooted.

Of the 9 counties that did not rank in the Republican first quarter in 1962 but did so in both 1957 and 1961, 6 are located in the same general area; they are Bee, Cameron, Goliad, Hidalgo, Live Oak, and Zavala. The other 3 (Colorado, Galveston, and Washington) have some Latin American population, but there the decline in relative Republican strength may be due to a much better mobilization of the liberal Democratic potential, particularly with Negro voters.

For the Republican Party, then, the 1962 election for the most part continued the geographical trends shown in earlier elections. Areas previously identified as being the most strongly Republican continued

[7] Because they are not identified in Figure G a listing is in order: Aransas, Bexar, Blanco, Brewster, Brooks, Calhoun, Dimmit, Fayette, Irion, Jim Wells, Kenedy, Kleberg, Medina, Nueces, Parker, Pecos, Refugio, Val Verde, Victoria, Wilson, and Zapata.

to hold that ranking, with adjacent counties showing similar tendencies. Republican pockets in East Texas and in the South Plains areas continued to grow and expand, and new ones in Central and West Central Texas may be developing. Such growth is undoubtedly pleasant for Republican leaders to contemplate, but the relative decline of Republican strength in South and Southwest Texas poses problems as well.

The bearing of the 1962 primaries on long-term liberal Democratic patterns is more difficult to analyze. Because the liberal vote in the 1961 special Senate election was split at least two and sometimes three and four ways, use of that election is not warranted. And yet, to utilize only the 1957 special Senate election vote for Ralph Yarborough and the 1962 gubernatorial second Democratic primary vote for Don Yarborough seems to leave an uncertain gap. Accordingly, the results of the 1960 presidential election are also pressed into service, the liberal Democratic vote being that for Kennedy and Johnson. Used alone, such a classification would be hazardous, but in conjunction with the other two elections it appears to be useful and reliable enough.

A tendency for liberal strength to ebb and flow more than that of the Republicans is indicated by the smaller number of counties that consistently provide relatively high percentages for liberal Democratic candidates. Only 12 counties ranked in the first quarter of the liberal candidate's vote in the 1957 special Senate, the 1960 presidential, and the 1962 second Democratic gubernatorial primary elections. As Figure H shows, there are two distinct geographical groupings. Five counties that so ranked in all three elections form a contiguous cluster in the Rolling Plains area of West Central Texas. Six counties with a similar rating form a much looser, noncontiguous block in East Central and Southeast Texas.

The importance of the two clusters as guides to liberal strength can be seen by adding to them the 23 counties that were classified as first-quarter liberal Democratic in 1957 and 1960 only. Nine of these counties fill out the contiguous block in West Central Texas; 2 others are on the southwestern side of the same core counties, although they scatter into the South Plains area. Seven of these counties that were first-quarter liberal in 1957 and 1960 only range loosely through East Central, Central, and South Central Texas in a northeast-southwestern direction. Three of the remaining counties are scattered over South Texas, with 2 others in North and Northeast Texas. Since these are the areas where Connally made some of his most impressive showings in 1962, their loss to the liberal candidate was quite significant. However, while 1962 suggests a more moderate cast to the political complexion of these 23 counties, it must be emphasized that they were pulled away from the liberal candidate only by virtue of the moderate appeal directed to them from Connally.

Another group of 8 counties ranked in the liberal first quarter in 1957 and in 1962, but slipped in 1960. The implication that "presidential Republicanism" may be a little stronger in these counties is strengthened by their geographical location, for 4 of the 8 are scattered over the Panhandle-South Plains area where we have already noted rising Republican strength.

Conspicuous by their absence from Figure H are 19 counties classed as first-quarter liberal Democratic in 1957. Most of them are located in the Panhandle, Plains, and Central Texas areas that were hard hit

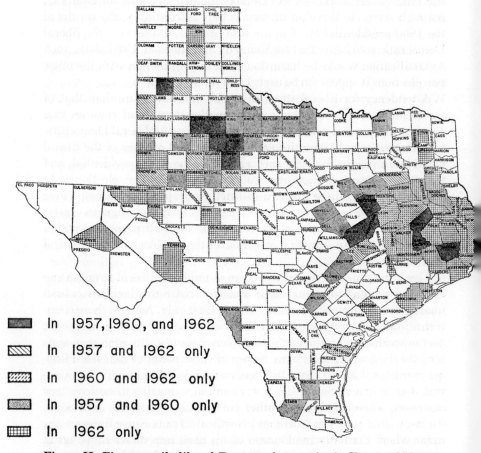

In 1957, 1960, and 1962

In 1957 and 1962 only

In 1960 and 1962 only

In 1957 and 1960 only

In 1962 only

Figure H. First-quartile liberal Democratic counties in Texas: 1957 senatorial and 1960 presidential elections and 1962 second Democratic primary.

by droughts that reached their climax in 1956 and early 1957. Presumably some of the liberal strength shown in those counties reflected support for the candidate who campaigned most vigorously on a platform of governmental assistance. Too, the decline for some was a matter of relatively little slippage, for 7 of the 19 ranked in the second quarter of the liberal vote in 1960 and 1962, and a number of others ranked in the second quarter in one of those two later elections. The record does indicate, however, that liberal strength has grown slower in those counties than elsewhere, despite their setting in areas tending to become more Republican. Although this appears somewhat contradictory of our hypothesis that leakage of conservative Democrats to the GOP will improve liberal showings, the explanation apparently is that the conservative shift to the GOP has progressed less rapidly in these 19 counties, presumably because to begin with they were somewhat more moderate.

Still another group of 9 counties is significant for a different reason. All ranked in the liberal Democratic first quarter in 1960 and 1962, but did not in 1957. All except 2 are in East and Southeast Texas. While their rankings in 1957 were perhaps affected by the fact that the conservative Democratic candidate (Martin Dies) was a former East Texas Congressman, these counties are not confined to his old district, and his liberal opponent, Ralph Yarborough, is a former East Texan too. The rankings in 1962 again may have been affected by the fact that Don Yarborough was regarded as an East Texan.

However, even with these cautionary notes in mind, it still seems quite possible that the presence of this group of counties heralds a turn back toward liberalism in rural East Texas. Several possible explanations of this apparent revival of liberal strength in an area once noted for its radicalism come to mind. It may be that Negroes in these counties are voting in greater numbers and with greater freedom than they were a few years ago, and their general orientation, we have noted repeatedly, is toward the liberal Democratic side. Another possibility is that East Texas voters and political leaders may be coming to feel that conservatism on racial issues has led them afield in economic matters; 1960 and 1962 may thus be seen as a response to the New Frontier program offered both by Kennedy and by Don Yarborough. Whether or not these are valid explanations remains to be seen, but one explanation applicable in other parts of the state seems to be ruled out here. It is very doubtful that growth of Republican sentiment has siphoned off conservative Democrats in numbers sufficient to bring about this change, in the first place because the Republican primary in 1962 drew only a tiny fraction of the voters, and secondly because turnout was considerably higher for the second Democratic primary than for the general election in a number of these counties.

The fifth set of counties are those that were ranked in the liberal Democratic first quarter only in 1962. Of the total of 34, 14 are in the western part of the state, with the most pronounced groupings in the South Plains area and adjacent to Ector County. Of the remainder, 14 are in East and East Central Texas, and 5 are scattered along the Gulf Coast region.

The rise of the West Texas counties in this group to ranking as first-quarter liberal Democratic counties appears to be related to the growth of Republicanism in that general area, draining off sizable numbers of conservative Democrats from the Democratic primary, and to some degree this growth also explains the behavior of the 5 Gulf Coast counties, especially Galveston and Jefferson. While this is undoubtedly a factor in certain of the East Texas counties among these 34 counties, notably Rusk, the fact that Republican performance is very uneven within the East Texas counties as a whole suggests other forces at work. Much the same sort of reasoning as that advanced in the preceding paragraph can be extended to these East Texas counties as well, but since performance in only one election is involved, only the most tentative sort of conclusions can be drawn.

Just as the counties that ranked in the liberal first quarter in 1962 help us to see areas of possible gain, so an examination of the 20 counties that were so ranked only in 1960 should help us to see an area of apparent weakness. With only five or six exceptions these counties are all located in South and Southwest Texas. They did not respond well to the campaigning of Ralph Yarborough in 1957 or Don Yarborough in 1962, which suggests strongly that a major explanation for their rise to first-quarter status in 1960 was the religion of John F. Kennedy. Their Latin American population cannot be determined with accuracy, but the one characteristic common to most of these counties is a sizable Latin American—and Catholic—population.

The 1962 elections thus apparently affected the liberal Democrats somewhat differently from the way they affected the Republicans. They showed the GOP gains to be in large measure by way of solidifying and expanding continuing spheres of influence. The 1962 primaries, by contrast, broke liberal Democratic ranks in North and Central Texas to an extent unknown for several years. At the same time, the primaries at least hold out the hope of a resurgent liberal movement in East Texas, based possibly on increased Negro support and on a subordination of feeling on racial issues to "pocketbook" issues among white persons.

Socio-Economic Characteristics of Republican and Liberal Democratic Counties

Our examination of the most Republican and the most liberal Democratic counties would not be complete if it stopped with the fixing of their geographic location. In fact, it would be misleading, because of the implication that regional sentiment provided the major motivation of voters in those counties. Although the 1962 primaries and elections remind us that regionalism still exerts some influence upon voter behavior, as evidenced by the vote in West Texas for Marshall Formby in the first Democratic primary and the vote for Don Yarborough in portions of East Texas in the second primary, a fuller understanding of the trends in Texas politics requires consideration of certain important social and economic characteristics associated with them.

What are some of these characteristics for the most Republican counties, defined as the 55 counties ranking in the first quarter of the Republican vote in at least two of the three elections covered in Figure G? And of the most liberal Democratic counties, defined as the 52 counties ranking in the first quarter of the vote for liberal Democratic candidates in at least two of the three elections covered in Figure H?

One of the most important clues to influences upon the voters constituting each of these two groups is provided by data on median family income. As Table 33 reveals, only about 10 per cent of the most liberal counties in Texas had a median family income of $5,000 or more in 1959; by contrast, 38.2 per cent of the most Republican counties were so classified. Of the 45 counties in the state with a median income over $5,000 annually, 21 were in the most Republican group, compared with only 5 in the most liberal one. Similar results are obtained when one shifts to the other end of the scale. Some 43 per cent of the most liberal counties had a median income in 1959 of less than $3,000, compared with only 14.5 per cent of the most Republican counties. Slightly more than one-third (22) of the state's 60 counties having median incomes below that figure are among the most liberal group, in contrast to the 8 most Republican counties falling below that level.

The significance of economic factors is also confirmed by the data of Table 34 pertaining to percentages of families earning less than $3,000 annually. The number of the most Republican counties where the percentage earning less than $3,000 a year was under 30 per cent was three times the number of most liberal counties in the same bracket. The number of the most liberal counties where the percentage earning less than $3,000 exceeded 50 per cent was almost three times the number of the most Republican counties in this bracket. In-

TABLE 33

Comparison of Median Family Income in Republican and
Liberal Democratic Counties

Median Family Income (1959)	Most Liberal Counties (51)[a]		Most Republican Counties (55)[b]		All Counties (251)	
	No.	%	No.	%	No.	%
$5,000 and over	5	9.8	21	38.2	45	17.9
Less than $3,000	22	43.1	8	14.5	60	23.9

Source: Income figures from U.S. Census reports.
[a] Includes 51 of the 52 counties fitting the "most liberal" classification as defined above. No income data were available for one county.
[b] Includes the 55 counties fitting the "most Republican" classification as defined above.

terestingly enough, within the most liberal category there was a pronounced grouping: 5 of the 8 counties that ranked in the liberal first
quarter in 1957 and 1960 but not in 1962 had less than 30 per cent
earning under $3,000 annually, as compared with only 3 of the remain-
ing 43 counties having that low a percentage.

Another characteristic adding to our understanding of these two
categories of counties involves percentages of urban and farm rural
population. Unfortunately for the purpose of comparison with our
earlier analysis of urban-rural differences, the United States Census
Bureau in 1960 changed significantly its definition of "farm rural"

TABLE 34

Distribution of Liberal and Republican Counties
According to Family Income

Per Cent Earning under $3,000 Annually (1959)	Most Liberal Counties (51)[a] No.	Most Republican Counties (55)[b] No.	All Counties (251)[c] No.
8.3–19.9	2	14	25
20–29.9	6	11	44
30–39.9	11	11	59
40–49.9	10	11	62
50–59.9	14	7	45
60–71.4	8	1	16

Source: Income data from U.S. Census returns.
[a] Includes all except one of the 52 counties fitting the "most liberal" classification as defined above. No income data were available for one county.
[b] Includes the 55 counties fitting the "most Republican" classification as defined above.
[c] No income data were available for 3 counties in the state.

and "nonfarm rural." Still, one can compare our most Republican and most liberal Democratic counties using the new definitions to obtain at least a general notion of the extent to which they differ. Table 35 presents the comparative distribution of the two groups of counties according to percentage of urban population.

TABLE 35

Distribution of Liberal and Republican Counties
According to Urban Population

Percentage of Urban Population	Most Liberal Counties (52) No.	Most Republican Counties (55) No.
None	20	19
13.8–39.9	17	2
40–59.9	8	13
60–79.9	5	10
80 and over	2	11

Source: Calculated from U.S. Census data.

Although in each case the number of counties with no urban population at all (by Census definitions) is about the same, the two columns of figures make clear that in general the most Republican counties are far more likely to have higher percentages of urban population. Thus, only 15 of the most liberal Democratic counties have over 40 per cent urban population; 34 of the most Republican counties exceed that figure.

A comparison of percentages of farm rural population in the two groups of counties is equally rewarding. As Table 36 indicates, there are three times as many Republican as liberal Democratic counties with less than 10 per cent farm rural population. Similarly, at the other extreme there are 9 liberal counties with 40 per cent or more farm rural population, compared with only one of the most Republican counties in that bracket.

Despite the differences in degree of urbanization and in percentages of farm rural population, the most Republican and most liberal Democratic counties have considerable similarity in manufacturing employment. The 1960 Census reported that 35 of the state's 254 counties had 20 per cent or more employed in manufacturing. Seven of these are classified as most liberal, 5 as most Republican. The Census also reported 59 counties with 10 to 19.9 per cent manufacturing employment. Twelve of these are classified as most liberal, 10 as most Republican. The most significant thing about these figures is not the

TABLE 36

Distribution of Liberal and Republican Counties
According to Farm Rural Population

Percentage of Farm Rural Population	Most Liberal Counties (52) No.	Most Republican Counties (55) No.
0–9.9	7	20
10–19.9	15	13
20–39.9	21	21
40 and over	9	1

Source: U.S. Census data.

similarity, however, but the fact that only 12 of the 35 counties with 20 per cent or more manufacturing employment fall into either of these two groups. While fuller study of this is required, it is probable that the explanation is rooted in the polarization likely to occur in the areas with high manufacturing employment. That is, our use of quartile rankings to establish the basic categories requires percentages for one group or the other that are not only consistent but also relatively high. High levels of manufacturing employment, one can hypothesize, help to generate forces in Texas that result in somewhat more even division of political strength than will be found in less industrialized counties.

Although figures for manufacturing employment do not significantly differentiate liberal Democratic from Republican counties, one other related set of Census figures is quite helpful for that purpose, namely, the percentage employed in white-collar occupations. As set forth in Table 37, a breakdown of such figures shows only one of the

TABLE 37

Distribution of Liberal and Republican Counties According to
Percentage Employed in White-Collar Occupations

Percentage Employed in White-Collar Occupations	Most Liberal Counties (52) No.	Most Republican Counties (54) No.	All Counties (253) No.
0–19.9	2	3	9
20–29.9	35	18	105
30–39.9	14	22	113
40–49.9	1	8	22
50 and over	0	3	4

Source: U.S. Census data. No figures available for one of the most Republican counties.

most liberal counties with more than 40 per cent employed in white-collar occupations, compared with 11 of the most Republican counties. At the opposite end of the scale, 37 of the most liberal counties had less than 30 per cent so employed, while only 21 of the most Republican counties were so classified.

What has been said to this point by no means exhausts all the relevant social and economic characteristics, but it does suffice to establish one major point above and beyond the implications of particular statistics. A really thorough understanding of Texas politics requires detailed consideration of such socio-economic factors as income, occupation, and place of residence. These factors have always been relevant to the study of politics, but they have an increasing importance as Texas continues the transition from a rural and agricultural society to a modern commercial and industrial one. To be sure, some voters still respond to the personality and campaign style of a candidate, and others vote in accordance with historical influences. Nevertheless, such responses seem to be of declining importance in Texas.

VI

CONCLUSIONS AND FUTURE PROSPECTS

Comparing recent with past developments in Texas political history one is impressed with the changes that have occurred in the nature of the issues, the modes of operation, and the relative strength of competing parties and factions. The pattern of the past was that of an amorphous one-party system with divisions resembling those of other states in the Old Confederacy, even to a similar, though less encompassing, concern with racial issues. Candidates for public office played up their personalities and relied primarily upon friendship-oriented campaign organizations. The Republican Party was a small and ineffectual group mainly interested in patronage, in which Negroes were a substantial element until the late 1920's. The prevailing temper of the dominant Democrats was conservatism occasionally relieved by sporadic and sputtering surges of early liberalism or rural radicalism. The most notable of the latter included the Populism of the 1890's, the long, checkered, and episodic Ferguson era from World War I to the thirties, and Governor Allred's administration during the mid-thirties.

From the New Deal came the origins of the state's gradual shift away from questions of race, personalities, and alcohol toward the more fundamental issue of economics. In 1944 the Texas Regulars kicked over the Democratic Party traces largely in reaction to President Roosevelt and the New Deal; and the 1948 bolt by the Dixiecrats, although pitched heavily to the race controversy, had some of the same motivation. As a matter of fact, the low vote for the Dixiecrats indicated that their chief error was in placing too much emphasis on the racial question. During the fifties this conservative reaction to—and against—New Deal-Fair Deal economics gained momentum to the point that it now must be considered a major motivating force.

Under the articulate leadership of Governor Allan Shivers the conservative Democrats were able to maintain a tight control over state politics during the first half of the fifties. By 1956, however, liberalism—which had been weakened but never obliterated—was revived and began to give the conservatives a hard run in Democratic primaries. This liberal resurgence, in turn, further hardened the positions of the more adamant conservatives to the point that by 1961 enough of them were willing to desert the Democratic Party and to support Republican John Tower in his successful bid for a seat in the United States Senate. Despite the defeat of Jack Cox his strong showing in the much-better attended 1962 gubernatorial election demonstrated that this shift was not a passing fancy.

The emergence of such groupings as those described above is a significant sign that the more traditional brand of factionalism tied to personalities and regionalism is being replaced by an economically oriented ideological politics. On the whole such conclusions are confirmed by the economic data offered on the most conservative and most liberal counties. On one hand, among the former were a significant number of livestock, large-farm counties with a relatively high income while, on the other hand, many of the liberally disposed counties tended to be of the crop, small-farm, low-income variety.

Of course, one cannot completely discount the more traditional motivations. In our preceding analysis of election returns there were occasional indications that some of the old attitudes and loyalties linger on—more so than in many Northern industrial states. The income differentials between the most conservative and most liberal counties were less sharp than a purely ideological thesis would suggest. In particular, a number of low-income counties have, on occasion, been less liberally inclined than one might expect. For example, in 1957 several such counties in East Texas temporarily endorsed conservative Democrat Martin Dies—the most plausible explanation being that he acquired a personal following because of his service to the region as a United States congressman. In a less pronounced manner a few normally liberal counties on either side of Connally's "home base" in Fort Worth favored him rather than liberal Don Yarborough in the first heat of the 1962 Democratic gubernatorial primary. Furthermore, the liberalism of a substantial proportion of liberal counties in East Texas and the Rolling Plains of West Central Texas may be due almost as much to Populist traditions and long-time loyalty to the national Democratic Party as to direct economic factors. Likewise, the conservatism of clusters of Southwest and South Central counties appears to be partially related to the influence of the German-settler tradition.

Yet, even regarding some of the cases cited above, there were significant tinges of ideological coloration. When taken as a group and examined over a span of years, the liberally disposed counties of East Texas and the Rolling Plains were strikingly consistent. Not only did they tend to support the liberal Democrats in state and national elections; they also gave such candidates much the same percentage of their total vote in election after election. On the other side, the Republicanism of the 16 German counties is no longer so much greater than that of a score of other counties. In fact, in the 1962 gubernatorial election 9 of the German counties failed to give Cox majorities. Moreover, in the same election the less Republican of the German counties were generally in a lower-income category than those which endorsed Cox. The Panhandle—the other area with a high degree of Republican propensities—demonstrates even more convincingly that economic motivations are gradually rising to the fore. At the very least, we can venture to say that the regional sentiments that do exist in such areas could not have survived had not traditional habits been reinforced by economic considerations moving voters to lean in the same direction.

Most important, in all of the preceding instances of lingering traditionalism the counties concerned are predominantly rural and static to declining in population growth. In the big cities, where a large and more critical proportion of the voters reside, there were strong signs of mounting ideological cleavages. One such indication was the greatly accelerated organizational activity by ideologically motivated groups. More convincing is the fact that from 1952 to 1962 both groups at the extremes of the ideological spectrum—the Republicans and the liberal Democrats—made sizable gains in the metropolitan centers. Furthermore, our cursory examination of precinct returns within Dallas and Houston revealed that voters in high-income, white-collar areas vote conservative by as much as 80 to 90 per cent while, in a less pronounced fashion, lower-income, blue-collar areas favored liberal Democrats.

In the not too distant past many political observers confidently asserted that urbanization as a whole automatically benefited the Democrats in general and the liberals in particular and pointed to a widening gap between urban and rural voting behavior. More recently, however, the independent and, in some instances, outright conservative behavior of suburbanites has given rise to reservations about liberal Democratic strength in metropolitan centers. And, studies on Southern metropolises have generally shown that in the South the conservatives and not the liberals have gained the most to date. More detailed investigations also have led to a little less emphasis on urban-rural differences in concrete political situations.

The nature of our findings leads us to support those who would caution against facile, one-sided explanations of the overall political effects of urbanization. Our analyses of the voting behavior of both the general public and state legislators presented as many examples of complementary as of conflicting relationships between cities and sur- rounding rural counties. Within the cities themselves there was a variety of behavior with those having more commercial, white-collar, native-white orientations tending to be either Republicans or conserva- tive Democrats. In other words, one must look more closely at the particular type of urbanization going on in specific areas before mak- ing generalizations. Furthermore, the three-way contest between Re- publicans, conservative Democrats, and liberal Democrats is now so close that a great deal depends upon their organizational status, namely, their effectiveness in organizing precincts block by block, ability to form firm coalitions with other groups, and relations with general community leaders.

Also significant are the changes occurring in the modes or styles of political operation. In several senses personalism in Texas politics has declined. It is doubtful, for example, that the traditional rural dema- gogue could be elected today. "Pappy" O'Daniel, the still living proto- type of this type of personalism, won four successive statewide races in the late thirties and early forties but failed miserably in his comeback attempts in 1956 and 1958. In sum, such personalities may still be in- fluential at the local, but not the state, level.

Somewhat less obviously, candidates are generally being forced to talk more about issues and less about personality factors. Of course, a considerable amount of campaign talk still centers around one's family and personal background, and efforts are still being made to solicit votes on the grounds that the candidate is a "local boy." Yet there is growing evidence that Texas voters—particularly middle-class electors in the cities—are tiring of persons who base their entire campaign on these or like appeals. That is, while the voters are not insisting that candidates take a rigid stand on one side or the other, they do desire the candidates to talk about the issues that concern them, particularly those of a broad, economic nature. The fate in the 1961 and 1962 elec- tions of Will Wilson and other candidates who generally avoided referring to big, controversial issues is proof of this observation.

The plight of Wilson and others like him points up the related fact that politicians can no longer rely entirely on friendship-oriented cam- paign organizations. If they want to win statewide races they must gain the confidence of one or more of the broader, more intensely mo- tivated organized groups.

All this does not mean that a candidate for national or statewide political office must side openly with one camp or the other in his public speeches. In fact, it is still advisable not to be labelled as a proponent of a particular economic interest such as that of organized labor or even the business community. However, in the smaller, more professional meetings with interest-group activists a candidate must demonstrate that he is aware of their grievances and demands and, though he need not promise that he will consistently vote their way, he must allay any suspicion that he will be an *a priori* opponent of their requests. Above all, unless he already has demonstrated influence, a person seeking election should avoid giving such group activists the impression of being "untrustworthy" or "indecisive." One of the quickest ways to alienate these people in meetings set up for the purpose of allowing them to see and question prospective candidates is to refuse to answer their pointed questions with such time-worn replies as "I am not going to be beholden to any group; I will serve all of the people." This type of reply may be good strategy in television speeches addressed to the general public, but it is very likely to antagonize professional political organizers when it is employed in their meetings. During the 1961 special Senate election campaigns both Jim Wright and Will Wilson did just this and accordingly lost a sizable number of organized votes that they might otherwise have had an opportunity to capture.

Nor should it be inferred that in this age of television the personal image of the candidate is not important. But he must somehow assure the voters that he is aware of the issues and has the ability to cope with them. Moreover, the increased use of television and of public relations firms has raised the costs of campaigning and, therefore, the candidate has an even greater need for the backing of organized groups capable of paying the bills.

These shifts to a loose, ideological framework and from personalized to organized methods of political warfare are significant. The most obvious change, however, has been in the relative power positions of the Republicans, conservative Democrats, and liberal Democrats. Most noteworthy has been the rise of Republican fortunes. During their uphill battle for recognition the Republicans have had some support in areas historically conditioned to vote Republican. One such area has been the Edwards Plateau-Hill Country region of Southwest Texas, including some German counties that have long been Republican prone —at least in presidential elections. Similarly, in the Panhandle are substantial numbers of electors with a background of Midwest-type Republicanism. After the 1961 Senate election it was obvious that the Republicans had support from a cluster of counties in the West Texas strip from Loving, Ward, and Winkler Counties on the west through

Tom Green and Runnels Counties on the east, and that they had established a small GOP beachhead in the heart of Democratic East Texas. In the 1962 elections the Republicans further consolidated and expanded their gains in each of these areas.

The aforementioned regions are predominantly rural in character. The most significant source of Republican votes, however, has been from the city, as a result of the erosion of Democratic Party loyalty under the impact of city life. About 60 per cent of Cox's tally in 1962 came from the 16 counties with over 100,000 population in 1960; no less than 40 per cent of his vote was located in the big 4 counties of Dallas, Harris, Tarrant, and Bexar.

This surge of Republican sentiment in metropolitan centers has been most apparent among conservative business and professional people— many of them former Democrats opposed to New Deal, Fair Deal, New Frontier programs and some of them out-of-state migrants who still retain their original Republican allegiances. Specifically, the most Republican-prone urban counties are Dallas, Midland, Ector, Potter, Harris, Taylor, and Lubbock.

Perhaps it is most appropriate to refer to present-day Texas as a "one and two-thirds party state." That is, in two out of three respects the Republican Party has a real chance to win elections. First, it has been statistically demonstrated that in statewide contests for national offices the GOP candidates are strong contenders. Specifically, in the cases of the presidency and at least one of the two United States Senate seats the Republican nominees must be rated as even with their Democratic opponents. Second, though they are still somewhat dependent upon low turnouts and rifts within the Democratic Party, GOP contenders in statewide elections for the top state offices of governor and, to a lesser degree, lieutenant governor can give the Democrats a close race. However, in local contests for positions in the United States House of Representatives, the Texas Legislature, and in city and county government the Republicans still lag far behind the Democrats. To be sure, there are GOP representatives from Dallas and Midland-Ector in the United States Congress, eight Republicans in the Texas House of Representatives, and a sprinkling of the Party's backers holding local offices, but, as yet, these successes represent but a small crack in an otherwise solid Democratic bulwark. And at the local level the hegemony of powerful community interests fearful of the disturbing effects of real party competition may act as a damper more effectively than at other levels.

The present situation may favor the growth of the Texas GOP as a militantly conservative group. But if in the future it does not broaden the basis of appeal beyond the rather narrow group of conservative

businessmen and professional people within the cities and of wealthy
cattlemen and large-scale farmers in rural areas like the Panhandle
and Southwest Texas its ultimate success is problematical. In particular the Republicans must give more attention to Latin American and
Negro voters. Had it not been for the overwhelmingly pro-Connally
vote among Spanish-speaking voters in Bexar, Cameron, Hidalgo, and
El Paso Counties Cox would have probably won in these urban areas,
which have shown Republican tendencies in the past. Recent an-
nouncements by Republican Party headquarters in the state indicate
that the Republicans are finally aware of the need to offer these minority groups more. Whether they go beyond the stage of pronouncements and token organization remains to be seen.

In summation, the Texas Republicans now have established more
than a beachhead. They have actually opened up two fronts in their
political warfare against the Democrats. Before they can win the war,
however, they must have more local reserves and must appeal to a
wider range of voters, particularly minority groups.

Within the Democratic Party, as well, significant changes have been
occurring. Until 1957 conservative elements dominated Party primaries though after 1954 their margins of victory gradually diminished.
During the early and mid-fifties the strength of conservative Democrats was widespread, as they drew support from important groups in
both rural and urban areas. Farm counties in a broad belt encompassing West and Southwest Texas and, to a lesser degree, counties in the
Panhandle and along the Gulf Coast provided conservative Democratic
nominees with substantial majorities. Among the most staunch supporters of the conservative version of Democracy, cattlemen and
large-scale farmers ranked especially high. In the urban areas the conservative Democratic candidates, with the backing of conservative
businessmen, professional people, and skilled technicians, generally
emerged victorious in all but McLennan, Nueces, Wichita, and Jefferson Counties. Except in Southwest Texas and the northeast corner of
the Panhandle the big switch to the Republican Party of the above
rural and urban groups—other than in presidential elections—did
not take place until 1961.

In 1958 liberal Ralph Yarborough overwhelmingly defeated conservative William Blakley in the race for a regular United States Senate seat, receiving majorities in all of the state's 12 metropolitan centers except Dallas. He even cut deeply into the Panhandle, a normally
conservative stronghold. Liberal jubilation was cut short, however,
when neither of the two liberal candidates reached the runoff in the
1961 Senate election and their combined total was far below that gar-

nered by Yarborough. In essence the chief liberal accomplishment of the period was forcing the conservative Democrats to moderate their position, with Governor Price Daniel leading this shift from the right toward the middle after he took office in 1957.

The strength of young, vigorous but relatively unknown Don Yarborough's showing in the 1962 Democratic runoff, despite his defeat, has given the liberals renewed hope of capturing control of the Democratic Party. This revitalization of the liberal camp springs from two sources. First, there were definite signs that liberal candidates were beginning to reap some of the political benefits from increased industrialization in some counties. The increase in the number of counties with sizable percentages of industrial workers found within the most liberal counties shown in Figure H and Yarborough's victories in the industrial cities of Houston, Galveston, and Beaumont-Port Arthur were especially noteworthy. Second, although a good many conservatives evidently stuck with Connally in the 1962 Democratic runoff, the ultraconservative shift to the Republican column did cut into conservative Democratic strength in some areas. In all probability Don Yarborough's narrow victories in Lubbock, Ector, and Tom Green Counties can be attributed largely to such defections. To a limited extent, along with the solid backing of industrial labor and Negroes, the shift away from the Democratic Party by Houston's ultraconservatives helped to produce that city's slight inclination toward Yarborough in the Democratic primaries. At the same time, the liberals appear to be holding on to and slightly expanding their traditional influence in East Texas and, to a lesser degree, the Rolling Plains of West Central Texas. Some gains were also made in scattered counties in the Panhandle and West Texas and along the Gulf Coast. With the exception of the Gulf Coast area, however, most of these counties are declining or static in population and, therefore, the total liberal vote gleaned from such regions is likely to decrease with the passage of time.

On the whole, the liberal Democrats can usually count on winning the countryside in East Texas and the Rolling Plains and the urban counties of McLennan, Wichita, Nueces, Jefferson, and Galveston. Depending on their ability to overcome differences of opinion among labor, intellectuals, and the Latin Americans they may also win, or at least make it close, in Bexar and El Paso Counties. With apt appeals to moderate Party loyalists and government employees as well as a closing of the ranks among the aforementioned groups the liberals can also finish ahead—from time to time at least—in Travis County; and with the assistance of Republican defections they can run strong races in Harris, Lubbock, Ector, and Tom Green Counties.

It is apparent that, at a minimum, the liberals have enough power to play the role of a balancing or at least negating third force in Texas politics; it is equally obvious, however, that they, like the Republicans, must eventually adjust their views to attract more middle-of-the-road swing voters and the racial-ethnic minorities, though among the latter they have an edge over the Republicans. Furthermore, since low-income groups are apparently inclined to vote less often and less consistently than high-income groups, liberal leaders must mount strong organizational drives to mobilize and to crystallize the votes of their supporters.

On first thought, the simultaneous growth of Republican and liberal strength might lead one to conclude that the conservative Democrats are caught in an inescapable political squeeze. Yet the electoral successes of Lyndon Johnson, Price Daniel, and now John Connally warn against counting them out of the future picture. Connally, in the 1962 elections, finished ahead in a broad band of counties down the center of the state from north to south—with a combination of pleas for party harmony, hard-nosed explanations of what Republican victories would mean in terms of patronage and Texas' influence in national politics, promises to status-conscious Latin and Negro leaders, a general appeal for avoiding extremism, and a well-financed and professionally smooth campaign organization. In intra-Democratic Party struggles with the liberals the conservative Democrats can probably count on winning the North, North Central, Far West, Southwest, and perhaps the South Central and South sections of the state. The cities of Dallas, Fort Worth, Amarillo, and Midland also appear to be safely under their control though they may very well side with the Republicans' brand of conservatism in the general election. Moreover, in almost all of the other cities the conservative Democrats have an equal chance with the liberals or can make it very close.

For the future probably the greatest asset of the conservative Democrats is that if they continue to moderate their stand they will have the inside track with middle-class swing voters, who along with the minorities hold the balance of power. Furthermore, although the pressures on the Democratic Party have undercut its more conservative element, they are at the same time forcing members to tolerate broader appeals. That is, since the Democratic Party must modify its position on some issues in order to regroup its forces against the GOP, moderate conservatives may benefit from a slight de-emphasis of dogmatic labels by inclusion of a wide range of viewpoints or by broad-gauged appeals directed at the issues of widest consensus. And, finally, although it may be difficult for the liberals to perceive, they must realize that by virtue of conservative adjustments and of their own inattention to minority-group demands for action, even urban Latins and Negroes can be persuaded occasionally to either join the conservatives or at least remain neutral during Democratic Party fighting.

Hence, if the conservatives remaining in the Democratic Party would follow a moderate course and adjust to the demands of status-conscious minorities, they could prevent a liberal takeover of the Party machinery. But they will need to give more attention to developing a philosophy of moderacy and must act upon it; mere opportunistic playing off of one group against another is likely to succeed only temporarily.

The places to watch in assessing the future chances of each of the state's competing political groups are the metropolitan centers—although any research must be broadly conceived so as to include the interdependent relationships between the core cities and surrounding rural counties. The particular items to look for are numerous. First, the effects of differing types of urbanization (e.g., commercial vs. industrial emphasis) must be examined with greater care. Second, the organizational techniques employed by each group, especially their degree of success in forging broad coalitions and penetrating into the total community power structure, should be noted. A third long-term factor of major significance will be the position of the minorities. Both the Negro and the Latin populations—particularly the latter—are on the move. Even if one admits that their change from nonparticipating or controlled status to active and uncontrolled standing may be gradual and episodic, they are nonetheless groups with considerable potential, and although they may lean more to the liberals they are quite flexible. Of course, if the Negroes and the Latin Americans are too narrowly absorbed with the racial-ethnic issues—especially in this age when other people are equally if not more concerned with broader economic or foreign-affairs issues—and if they do not make a united choice in any given contest, their potential power can be dissipated.

Finally, there is the question of whether the process of political polarization will be further accelerated and, if it is, whether this movement will lead to more or less ideological tension. Some observers have assumed that the creation of a two-party system will heighten such inclinations. Although it would probably give rise to more attention to issues and greater action, the emergence of a full-blown two-party system might actually operate to reduce rather than increase the ideological tensions now evident in Texas politics. As indicated, Democratic Party leaders in particular are under pressure to compromise the differences between warring factions.

Despite its great variety and outward appearance of uniqueness Texas politics may very well—belatedly to be sure—evolve in much the same manner as politics has in states north of the Mason-Dixon line. During the 1930's and 1940's politics in the Northern states was characterized by political cleavages based on loose ideological differences in general and sharp clashes of economic interest in particular. But, with the marked rise in white-collar jobs and suburban living and with the gradual increase in an awareness of more encompassing foreign-policy issues, the 1950's saw a decline in ideological voting along worker versus businessman, city versus rural lines. At present, Texas is going through the stage in which economically oriented ideological clashes are rapidly displacing the personal and regional divisions of the past. In all probability this ideological polarization has not yet reached its peak in Texas. But, it may do so soon and the next stage of greater moderation and broader perspective may begin.

The past decade has truly been one of considerable change in Texas politics; the likelihood is that the decades to follow will bring even more interesting and momentous changes.

POSTSCRIPT

The hazards of political prognostication were never better illustrated than by the events that transpired after this manuscript was sent to the printers. The assassination of President Kennedy in Dallas on November 22, 1963, and the immediate accession of Lyndon Johnson to the Presidency are likely to have important consequences for politics in Texas and in the nation as a whole. Though these consequences can be perceived but dimly at this time (January, 1964), they are potentially so far reaching that some speculation on them cannot be avoided. Probably the most useful course of action would be to distinguish between short-range and long-range impact.

Within the short range, it seems likely that the accession of Johnson to the Presidency will again make Texas safe for the Democratic Party in 1964, assuming—as one is entitled to do—that President Johnson will be renominated by the Democrats for the nation's highest office. It seems probable too that a bid by Governor Connally (himself wounded by Kennedy's assassin) for a second term will be resisted less strenuously than was his first, both in the Democratic primary and in the general election. Opposition to the Governor from both liberal Democrats and Republicans may be forthcoming, but it is unlikely to reach the intensity that might have been expected had President Kennedy lived. Sharing involuntarily in the martyrdom of Kennedy, the Governor is no longer open to attack by liberals for not supporting the late President's programs, or by Republicans for affiliation with the party of the "New Frontier."

By a process of similar reasoning, it seems likely that another short-run effect will be to ease Ralph Yarborough's campaign for renomination and re-election to the United States Senate. Although he will unquestionably have opposition in both contests, the altered situation seems to favor him. In the Democratic primary it will be hard to attack Yarborough for adhering to the principles of the national Democratic

Party now that Lyndon Johnson is its leader; in the general election Yarborough is sure to benefit from the presence of Johnson at the head of the Democratic ticket (again, assuming he is the nominee).[1]

If there is a temporary reaffirmation of Democratic Party spirit, which faction will benefit? It has generally been assumed that conservative Democrats will be the beneficiaries, on the expectation that the conservative shift to the Republican Party will be halted, or perhaps reversed. That the conservative Democratic faction will thus gain a "new lease on life" is fairly certain, but one should not overlook certain advantages that will accrue to the liberal faction as well. The most important of these are derivatives of the sudden availability of presidential coattails—coattails, be it remembered, that belong to a native son who was already a powerful figure in the state even prior to taking the Presidency. Although there will no doubt be changes of emphasis, President Johnson (if a candidate in 1964) will be running on much the same platform as that of his predecessor, and thus the goals of Texas liberals can be expected to acquire a respectability and legitimacy often denied in the past. One may very well see, then, a tendency in the short run for ideological differences to be soft-pedaled and a corresponding increase in the importance of factors touching region, candidate personality, and so on.

And what will be the immediate impact on Republicans? As already suggested, the GOP will probably see a decline in its strength in presidential, senatorial, and gubernatorial elections, although the extent of this decline may be easily overestimated.[2] A priori, it seems likely

[1] Although President Johnson might conceivably move to purge Ralph Yarborough for reasons growing out of their past differences in factional brawls as well as their conflicts over patronage, this seems unlikely. A number of reports indicate that a modus vivendi between then Vice President Johnson and Senator Yarborough was being worked out during President Kennedy's visit in Texas, and in the post-assassination period both Johnson and Yarborough in several ways indicated that their relationship had significantly improved. Even if President Johnson should desire Yarborough's defeat in the Democratic primary, any except the most subtle moves in that direction would seem to be very risky politics. Thus, whether because of a genuine reconciliation, or because of political expediency, presidential movement against Yarborough is not expected.

[2] Two postassassination elections in Texas provide some slight help in evaluating GOP fortunes. A special election in the Tenth Congressional District to fill a vacancy caused by the appointment of incumbent Homer Thornberry to a federal judgeship was held November 9, before the assassination. The front-runner in the "nonpartisan" election was conservative Democrat J. J. "Jake" Pickle (35.0 per cent), followed closely by even more conservative Republican Jim Dobbs (33.3 per cent), and by moderate liberal Jack Ritter (31.7 per cent). The runoff between the conservative Democrat and the Republican was held December 17 after the tragedy in Dallas. The former polled 62.9 per cent of the vote, the latter 37.1 per cent. At least three consequences of the intervening tragedy seem visible: (1) Republican Dobbs was forced to alter the nature of his campaign (the earlier theme was articulated by a poster

that the unfavorable consequences for the GOP will progressively lessen as the relationship of local offices to national politics becomes more remote. (It should be remembered, however, that Republican support has usually been weaker in the more remote elections.) Particularly in those areas (e.g., Dallas County) where Republican strength is based on a well-developed partisan spirit and on effective organization rather than confined to the exploitation of differences in the Democratic Party, the impact may be modest indeed.

The long-range picture is a much cloudier one. It is within the realm of possibility that President Johnson will be able to heal permanently the split in the Democracy and to develop for the Party in Texas an image that will reduce the appeal of the GOP. To do this successfully, he must give the Texas Democratic Party a moderate or slightly conservative cast. Since the national Democratic Party has—and is likely to retain—a very definite liberal complexion, it may be impossible for President Johnson to engineer a significantly different image for the Party in his home state.

If, as seems likely, it should prove impossible to divorce the Democratic Party within the state from the liberalism of the national Party, what then? Again, it is within the realm of possibility that Texas voters will nevertheless crowd under the Democratic tent as they were accustomed to do for so long. However, if our analysis of the Texas political scene has any validity at all, this seems an unlikely eventuality. Instead, we can expect over an extent of time that the basic social and economic forces that have been propelling voters along conservative paths will reassert themselves, and the logic of the situation will again dictate a turn from the liberalism of the Democratic Party to the conservatism of the GOP.

---

message that quickly disappeared after November 22—"Scratch Lyndon's Boy, Jake"); (2) liberals refused to support the Republican (who was in any case considerably more conservative than Pickle); and (3) turnout in the second contest was 5 per cent above that for the first one. It appears that the death of the President made it more difficult for Republicans to exploit factional differences, and increased the margin of the Democratic victory, but the increase was probably modest (after all, the same Republican candidate had in 1962 polled only 35.9 per cent against the long-time incumbent who generally voted in a moderate to liberal fashion).

The second postassassination election that deserves mention was for Houston municipal offices. Held December 10, the runoff municipal contests were still under the shadow of the November tragedy, and therefore quite subdued—due both to the reluctance of candidates to engage in "politics as usual" during a period of mourning and to the stiff competition for attention of the public and the mass media. The results showed little impact of the events of November. In fact, the one avowed Republican on the ballot (for a City Council position) won handily over his Negro runoff opponent, and in doing so polled a vote entirely comparable to that of the other winners.

Thus, the Johnson Administration seems likely to produce but a temporary interruption to the process of political realignment in Texas. Republicans will have to live temporarily on the memory of the rich harvests of the past and the dreams of the future, and to strive desperately to consolidate and preserve past gains. But, as the memories of November 22 fade, and as the novelty of a Texan at the head of the national Democratic Party wears off, a revival of the tendencies we have tried to trace in this study will almost certainly come. Factional feeling among Democrats will again emerge, and the dissatisfaction of conservative-minded voters with the tendencies of the national Democratic Party—even with Lyndon Johnson at its head—will begin to mount again. From that point on, the script will be a familiar one.

In sum, one can expect the death of President Kennedy to produce in Texas politics a temporary "era of good feeling" during which factional and ideological differences will be somewhat muted. As the era advances, however, one can also expect a resumption of the battle along lines we have attempted to trace in this book.

APPENDIXES

A. Explanation of Process for Determining Quartiles

County election returns in raw figures and in percentages are readily available in the *America Votes* series edited by Richard Scammon for the Governmental Affairs Institute of the University of Pittsburgh. To publish in this volume the results for all Texas counties would therefore be an unjustified duplication. However, despite the frequent use in election studies of quartiles as a preliminary classificatory measure, no work has reported quartiling results. Therefore, to facilitate further studies we have listed below the county voting percentages used to identify the quartiles for a number of elections.

Inasmuch as we could not wait for the publication of county returns and percentages, we made all the necessary calculations ourselves, using either the raw figures from the *Texas Almanac* or the official county returns obtained from the Secretary of State's office. It is therefore possible that some of our results might diverge from those published by others, but we believe that any such instances would be few and insignificant. Reliance on our own computations did, however, cause one minor complication. For some of the earlier elections we rounded the percentages for each county to the nearest whole number and did not carry out the numbers to decimal places. In some instances a number of counties were found to have the same percentage figure used as the breaking point. In such cases we resorted to an artificial but seemingly acceptable procedure, that of making the break on an alphabetical basis. Thus, if the first quarter had to be broken somewhere within the 37 per cent range, the necessary number of counties would be counted off in reverse alphabetical order. (The specific letters at which the quartiles were divided are indicated in parenthesis in the following listing.) However, for the most important elections—1957, 1960, 1961, and 1962—we avoided this problem by carrying the percentages to one or two decimal places.

Because the 254 Texas counties do not break neatly into four equal quarters, we usually provided two quarters of 63 counties each and two of 64 counties each. In some elections not all counties submitted official returns, and in those cases the quarters are calculated on the basis of the actual total of reporting counties.

Most of the figures below are for elections in which the vote was divided between only two candidates or only two parties. Since the quartile results for one candidate can be determined by reversing the results for the other (to the nearest whole per cent), we have not recorded both figures.

QUARTILES FOR LIBERAL CANDIDATES IN DEMOCRATIC PRIMARIES
(To obtain conservative quartiles simply reverse the ranking)

ELECTION	QUARTILE
1952 first Democratic gubernatorial primary (Ralph Yarborough)	1st—41% (Q) and over 2nd—33% to 41% (P) 3rd—24% (S) to 32% 4th—24% (R) and under
1954 second Democratic gubernatorial primary (Ralph Yarborough)	1st—54% (T) and over 2nd—46% (T) to 54% (S) 3rd—38% (F) to 46% (S) 4th—38% (E) and under
1956 second Democratic gubernatorial primary (Ralph Yarborough)	1st—58% (Col) and over 2nd—53% to 58% (Cok) 3rd—45% (D) to 52% 4th—45% (C) and under
1958 first Democratic senatorial primary (Ralph Yarborough)	1st—65% (Mo) and over 2nd—61% to 65% (Mi) 3rd—54% (M) to 60% 4th—54% (L) and under
1962 second Democratic gubernatorial primary (Don Yarborough)	1st—55.1% and over 2nd—48.7% to 55.09% 3rd—42.4% to 48.6% 4th—42.38% and under

QUARTILES FOR SPECIFIED CANDIDATES IN SPECIAL SENATORIAL ELECTIONS.

ELECTION	QUARTILE
1957 special Senate election (Liberal Democrat Ralph Yarborough)	1st—53.5% and over 2nd—44.3% to 53.4% 3rd—35% (T) to 44.2% 4th—35% (H) and under
1957 special Senate election (Conservative Democrat Martin Dies, Sr.)	1st—40% and over 2nd—33% (He) to 39% 3rd—26% (I) to 33% (Ha) 4th—26% (H) and under
1957 special Senate election (Republican Thad Hutcheson)	1st—24.4% and over 2nd—17% (I) to 24.3% 3rd—11% (Z) to 17% (H) 4th—11% (W) and under
1961 first special Senate election (Republican John Tower)	1st—35.8% and over 2nd—26.0% to 35.79% 3rd—19.65% to 25.99% 4th—19.6% and under

QUARTILES FOR DEMOCRATIC CANDIDATES IN PRESIDENTIAL ELECTIONS
(To obtain Republican quartile figures simply reverse the ranking)

1952 presidential election
(Democratic candidate
Adlai Stevenson)

1st—58% (D) and over
2nd—49% (Hu) to 58% (C)
3rd—42% to 49% (Ha)
4th—41% and under

1956 presidential election
(Democratic candidate
Adlai Stevenson)

1st—56% (M) and over
2nd—49% to 56% (L)
3rd—40% (St) to 48%
4th—40% (So) and under

1960 presidential election
(Democratic candidate
John F. Kennedy)

1st—61.93% and over
2nd—54.92% to 61.92%
3rd—47% to 54.91%
4th—46.99% and under

QUARTILES FOR REPUBLICAN CANDIDATE IN GUBERNATORIAL ELECTION
(To obtain Democratic quartiles simply reverse the ranking)

1962 gubernatorial election
(Republican Jack Cox)

1st—48.2% and over
2nd—41.0% to 48.1%
3rd—35.0% to 40.9%
4th—34.9% and under

B. Counties in First Quartile of Vote for Liberal Democratic, Conservative Democratic, and Republican Candidates in 1957 Special Senate Election

COUNTIES IN FIRST QUARTILE OF VOTE FOR LIBERAL DEMOCRAT RALPH
YARBOROUGH IN 1957 SPECIAL SENATE ELECTION

(53.5% and above)

Andrews	Fannin	Martin
Archer	Fisher	Maverick
Armstrong	Foard	Milam
Bailey	Franklin	Mitchell
Bastrop	Frio	Moore
Baylor	Grayson	Navarro
Bell	Hall	Nolan
Borden	Hardin	Oldham
Briscoe	Haskell	Robertson
Brooks	Henderson	San Jacinto
Burnet	Hill	San Saba
Caldwell	Hockley	Starr
Carson	Hood	Stonewall
Castro	Kent	Swisher
Clay	King	Terry
Concho	Knox	Throckmorton
Coryell	Lamb	Trinity
Cottle	Lee	Van Zandt
Crosby	Limestone	Wheeler
Dallam	Llano	Wilson
Dickens	Lynn	

Counties in First Quartile of Vote for Conservative Democrat Martin Dies

(40% and above)

Anderson	Hudspeth	Reagan
Angelina	Hunt	Red River
Austin	Jasper	Reeves
Bee	Jim Hogg	Roberts
Bowie	Kaufman	Rockwall
Camp	Lamar	Runnels
Cass	Lavaca	Rusk
Chambers	Leon	Sabine
Cherokee	Liberty	San Augustine
Coleman	Marion	Shackelford
Cooke	McMullen	Shelby
Culberson	Morris	Smith
Delta	Motley	Stephens
Fort Bend	Nacogdoches	Sterling
Freestone	Newton	Titus
Glasscock	Ochiltree	Tyler
Gregg	Orange	Upshur
Hamilton	Panola	Webb
Hardeman	Polk	Wilbarger
Harrison	Presidio	Willacy
Hopkins	Rains	Wood

COUNTIES IN FIRST QUARTILE OF VOTE FOR REPUBLICAN THAD HUTCHESON

(24.4% and above)

Aransas	Gillespie***	Midland**
Austin	Goliad**	Nueces
Bandera**	Gray	Ochiltree
Bee	Guadalupe**	Parker
Bexar*	Hansford	Pecos
Blanco	Harris	Potter
Brewster	Hidalgo	Randall
Brooks	Irion	Real**
Calhoun	Jim Wells	Refugio
Cameron	Kendall***	Roberts
Colorado*	Kenedy***	Schleicher
Comal**	Kerr**	Sutton**
Crockett	Kimble	Terrell*
Dallas	Kleberg	Tom Green
Deaf Smith	Lipscomb	Uvalde**
De Witt	Live Oak*	Val Verde
Dimmit	Mason*	Victoria*
Ector	Matagorda	Washington
Edwards**	McMullen	Wilson
Fayette	Medina*	Zapata
Galveston	Menard	Zavala

Note: Five of the first-quartile Republican counties (Austin, Bee, McMullen, Ochiltree, and Roberts), also appear in the first quartile of the conservative Democratic vote and two others (Brooks and Wilson) are found also in the first quartile of the liberal Democratic tally. Therefore, we have designated the most Republican counties as follows:

    * Counties that gave Hutcheson more than 50 per cent of their vote.

    ** Counties that gave Hutcheson plurality and 40–49 per cent of their vote.

    *** Counties that gave Hutcheson a plurality but less than 40 per cent of vote.

C. Counties in First Quartile of Vote for Liberal Democratic and Conservative Democratic Candidates in 1962 Democratic Runoff Primary for Governor

COUNTIES IN FIRST QUARTILE OF VOTE FOR LIBERAL DEMOCRAT DON YARBOROUGH IN 1962 DEMOCRATIC RUNOFF PRIMARY FOR GOVERNOR

(55.1% and above)

Anderson	Henderson	Orange
Andrews	Houston	Polk
Angelina	Howard	Robertson
Bailey	Hutchinson	Rusk
Borden	Irion	Sabine
Brazoria	Jackson	San Augustine
Burleson	Jasper	San Jacinto
Carson	Jeff Davis	San Patricio
Castro	Jefferson	Schleicher
Cherokee	Kent	Scurry
Crane	Lee	Stonewall
Crosby	Leon	Swisher
Dickens	Liberty	Terrell
Ector	Limestone	Titus
Fisher	Loving	Trinity
Freestone	Madison	Tyler
Gaines	Milam	Upshur
Galveston	Montgomery	Walker
Garza	Nacogdoches	Waller
Grimes	Newton	Winkler
Hardin	Nolan	Yoakum

COUNTIES IN FIRST QUARTILE OF VOTE FOR CONSERVATIVE DEMOCRAT
JOHN CONNALLY IN 1962 DEMOCRATIC RUNOFF
PRIMARY FOR GOVERNOR

(57.6% and above)

Armstrong	Hardeman	Ochiltree
Atascosa	Hartley	Palo Pinto
Bandera	Jim Hogg	Randall
Baylor	Karnes	Real
Bexar	Kaufman	Reeves
Caldwell	Kendall	Roberts
Comal	Kenedy	Rockwall
Cottle	Kerr	Sherman
Culberson	Kimble	Starr
Dallas	King	Sutton
Delta	Kinney	Tarrant
Dimmit	Knox	Taylor
Duval	Lampasas	Throckmorton
Edwards	La Salle	Uvalde
Fannin	Lipscomb	Val Verde
Foard	Lynn	Webb
Frio	Marion	Wilbarger
Gillespie	Maverick	Willacy
Gonzales	McMullen	Wilson
Guadalupe	Medina	Zapata
Hansford	Midland	Zavala

D. Counties in First Quartile of Vote for Democratic and Republican Candidates in 1962 Gubernatorial Election

COUNTIES IN FIRST QUARTILE OF VOTE FOR DEMOCRAT JOHN
CONNALLY IN 1962 GUBERNATORIAL ELECTION

(65.5% and above)

Archer	Fisher	Lynn
Bastrop	Foard	Maverick
Baylor	Franklin	Milam
Bell	Frio	Mitchell
Briscoe	Gonzales	Navarro
Brooks	Hall	Newton
Burleson	Haskell	Rains
Caldwell	Hill	Red River
Camp	Hopkins	Robertson
Castro	Houston	Rockwall
Childress	Jim Hogg	Sabine
Clay	Jim Wells	San Augustine
Coryell	Kenedy	San Jacinto
Cottle	Kent	San Saba
Crosby	King	Stonewall
Delta	Kinney	Swisher
Dickens	Knox	Throckmorton
Duval	Lamar	Webb
Ellis	La Salle	Williamson
Falls	Lavaca	Wilson
Fannin	Leon	Zapata

COUNTIES IN FIRST QUARTILE OF VOTE FOR REPUBLICAN JACK COX
IN 1962 GUBERNATORIAL ELECTION

(48.2% and above)

Austin*	Harris	Randall
Bailey	Harrison	Reagan*
Bandera	Hemphill	Real
Comal	Hutchinson	Roberts
Cooke	Kendall	Runnels
Crockett	Kerr	Rusk
Culberson	Kimble	Schleicher
Dallas	Lipscomb	Sherman
Deaf Smith	Loving	Smith
De Witt	Lubbock	Stephens
Ector	Mason	Sterling
Edwards	Matagorda*	Sutton*
Floyd*	McMullen	Tarrant*
Gillespie	Menard	Taylor
Glasscock	Midland	Terrell
Gray	Mills*	Tom Green
Gregg	Ochiltree	Upton
Guadalupe	Oldham*	Uvalde
Hale	Panola	Ward
Hamilton	Parmer	Winkler
Hansford	Potter	Yoakum*

* Denotes counties that gave Cox less than 50 per cent of their vote.

E. Classification of Texas Counties According to Urban-Rural Scale

CATEGORY I: Metropolitan Counties (12)
Bexar, Dallas, El Paso, Harris, Jefferson, Lubbock, McLennan, Nueces, Potter, Tarrant, Travis, Wichita

CATEGORY II: Large Urban Counties (17)
Bell, Brazos, Cameron, Denton, Ector, Galveston, Grayson, Gregg, Hidalgo, Howard, Midland, Orange, Smith, Taylor, Tom Green, Victoria, Webb

CATEGORY III: Intermediate Urban Counties (22)
Andrews, Bee, Brown, Calhoun, Comal, Cooke, Dawson, Gray, Hays, Hutchinson, Jim Wells, Kleberg, Lamar, Matagorda, Maverick, Nolan, Reeves, Scurry, Uvalde, Val Verde, Wilbarger, Winkler

CATEGORY IV: Small Urban Counties (7)
Bowie, Brazoria, Montgomery, Moore, Palo Pinto, San Patricio, Willacy

CATEGORY V: Agri-Urban Counties (20)
Anderson, Angelina, Cherokee, Collin, Ellis, Guadalupe, Hale, Harrison, Hockley, Hopkins, Hunt, Johnson, Kaufman, Nacogdoches, Navarro, Parker, Terry, Titus, Walker, Williamson

CATEGORY VI: Nonfarm Rural-Urban Counties (27)
Aransas, Brewster, Brooks, Chambers, Crane, Crockett, Culberson, Dallam, Dimmit, Hardin, Jim Hogg, Kerr, Kinney, La Salle, Liberty, Pecos, Presidio, Randall, Reagan, Refugio, Stephens, Sutton, Terrell, Upton, Ward, Young, Zavala

CATEGORY VII: Nonfarm Rural Counties (65)
Archer, Bastrop, Baylor, Burnet, Caldwell, Carson, Childress, Cochran, Coke, Coleman, Colorado, Coryell, Deaf Smith, De Witt, Duval, Eastland, Edwards, Erath, Fort Bend, Frio, Gaines, Garza, Hansford, Hardeman, Hemphill, Hill, Irion, Jack, Jackson, Jasper, Jeff Davis, Jones, Kimble, Lampasas, Limestone, Lipscomb, Llano, Loving, McCulloch, Medina, Menard, Mitchell, Montague, Morris, Ochiltree, Oldham, Polk, Real, Roberts, Robertson, Runnels, Sabine, Schleicher, Shackelford, Sherman, Starr, Sterling, Trinity, Tyler, Waller, Wharton, Wheeler, Yoakum, Zapata. Rusk is also included in this group, although it does not conform perfectly to the description.

CATEGORY VIII: Farm Rural Counties (84)

Armstrong, Atascosa, Austin, Bailey, Bandera, Blanco, Borden, Bosque, Briscoe, Burleson, Callahan, Camp, Cass, Castro, Clay, Collingsworth, Comanche, Concho, Cottle, Crosby, Delta, Dickens, Donley, Falls, Fannin, Fayette, Fisher, Floyd, Foard, Franklin, Freestone, Gillespie, Glasscock, Goliad, Gonzales, Grimes, Hall, Hamilton, Hartley, Haskell, Henderson, Hood, Houston, Hudspeth, Karnes, Kendall, Kenedy, Kent, King, Knox, Lamb, Lavaca, Lee, Leon, Live Oak, Lynn, McMullen, Madison, Marion, Martin, Mason, Milam, Mills, Motley, Newton, Panola, Parmer, Rains, Red River, Rockwall, San Augustine, San Jacinto, San Saba, Shelby, Somervell, Stonewall, Swisher, Throckmorton, Upshur, Van Zandt, Washington, Wilson, Wise, Wood

F. Socio-Economic Characteristics of Metropolitan Counties in Texas, 1960

Social Characteristics of Metropolitan Counties in Texas, 1960

County	Population					
	Total	Per cent Increase (1950–1960)	Per cent Urban	Per cent Nonwhite	Per cent Foreign Stock[a]	Per cent Born in Texas[b]
	(1)	(2)	(3)	(4)	(5)	(6)
Bexar	687,151	37.3	93.4	6.9	22.5	74.6
Dallas	951,527	54.8	97.5	14.7	6.1	71.2
El Paso	314,070	61.1	89.2	3.3	38.1	56.5
Harris	1,243,158	54.1	94.5	20.1	8.9	70.1
Jefferson	245,659	25.9	95.9	23.4	5.5	63.3
Lubbock	156,271	54.7	87.0	8.0	5.8	77.7
McLennan	150,091	15.3	80.5	16.1	7.8	81.4
Nueces	221,573	33.9	88.7	4.7	17.5	77.0
Potter	115,580	57.5	97.7	6.9	4.7	56.5
Tarrant	538,495	49.1	94.6	11.1	4.8	71.4
Travis	212,136	31.8	88.2	12.8	10.7	79.7
Wichita	123,528	25.4	95.4	7.4	5.4	61.5

Sources: Columns 1, 2, and 4 are taken from U.S. Bureau of the Census, *Census of Population: 1960. General Population Characteristics, Texas.* Final Report PC(1)–45B, Table 13, pp. 59–62. The data in columns 3, 5, and 6 are derived from *Census of Population: 1960. General Social and Economic Characteristics, Texas.* Final Report PC(1)–45C, Table 35, pp. 319–321.

[a] Combines "foreign born" category with "native born of foreign or mixed parentage."

[b] The figures in this column are percentages of the native population and not percentages of total population (i.e., "foreign stock" is excluded).

Economic Characteristics of Metropolitan Counties in Texas, 1960

County	Per cent Employed in Manufacturing	Per cent Employed in White-Collar Occupations	Median Family Income (dollars)	Per cent Earning Under $3,000	Percent Earning $10,000 and over
Bexar	11.0	46.0	4,766	27.2	11.0
Dallas	22.2	50.8	6,188	16.3	19.1
El Paso	16.2	48.1	5,157	22.1	12.7
Harris	21.7	46.0	6,040	18.1	17.6
Jefferson	30.1	39.3	6,001	20.0	13.8
Lubbock	9.7	46.3	5,425	20.0	14.6
McLennan	18.6	42.8	4,684	29.8	9.3
Nueces	13.4	43.3	4,908	28.4	12.0
Potter	11.7	44.5	5,570	16.1	13.4
Tarrant	26.5	47.2	5,697	18.7	14.0
Travis	7.5	52.5	5,058	24.8	13.3
Wichita	9.8	47.9	5,322	19.8	12.3

Source: *Census of Population: 1960. General Social and Economic Characteristics, Texas.* Final Report PC(1)–45C, Table 36, pp. 322–324.

G. Geopolitical Regions of Texas.

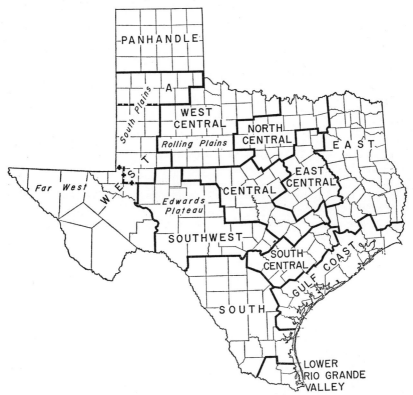

In examinations of roll-call voting patterns in the Texas Legislature (1) counties within Area A, enclosed by solid and dashed lines, are combined with the Panhandle counties, and (2) the other South Plains counties and Far West Texas are combined under the heading of "West Texas," which extends north to the dashed line. In analyses of voting in state and national elections the South Plains, extending north to the solid line, and Far West Texas are referred to individually; these two areas are separated by the crossed line.

SELECTED BIBLIOGRAPHY

PUBLICATIONS OF THE UNITED STATES DEPARTMENT OF COMMERCE BUREAU OF THE CENSUS

Census of Manufactures: 1954. III, *Area Statistics, Texas.* Washington, D.C.: Government Printing Office, 1957.

Census of Manufactures: 1958. III, *Area Statistics, Texas.* Washington, D.C.: Government Printing Office, 1961.

Census of Population: 1950. II, Part 43. Washington, D.C.: Government Printing Office, 1952.

Census of Population: 1960. General Population Characteristics, Texas. Final Report PC(1)–45B. Washington, D.C.: Government Printing Office, 1962.

Census of Population: 1960. General Social and Economic Characteristics, Texas. Final Report PC(1)–45C. Washington, D.C.: Government Printing Office, 1962.

County and City Data Book: 1956. Washington, D.C.: Government Printing Office, 1957.

Historical Statistics of the United States from Colonial Times to 1957. Washington, D.C.: Government Printing Office, 1960.

Summary of Social and Economic Characteristics of the United States: 1960. Washington, D.C.: Government Printing Office, 1962.

BOOKS AND MONOGRAPHS

Adrian, Charles R. *State and Local Governments.* New York: McGraw-Hill, 1960.

Baker, G. E. *Rural Versus Urban Political Power.* Garden City, New York: Doubleday & Company, 1955.

Benton, Wilbourn E. *Suffrage and Elections.* Arnold Foundation Monograph VII. Dallas: Southern Methodist University, Arnold Foundation, 1960.

———. *Texas: Its Government and Politics.* Englewood Cliffs, New Jersey: Prentice-Hall, 1961.

Berelson, Bernard P., Paul F. Lazarsfeld, and William N. McPhee. *Voting: A Study of Opinion Formation in a Presidential Campaign.* Chicago: University of Chicago Press, 1954.

Campbell, Angus, Phillip E. Converse, Warren E. Miller, and Donald E. Stokes. *The American Voter.* New York: John Wiley & Sons, 1960.

Donnelly, Thomas C. (editor). *Rocky Mountain Politics.* Albuquerque: University of New Mexico Press, 1940.

Epstein, Leon D. *Politics in Wisconsin.* Madison: University of Wisconsin Press, 1958.

Ewing, Cortez A. M. *Primary Elections in the South.* Norman: University of Oklahoma Press, 1953.

Fenton, John H. *Politics in the Border States*. New Orleans: Hauser Press, 1957.

Feurmann, George. *Reluctant Empire*. Garden City, New York: Doubleday & Company, 1957.

Havens, Murray C. *City Versus Farm*. University, Alabama: Bureau of Public Administration, 1957.

Goodwyn, Frank. *Lone-Star Land: Twentieth Century Texas in Perspective*. New York: Alfred A. Knopf, 1955.

Heard, Alexander. *A Two-Party South?* Chapel Hill: University of North Carolina Press, 1952.

Heard, Alexander, and Donald S. Strong. *Southern Primaries and Elections, 1920–1949*. University, Alabama: University of Alabama Press, 1950.

Kardiner, Abram, and Lionel Ovesey. *The Mark of Oppression*. New York: W. W. Norton & Company, 1951.

Key, V. O., Jr. *American State Politics: An Introduction*. New York: Alfred A. Knopf, 1956.

———. *Southern Politics in State and Nation*. New York: Alfred A. Knopf, 1949.

Lane, Robert E. *Political Life*. Glencoe, Illinois: Free Press, 1959.

Levin, Murray B. *The Alienated Voter: Politics in Boston*. New York: Holt, Rinehart, and Winston, Inc., 1960.

Lockard, Duane. *New England State Politics*. Princeton, New Jersey: Princeton University Press, 1959.

Lubell, Samuel. *The Future of American Politics*. Second edition. Garden City, New York: Doubleday Anchor Books, 1956.

———. *The Revolt of the Moderates*. New York: Harper & Brothers, 1956.

MacCorkle, Stuart, and Dick Smith. *Texas Government*. Fourth Edition. New York: McGraw-Hill, 1960.

Martin, Roscoe. *The People's Party in Texas: A Study of Third-Party Politics*. Austin: University of Texas, Bulletin No. 3308, 1933.

McCleskey, Clifton. *The Government and Politics of Texas*. Boston: Little, Brown & Company, 1963.

McKay, Seth S. *Texas Politics, 1906–1944: With Special Reference to the German Counties*. Lubbock: Texas Tech Press, 1952.

Members of the Legislature of Texas from 1846–1939. Austin: Office of the Chief Clerk, Texas House of Representatives, 1939.

Myrdal, Gunnar. *An American Dilemma*. New York: Harper & Brothers, 1944.

Ogden, Frederick D. *The Poll Tax in the South*. University, Alabama: University of Alabama Press, 1958.

Price, Hugh D. *The Negro and Southern Politics*. New York: New York University Press, 1957.

Price, Margaret. *The Negro and the Ballot in the South*. Atlanta: Southern Regional Council, 1959.

———. *The Negro Voter in the South*. Atlanta: Southern Regional Council, 1957.

Report on the Conference of Business and Professional Leaders. Dallas, 1960.

Report of the United States Commission on Civil Rights, 1959. Washington, D.C.: Government Printing Office, 1959.
Report of the United States Commission on Civil Rights, 1961. Washington, D.C.: Government Printing Office, 1961.
Richardson, Rupert H. *Texas: The Lone Star State.* Second edition. Englewood Cliffs, New Jersey: Prentice-Hall, 1958.
Sarasohn, Stephen B., and Vera Sarasohn. *Political Party Patterns in Michigan.* Detroit: Wayne State University Press, 1957.
Schattschneider, E. E. *Party Government.* New York: Rinehart & Company, 1940.
Strong, Donald S. *Urban Republicanism in the South.* University, Alabama: Bureau of Public Administration, 1960.
Texas Almanac. Dallas: Dallas Morning News, published biennially since 1857 except for temporary interruptions.
Texas Manufacturers Association. *How To Be Influential in Politics.* Houston, 1953.
———. *1958 Statement of Guiding Principles and Program.* Houston, 1958.
Vines, Kenneth N. *Two Parties for Shreveport.* New York: Henry Holt and Company, Eagleton Foundation Case Study, 1959.
Weeks, O. Douglas. *Texas in the 1960 Presidential Election.* Austin: Institute of Public Affairs, 1961.
———. *Texas One-Party Politics in 1956.* Austin: Institute of Public Affairs, 1957.
———. *Texas Presidential Politics in 1952.* Austin: Institute of Public Affairs, 1953.
Winkler, E. W. *Platforms of Political Parties in Texas.* Austin: University of Texas, Bulletin No. 53, 1916.
Woodward, C. Vann. *The Strange Career of Jim Crow.* New York: Oxford University Press, 1955.

PERIODICALS

Campbell, Angus, and Warren Miller. "The Motivational Basis of Straight and Split Ticket Voting," *American Political Science Review,* LI (1957), 293–312.
Congressional Quarterly Weekly Report, published by the Congressional Quarterly, Inc., Washington, D.C.
Converse, Phillip E., Angus Campbell, Warren E. Miller, and Donald E. Stokes. "Stability and Change in 1960: A Reinstating Election," *American Political Science Review,* LV (June, 1961), 269–280.
Dickson, Fagan. "The Texas Poll Tax," *Texas Bar Journal,* XI (1948), 1–12.
Doherty, H. J. "Liberal and Conservative Voting Patterns in Florida," *Journal of Politics,* 14 (1952), 403–417.
"Dynamic Men of Dallas, The," *Fortune,* February, 1949, pp. 99 ff.
Epstein, Leon D. "A Two-Party Wisconsin," *Journal of Politics,* 18 (1956), 427–458.
Friedman, Robert S. "The Urban-Rural Conflict Revisited," *Western Political Quarterly,* XIV (1961), 481–495.
Hardeman, D. B. "Shivers of Texas: A Tragedy in Three Acts," *Harper's Magazine,* 213 (1956), 49–56.

Heberle, R., and A. L. Berhardt, "Factors Motivating Voting Behavior in a One-Party State," *Social Forces*, 27 (1949), 343–358.

Holloway, Harry. "The Negro and the Vote: The Case of Texas," *Journal of Politics*, 23 (1961), 522–556.

Masters, Nicholas A., and Deil S. Wright. "Trends and Variations in the Two-Party Vote: The Case of Michigan," *American Political Science Review*, LII (1958), 1078–1090.

McClosky, Herbert. "Conservatism and Personality," *American Political Science Review*, LII (1958), 27–45.

McClosky, Herbert, Paul J. Hoffman, and Rosemary O'Hara. "Issue Conflict and Consensus Among Party Leaders and Followers," *American Political Science Review*, LIV (1960), 406–427.

Miller, Warren E. "One-Party Politics and the Voter," *American Political Science Review*, L (1956), 707–725.

Price, Hugh D. "The Negro and Florida Politics," *Journal of Politics*, 17 (1955), 198–220.

Prothro, James W., Ernest Q. Campbell, and Charles M. Grigg. "Two-Party Voting in the South: Class Versus Party Identification," *American Political Science Review*, LII (1958), 131–139.

Ranney, Austin, and Willmore Kendall. "The American Party Systems," *American Political Science Review*, XLVIII (1954), 477–485.

Rhyne, Edwin H. "Political Parties and Decision Making in Three Southern Counties," *American Political Science Review*, LII (1958), 1091–1107.

Schlesinger, Joseph A. "Stability in the Vote for Governor," *Public Opinion Quarterly*, 24 (1960), 85–91.

———. "A Two-Dimensional Scheme for Classifying the States According to the Degree of Inter-Party Competition," *American Political Science Review*, XLIX (1955), 1120–1128.

Sindler, Allan P. "Bifactional Rivalry as an Alternative to Two-Party Competition in Louisiana," *American Political Science Review*, XLIX (1955), 641–662.

Southern School News, published monthly by the Southern Educational Reporting Service in Nashville, Tennessee.

"Spanish-Americans in Politics," *Congressional Quarterly Weekly Report*, June 23, 1961, 1042–1043.

Standing, William H., and James A. Robinson. "Inter-Party Competition and Primary Contesting: The Case of Indiana," *American Political Science Review*, LII (1958), 1066–1077.

Strong, Donald S. "The Poll Tax: The Case of Texas," *American Political Science Review*, XXXVIII (1944), 693–709.

———. "The Presidential Election in the South, 1952," *Journal of Politics*, 17 (1955), 343–388.

———. "The Rise of Negro Voting in Texas," *American Political Science Review*," XLII (1948), 510–522.

Texas Observer, published weekly from December, 1954, to December, 1962, and biweekly since December, 1962, in Austin, Texas.

Weeks, O. Douglas. "The League of United Latin American Citizens: A Texas-Mexican Civic Organization," *Southwestern Political and Social Science Quarterly*, 10 (1929), 257–278.

————. "Republicanism and Conservatism in the South," *Southwestern Social Science Quarterly*, 36 (1955), 248–256.

————. "The Texas-Mexican and the Politics of South Texas," *American Political Science Review*, XXIV (1930), 606–627.

"Where the 335,000 Workers in Dallas County Live and Work," Austin: Texas Employment Commission, 1958.

Wilson, James Q. "How the Northern Negro Uses His Vote," *The Reporter*, 22 (1960), 20–22.

UNPUBLISHED MATERIALS

Budd, H. E. "The Negro in Texas Politics, 1867–1898." Unpublished M.A. thesis. Austin, University of Texas, 1925.

Ellison, William M., Jr. "Negro Suffrage in Texas and Its Exercise." Unpublished M.A. thesis. Greeley, Colorado, Colorado State College, 1943.

Grossman, Mitchell. "Multi-Factional Politics in San Antonio and Bexar County, Texas." Unpublished typescript. Austin, University of Texas, 1959.

Sanford, William R. "History of the Republican Party of Texas." Unpublished M.A. thesis. Austin, University of Texas, 1954.

Tinsley, James. "The Progressive Movement in Texas." Unpublished Ph.D. dissertation. Madison, University of Wisconsin, 1953.

INDEX

AFL-CIO, Texas: as liberals, 5 n, 11, 136, 139; on minorities, 12, 139; president of, 13; scoreboard of, 73 n, 82, 136; on organized labor, 81–83, 85; political participation of, 106; headquarters of, 108. See also labor, organized

Africa, South: 126

aged: care for, 6

agriculture: and GOP, 32, 35, 60, 64, 174; in the Panhandle, 32; and conservative Democrats, 75, 76, 77, 79, 174; and liberals, 97, 138, 139; and Negroes, 111, 117. See also agri-urban area; cattle industry; farmers

agri-urban area: definition of, 41; elections in, 80; population in, 102. See also agriculture

Alger, Bruce: 22 n, 25, 52

Allred, James: 91, 168

Amarillo, Texas: Republicans in, 32, 47, 61; industry in, 44, 84; conservatives in, 103, 176. See also Potter County

"American Creed": 44–45

American GI Forum: 135, 137, 138

American Party: 27

American Voter, The: xvi–xvii

America Votes: 185

Anderson County: 189, 191, 195

Andrews County: 188, 191, 195

Angelina County: 189, 191, 195

Anglo Americans: and Negroes, 109–110, 123; and poll tax, 112, 138; and Latins, 127, 135; and GOP, 130, 154

antitrust actions: by Jim Hogg, 91

Aransas County: 158 n, 190, 195

Archer County: 188, 193, 195

Arizona: 25

Armstrong County: 34, 35, 188, 192, 196

Atascosa County: 133, 192, 196

Atlanta, Georgia: 125 n

attorney general, Texas: 140

Austin, Texas: 99; white-collar workers in, 85; liberal vote in, 103, 107; Latin Americans in, 107–108; Negroes in, 107–108, 112–117 passim, 120–121; AFL-CIO in, 108. See also Travis County

Austin Commission on Human Relations: 118 n

Austin County: 38, 189, 190, 194, 196

Bailey County: 188, 191, 194, 196

ballot, absentee: 119

—, party-column: 16, 18

Bandera County: 190, 192, 194, 196

banking interests: and Daniel, 7, 92

Barry, Desmond: 152

Bastrop County: 145, 188, 193, 195

Baylor County: 188, 192, 193, 195

Beaumont, Texas: Republicans in, 61; liberals in, 103, 139, 175; Negroes in, 112 n. See also Jefferson County

Bee County: 158, 189, 190, 195

Belden Poll: 153, 154

Bell County: 188, 193, 195

Bexar County: 30; conservatives in, 4 n, 103, 138, 192; liberals in, 13, 53, 104, 107, 108, 175; poll taxes in, 19, 138; Republicans in, 22 n, 25, 26, 43, 48, 49, 53, 61, 131 n, 158, 158 n, 173, 190; and Germans, 38, 81; economic characteristics of, 44, 52, 53, 84, 85, 104, 105, 198; organized labor in, 53, 85; Negroes in, 53, 106, 112–117 passim; Latins in, 53, 81, 104, 106, 108, 127, 129, 130, 131, 174; ideological positions within, 82, 83; support for Ralph Yarborough in, 88; support for Connally in, 144, 146; support for Cox in, 150; as metropolitan area, 195, 197, 198; social characteristics of, 197

Bexar County Democratic Coalition: 4

Bexar County Legislative Group: 4 n

Birch Society, John: 3, 141, 142

Black-and-Tan: 27

Blackland Prairie: 110

Blakley, William: and liberals, 13, 45, 151; and Texas Observer, 13; 1961 vote for, 27; 1961 candidacy of, 28–29, 31–32, 45, 92, 174; conservatism of, 32, 68; urban support for, 43, 108; supports Kennedy-Johnson, 45; Latin support for, 129

Blanco County: 158 n, 190, 196

blue-collar workers. See workers, blue-collar

Borden County: 188, 191, 196

Bosque County: 196

bosses, political. See leadership

Bowie County: 189, 195

Brazoria County: 191, 195